The Currency Game
Exchange Rate Politics
in Latin America

Jeffry Frieden and Ernesto Stein
Editors

Distributed by the Johns Hopkins University Press
for the Inter-American Development Bank

Washington, D.C.
2001

To order this book, contact:
IDB Bookstore
Tel: 1-877-PUBS IDB/(202) 623-1753
Fax: (202) 623-1709
E-mail: idb-books@iadb.org
www.iadb.org/pub

**Cataloging-in-Publication data provided by the
Inter-American Development Bank
Felipe Herrera Library**

The currency game : exchange rate politics in Latin America / Jeffry Frieden and Ernesto Stein, editors.

    p. cm.   Includes bibliographical references.
    ISBN: 1886938873

    1. Foreign exchange—Latin America.   2. Foreign exchange rate—Latin America.   3. Balance of payments—Latin America.   4. Inflation (Economics).   I. Frieden, Jeffry A. II. Stein, Ernesto. III. Inter-American Development Bank.

332.456 C325—dc21
Library of Congress Card Number   2001 131396

Latin American Research Network
Inter-American Development Bank

The Inter-American Development Bank created the Latin American Research Network in 1991 in order to strengthen policy formulation and contribute to the development policy agenda in Latin America.

Through a competitive bidding process, the network provides grant funding to leading Latin American research centers to conduct studies on economic and social issues selected by the Bank in consultation with the region's development community.

Most of the studies are comparative, which allows the Bank to build its knowledge base and draw lessons from experiences in macroeconomic and financial policy, modernization of the state, regulation, poverty and income distribution, social services, and employment. This book is based on a study of the political economy of exchange rate policy in Latin America that included research from Argentina, Brazil, Chile, Colombia, Peru and the Caribbean.

Individual country studies are available as working papers and are also available in PDF format on the Internet at http://www.iadb.org/oce/ RED_working_papers.cfm

Acknowledgments

The studies in this book were financed by the Latin American Research Network of the Inter-American Development Bank and would not have been possible without the collaboration of many friends and colleagues. The authors would like to thank the following for their comments and collaboration on the individual studies: Mauricio Cardenas, Momi Dahan, Suzanne Duryea, Eduardo Fernández-Arias, Ricardo Hausmann, Alberto Isgut, Andres Velasco, Robert Tchaidze, Felipe Barrera, Alberto Carrasquilla, Roberto Junguito, Armando Montenegro, Miguel Urrutia, Eduardo Wiesner, Jorge Streb, Marcelo Neri, Carla Bernardes, Gabriela Domingues, Juliana Pessoa de Araújo, Marcelo Pinheiro, Altamir Lopes, Ricardo Markwald, René Garcia, Ilan Goldfajn, Claudio Bravo, Daniel Cerquera, Virgilio Galdo, Helia Henríquez, and Norman Loayza.

We would also like to thank all those who participated in the Research Network project on the political economy of exchange rate policy, the LACEA-PEG meeting in Cartagena in 1998, and in the Fundación Getulio Vargas (FGV), PUC-Rio, IDB Workshop.

Further thanks are extended to CNPq for a research fellowship, and to PRONEX/CNPq for additional financial support in the Brazilian study. Raquel Gómez and Aglae Parra provided valuable administrative support, while Rita Funaro and John Dunn Smith contributed their editorial expertise.

Preface

Exchange rate policy figures prominently on the current Latin American agenda. The pros and cons of fixed and floating regimes, regional currencies, dollarization and other arrangements are all being discussed. In this context, the information and analysis compiled in *The Currency Game* is a valuable and timely resource.

Latin Americans as well as analysts of Latin America have long understood the central role of currency policies in the economic development of the region. Yet there has been surprisingly little research on the sources of national exchange rate policies. *The Currency Game* provides a deeper and more systematic understanding of exchange rate issues by analyzing the political economy of currency policy in Latin America and the Caribbean. It looks at the economic and political strategies that often lie behind exchange rate decisions, as well as the winners and losers that result from policy moves. It assesses the impact of economic structure, macroeconomic conditions, political institutions, interest groups, and electoral politics on the making of exchange rate policy in the region.

Written by a distinguished group of economists and political scientists from around the hemisphere, the essays in this book include analytical perspectives, a cross-national statistical study, and a series of detailed country studies prepared under the direction of Jeffry Frieden and Ernesto Stein. The current debate in Latin America over exchange rate policy is politically charged. This book brings important new theoretical insights and empirical evidence to that debate in order to best address a policy issue critical to the future of Latin American development.

Guillermo Calvo
Chief Economist
Inter-American Development Bank

Contents

Chapter One
The Political Economy of Exchange Rate Policy
in Latin America: An Analytical Overview
Jeffry Frieden and Ernesto Stein   1

Chapter Two
Politics and Exchange Rates: A Cross-Country Approach
Jeffry Frieden, Piero Ghezzi and Ernesto Stein 21

Chapter Three
From Redistribution to Stability: The Evolution of Exchange Rate
Policies in Argentina, 1950-98
Eugenio Díaz-Bonilla and Hector E. Schamis 65

Chapter Four
The Dilemma of Inflation vs. Balance of Payments:
Crawling Pegs in Brazil, 1964-98
Marco Bonomo and Maria Cristina T. Terra 119

Chapter Five
Something for Everyone: Chilean Exchange Rate Policy since 1960
José De Gregorio 157

Chapter Six
A Long-lasting Crawling Peg:
Political Determinants of Exchange Rate Policy in Colombia
Juan C. Jaramillo, Roberto Steiner and Natalia Salazar 199

Chapter Seven
Exchange Rates and Interest Groups in Peru, 1950-1996
Alberto Pascó-Font and Piero Ghezzi 249

CHAPTER ONE

The Political Economy of Exchange Rate Policy in Latin America: An Analytical Overview

Jeffry Frieden and Ernesto Stein[1]

Exchange rates have been central to the course of economic development in Latin America for decades. From the heyday of import substitution in the 1960s to the rapid expansion of foreign debt in the 1970s, and from the debt crisis and its troubled aftermath to the rekindling of growth and borrowing in the 1990s, the exchange rate has been crucial to the mix of government policies that has shaped the region. Indeed, many analysts regard exchange rate policy as a major determinant of other economic outcomes, such as adjustment to the oil shocks of the 1970s and the debt crisis of the 1980s (Sachs, 1985). And currency policies have themselves been at the center of some of the region's most prominent economic processes and events, including liberalization in the Southern Cone between 1976 and 1982, the Mexican crises of 1982 and 1994, Argentina's adoption of a currency board in 1991, Brazil's 1999 currency crisis, and ongoing discussions of dollarization.

It is thus surprising that there is so little analysis of how political economy affects the exchange rate policies of Latin American governments. Currency policy is made by governments, and governments operate in a political environment, yet a *political economy* of exchange rate policy is barely in its infancy. There are no generally accepted theories that explain why governments choose certain currency policies, and no developed body of empirical work that shows the relationship of economic and political factors in the determination of currency policy. In contrast, scholars have long

---

[1] Jeffry Frieden is Professor of Government at Harvard University. Ernesto Stein is Senior Economist with the IDB Research Department.

worked with well-developed theories of the distributional implications of different trade policies,[2] and more recent work has focused on how electoral and other political institutions affect the making of trade policy.[3]

This book analyzes the political economy of exchange rate policy in Latin America. It brings together the work of economists and political scientists interested in the interaction of economic and political factors in the making of exchange rate policy. The basis of the book is a series of arguments about the potential determinants of currency choices by national governments. While purely economic factors are of course important—especially economic structure, trade patterns, and exogenous economic conditions—the focus here is on the political and political economy considerations that have typically been underrepresented in the literature. These include the role of interest groups, electoral competition, and the timing of elections. These considerations are evaluated both with statistical analyses and in-depth studies of important national experiences.

Analyzing the Political Economy of Exchange Rates

The contrast between the amount of literature on trade policy and that on the political economy of exchange rate policy is striking. Economists and political scientists have carried out rigorous analyses of the political economy of trade for over 60 years, and the large body of work on the subject has given rise to some more or less generally accepted principles. Analysts typically agree on the tradeoffs facing policymakers between the distributional and welfare effects of protection. There are powerful (if contending) theories about the distributional impact of different trade policies; well-developed models of the interaction of distributional, electoral, institutional and other factors; and a wealth of empirical studies evaluating these approaches. No such background is available for the study of the making of exchange rate policy.

This chapter presents a consensual view, drawn from what literature is available,[4] on the crucial building blocks of the political economy of

---

[2] Indeed, there is a proliferation of such theories, including the Heckscher-Ohlin/Stolper-Samuelson approach, the specific-factors or Ricardo-Viner view, and more recent perspectives emphasizing imperfect competition.

[3] Lohmann and O'Halloran (1994), Rogowski (1987), and Persson and Tabellini (2000).

[4] See Bernhard and Leblang (1999), Clark and Reichert (1998), Collins (1996), Edison and Melvin (1990), Edwards (1996), Eichengreen (1995), Frieden (1994), Hefeker (1996), and Klein and Marion (1997).

exchange rate policy: the tradeoffs faced by governments, and the distributional, macroeconomic, institutional and other socioeconomic factors that affect the choices policymakers make as they address these tradeoffs.

Decisions on an exchange rate regime involve choosing the degree to which the currency is allowed to float freely or be fixed against some other currency. There is a wide spectrum of choices, ranging from a completely free float to a variety of managed floats, degrees of fixity ranging from a target zone to a peg, and a currency board or dollarization. The focus in this book on policies that address the level of the exchange rate is bound to raise eyebrows among economists. But theory and experience indicate that nominal exchange rate movements can have substantial real effects on relative prices, and that governments can and do affect their real exchange rates—within limits, of course. Although decisions on the exchange rate regime and level are closely linked, they can be thought of separately for purposes of analysis. In making these choices, policymakers have to consider the costs and benefits of their actions, and the tradeoffs they entail.

With regard to the exchange rate regime, the principal tradeoff is between *stability* and *flexibility*. Governments value two types of monetary stability. The most direct impact of the exchange rate regime is on *currency stability*, which is of value inasmuch as predictable exchange rates reduce the risk attached to cross-border economic activity.[5] All else being equal, governments would prefer stable exchange rates, which tend to be associated with fixed regimes. Fixed exchange rates can also lead to *monetary stability*, i.e., low inflation, through two different channels. First, a fixed rate makes it difficult for tradables prices to rise without drawing in competing imports. Second, the choice of a fixed rate can serve as a visible signal of government intentions, as policymakers tie their own hands as a commitment device.

Yet this domestic and international monetary stability can only be attained at the cost of giving up national policy flexibility. A fixed currency regime makes it impossible, without abandoning the parity, to use the exchange rate as a policy instrument, and it also makes it difficult or impossible to use interest rates for macroeconomic policy purposes (the difficulty varies with the degree of capital mobility). This has two related implications for policymakers. First, it reduces maneuvering room for dealing with macroeconomic distress: they cannot devalue in the face of payments deficits, or lower interest rates in a recession. Second, it reduces their ability to

---

[5] Certainly economic agents can hedge against these risks, but this possibility is especially limited in small developing countries where forward markets are often underdeveloped.

respond to distributional pressures for supportive policy: the government cannot devalue to satisfy complaints from importers or exporters about foreign competition, and it cannot lower interest rates to appease debtors. Obviously, this is not necessarily bad. In fact, policymakers may want to tie their own hands, removing inflation from the list of problems for which voters can blame them. However, this also means that they cannot use exchange rate policy to satisfy their constituents, which may be politically costly.

There is an analogous set of tradeoffs for the level of the exchange rate. A weaker real exchange rate stimulates demand for local tradable products, whether in domestic or foreign markets. It can therefore help reduce trade and payment deficits, and invigorate the tradable sectors of the economy. For exporters, it has the direct effect of raising the local currency earnings derived from foreign sales. On the other hand, a weaker real exchange rate reduces national purchasing power, making consumers worse off. The two desirable goals—stimulating local manufacturing, agricultural and raw materials sectors, and increasing local purchasing power—are mutually exclusive with regard to the level of the exchange rate. The benefit of increasing the competitiveness of national producers comes at the cost of reducing the real income of national consumers, and vice versa.

There are, then, two sets of tradeoffs. With regard to the regime (fixed or floating), the choice is either monetary stability or credibility versus monetary flexibility. And with regard to the level (depreciated or appreciated), the choice is competitiveness versus purchasing power. An even simpler setup could collapse the two into a choice between "credibility" and "competitiveness;" i.e., between a fixed currency with strong anti-inflationary effects but no ability to affect relative prices, and a more flexible currency with a tendency to depreciate in order to maintain local price competitiveness. Governments must weigh the costs and benefits of the various choices. The ways in which these choices are weighed depends on the structure of the national economy, and on the character of the domestic political economy.

Economic Structure

An economy with a greater need for an independent monetary policy, and a greater ability to pursue one, is more likely to choose a floating rate. As indicated by the longstanding literature on optimal currency areas, this implies that economies subjected to exogenous shocks uncorrelated with those faced by potential anchor countries, and with little mobility of factors between themselves and potential anchor countries, will be more likely to float. By the same token, extremely open economies will be more likely to fix, for two reasons. First, highly open economies typically find the exchange rate less effective as a policy tool—the real impact of a nominal depreciation, for example, is rapidly eroded as import prices rise and are transmitted through the economy. Second, a very large proportion of economic agents in such economies are sensitive to exchange rate risk and will be sympathetic to attempts to reduce it. Empirical evidence indicates that these last considerations are especially relevant at very high levels of openness, typical of the small European countries or the small nations of the Caribbean, for which total trade is often in excess of 100 percent of GDP.

Macroeconomic Conditions

Countries with long histories of persistent high inflation might be especially tempted to use a fixed exchange rate to bring down inflation. However, this interest will be tempered by the fact that fixing the currency in conditions of high inflation typically leads to a real appreciation, with undesirable effects on tradables producers and the balance of payments. So the anti-inflationary advantages of a fixed exchange rate have to be weighed against the disadvantages of a transitional real appreciation. These last disadvantages may be moderated by a high degree of indexation, or by great wage and price flexibility, either of which substantially reduces the likelihood of a real appreciation. If, as has been the case in many episodes of hyperinflation in Latin America, wages, prices and contracts are indexed to the dollar, fixing against the dollar is unlikely to cause a substantial real appreciation. And since indexation tends to rise as inflation rises, typically becoming close to full in conditions of hyperinflation, it can be hypothesized that under hyperinflationary conditions, anti-inflationary motives predominate over concern about a real appreciation. Conversely, when inflation is moderate, avoiding a real appreciation tends to outweigh bringing inflation down, given the typically limited nature of indexation in these conditions. This would give the relationship between inflation and exchange rate regime choice a U-shape, with fixed rates most likely to be adopted in conditions of either very low or extremely high inflation.

Interest Groups

The exchange rate has powerful effects on relative prices, and thus on the interests of different groups. An appreciated currency raises the relative price of nontradables, while a depreciated currency raises the relative price of tradables, so preferences on the level of the real exchange rate are clear. With regard to the regime, tradables producers are likely to oppose a fixed rate, for two reasons. First, as already discussed, the adoption of a fixed rate in conditions of high inflation, such as has characterized much of Latin America, usually leads to a transitional real appreciation, with detrimental effects on tradables producers. This is the common experience of most exchange rate-based stabilization programs. Second, a fixed rate eliminates the possibility of a depreciation to maintain or restore the competitiveness of tradables producers.[6] Because these producers are often involved in cross-border transactions, they may also be concerned with the volatility that a floating rate can bring. They may thus prefer a regime such as a backward-looking crawling peg, which tends to both reduce volatility and maintain the competitiveness of the real exchange rate. The most prominent supporters of a fixed rate are likely to be those heavily committed to cross-border contracts that involve an intertemporal dimension, particularly in countries, such as many in Latin America, where forward markets are limited. These would typically include the commercial and financial sectors, and foreign currency debtors. The clearest predictions from interest group approaches, then, are that on distributional grounds tradables producers will prefer a depreciated, floating rate, while those heavily engaged in cross-border activities, such as finance, commerce, and foreign debtors, will prefer a fixed rate.

Political Institutions

A fixed exchange rate requires that the government respond to exogenous shocks with domestic adjustment measures, and rules out the use of active exchange rate policy or monetary policy to stimulate the national economy. It also requires that fiscal policy be under control. Therefore, relatively weak governments will be unlikely to be able to sustain a fixed rate. They will be less able to resist the fiscal demands of sectoral and other groups, as they will lack the political support necessary to impose adjustment. In addition, they may have strong motives to use the exchange rate to improve short-term macroeconomic conditions. Thus, minority or coalition governments, divided governments, and other governments in a weak political position may be less likely to opt for a fixed rate. On the other end of the political spectrum, dictatorships and other authoritarian regimes are likely to be better able to undertake the adjustment measures necessary to maintain a fixed rate.

---

[6] It also eliminates the possibility of a nominal appreciation that would favor nontradables producers, but this is quite rare. The asymmetry, while of theoretical interest, is virtually universal and can simply be assumed to hold.

Electoral Considerations

There are a number of reasons why elections may have an effect on exchange rate policy. The income effect associated with depreciation reduces the purchasing power of the population. This can make depreciation unpopular, and therefore politicians may want to avoid it at election time. Devaluations may also be unpopular because they generate inflation.[7] One specific possibility is that governments may be tempted to launch exchange rate-based stabilization programs during the period prior to an election. In addition to reducing inflation, these stabilization programs tend to generate an economic boom in the short run, followed by a recession.[8] In high inflation economies, the combination of inflation reduction and economic boom may be appealing as an election approaches.[9] These arguments point in the same direction: the rate of depreciation may be expected to decline prior to elections, and to accelerate once elections have taken place. In terms of the real exchange rate, a government facing elections may be expected to attempt to effect a real appreciation, perhaps by lagging (or fixing) the nominal exchange rate behind inflation, with an inevitable real depreciation to follow.

These, then, are the expectations regarding the analysis of the political economy of exchange rates in Latin America. The chapters that follow, which are summarized in the next section, subject the issue to close empirical investigation in the context of these analytical expectations.

---

[7] Stein and Streb (1998) have developed a model in which devaluation acts as an inflation tax, and governments differ with regard to their competence. Competence is associated with the capacity of the incumbent to deliver a given bundle of public goods with less tax resources. Under an imperfect information setting, governments reduce the rate of devaluation (and thus the inflation tax rate) in the run-up to elections, in order to convey a signal about their competence and increase their chances of reelection.

[8] See Kiguel and Liviatan (1991) and Calvo and Végh (1990).

[9] Stein and Streb (1999) discuss several examples of such programs launched in the run-up to elections, and some of the country studies in this book provide additional examples. The chapter on Brazil presents an analytical framework in which politicians have a loss function defined in terms of the current account and inflation, but place different weights on these two objectives. Thus, the politicians tend to cater to two different groups in the population: workers, who place more weight on the inflation objective, and tradables producers, who care primarily about competitiveness. However, as elections approach, and in the presence of unobserved shocks, even those who favor the tradables sector have incentives to appear driven by inflation rather than competitiveness concerns, as workers outnumber tradables producers and can define the result of the election.

The Political Economy of Exchange Rates in Latin America

This book assesses the importance of factors that determine exchange rate policy in Latin America. Chapter Two is a cross-national statistical study that looks at a large number of Latin American and Caribbean nations over a 35-year period. The remaining chapters are case studies of Argentina, Brazil, Chile, Colombia and Peru. All the country studies include a descriptive analysis of the evolution of exchange rate policy since the 1960s, complemented by quantitative analysis. These analyses differ between countries in terms of the questions they ask, the methodology used to answer these questions and, of course, the results.

The five countries studied have gone through highly varied exchange rate experiences on several dimensions. While some countries have experienced few changes in their exchange rate regime during the period under study, others have had a variety of regimes, in some cases repeatedly. While some countries have shown great concern regarding the level of the exchange rate for competitiveness purposes, others have generally given more importance to macroeconomic stability in designing exchange rate policies. In several cases, the policy emphasis has swayed from macroeconomic stability to competitiveness and back, depending on external conditions, as well as on the country's economic and political developments.

This diversity of experiences naturally leads to different methodological choices in trying to learn about the political economy determinants of exchange rate policy. In Chile and Peru, where the exchange rate regime has undergone numerous changes over time, explaining the choice of regime and its level becomes an interesting experiment. For these two countries, as well as for the cross-country analysis, different models of qualitative dependent variables are used to study the political economy determinants of exchange rate regimes. In other countries where the regime has been constant for prolonged periods, it is more productive to focus not on the regime but rather on such exchange rate outcomes as the level of the real exchange rate or the degree of misalignment from equilibrium levels. This is the case in Brazil and Colombia, which have primarily been on backward-looking crawling peg regimes since 1967. The Argentine study takes a somewhat different methodological route, using various time series techniques to emphasize the change in the relevant tradeoffs underlying exchange rate policy, which have shifted from the politics of redistribution during the import-substitution industrialization (ISI) period to the politics of inflation.

Credibility vs. Competitiveness and Other Tradeoffs

Center stage throughout this book is the tradeoff in exchange rate policy between competitiveness (achieved through a depreciated real exchange rate) and macroeconomic stability (achieved through a fixed nominal and/or appreciating real exchange rate). In many instances, the nature of the tradeoff and the choices made along the way have changed over time. The chapter on Chile, for example, highlights shifts between pro-competitiveness and anti-inflationary stances. This was illustrated by the shift toward inflation fighting as the crawling peg was replaced by fixed exchange rates in 1979, only to go back to a pro-competitiveness stance (and a crawling peg regime) after the 1982 crisis.

The conflict between credibility and competitiveness was not always the main tradeoff in exchange rate policy. In Argentina, exchange rate policy evolved from being mostly a distributional issue during the height of the ISI period to being an issue dominated by conflicting concerns about macroeconomic stability and competitiveness. In the closed economy that characterized ISI, spells of appreciated real exchange rates were associated primarily with the goal of maintaining low prices for intermediate inputs, food, and capital goods. Given the heavily protected domestic market, the impact of the appreciated peso on local finished goods producers was essentially irrelevant. Although sometimes related to balance of payments constraints, devaluations were primarily associated with distributional conflict, and specifically with real wage reductions. In fact, before liberalization began in 1978, devaluations reduced real wages substantially. As the Argentine economy was liberalized during the 1980s, the competitiveness-credibility tradeoff emerged more strongly. Most particularly, the link between devaluations and inflation became much more direct, so that those concerned about inflation focused on the value of a real appreciation as an anti-inflationary tool. The Argentine study provides evidence, then, of a significant change in the very character of exchange rate politics as economies become more open, and as inflation becomes a more politically salient issue.

Economic Structure

The case studies in this book are not comparative, and as such they are not well suited to assess the impact of economic structure on exchange rate policy. In fact, the five countries studied are all of medium to large size by Latin American standards, have large manufacturing and primary exporting sectors, and went through long periods of import substitution followed by substantial trade liberalization. The principal comparative evidence in this book, therefore, is in the cross-country chapter, where a strong finding is that a high degree of economic openness is in fact associated with a greater likelihood of a fixed rate. Although the result is due in part to the tendency of the very open economies in and around the Caribbean basin to fix their exchange rates, it is robust to the exclusion of these countries. Another comparative expectation was that national sensitivity to terms of trade shocks would be associated with a greater likelihood of floating. Surprisingly, the *opposite* relationship holds: countries whose terms of trade are particularly variable are in fact *less* likely to float their currencies. This is a puzzle not explained by the existing literature.

Macroeconomic Conditions

The country studies provide suggestive evidence about the impact of inflation on exchange rate policy. Conditions of moderate inflation typically were associated in all five countries with exchange rate regimes with some degree of flexibility—backward-looking crawling pegs, target zones, or managed floats. In almost all instances, hyperinflation led to the use of a fixed exchange rate to bring monetary conditions under control. This pattern appears to hold both across countries and over time. Argentina and Chile attempted exchange rate-based stabilization programs in the late 1970s to deal with high inflation. At the same time, countries with more moderate inflation, such as Colombia and Brazil, operated under crawling pegs. But as Brazil and Argentina ratcheted into hyperinflation during the 1980s, they turned to fixing the exchange rate to bring inflation down—this time, with substantial success. Chile, on the other hand, having essentially ended hyperinflation and settled into mild inflation, moved back to a more flexible currency.

There is a strong correlation between moderate inflation and flexibility, and hyperinflation and fixing.[10] This tends to support the expectations of the U-shaped relationship mentioned above: regimes that allow some flexibility are more likely with moderate inflation, while fixing is more likely with very low inflation or hyperinflation. This is also in part borne out by the cross-national study: in particular, the statistical evidence

---

[10] Peru, however, is an interesting counter-example. As shown in the chapter on Peru, hyperinflation was defeated without the active use of a nominal exchange rate anchor. This was probably out of necessity, as the country had essentially run out of reserves and could not credibly commit to a fixed rate. And once the program was successful, there was little reason to alter it. In any case, Peru does not fit the pattern described here.

is strong that, in times of hyperinflation, countries tend to adopt fixed exchange rate regimes.

Interest Groups

The impact of interest groups on exchange rate policy has evolved over time, primarily because of the trend toward trade liberalization in all the countries considered. In some cases financial liberalization seems to have played an important role as well. Because of the many specific tariffs and subsidies in place during the import substitution period, tradables producers tended to focus their demands on targeted measures that would affect their own profitability without directly implicating the exchange rate. These tariffs and subsidies made it possible for governments to respond to the demands of interest groups without affecting overall exchange rate policy, or to compensate those sectors otherwise hurt by changes in that policy. Indeed, given the prohibitive protection afforded many manufacturers, the level of the exchange rate was close to irrelevant—and an appreciated currency could even be favorable, as it kept input prices low. With the advent of trade liberalization and the dismantling of these specific measures the role of interest groups as a determinant of exchange rate policy became more important. And manufacturers, no longer protected by trade barriers, had much stronger incentives to push for a weaker real exchange rate.

The Colombian chapter illustrates the changes over time in the role of interest groups in exchange rate policy. The country's coffee sector was subject to export taxes (in the context of a stabilization fund) broadly related to international coffee prices and to the exchange rate. The relationship between prices paid to producers and the external price of coffee thus determined an implicit exchange rate applicable only to coffee. According to the authors, the sector was inclined to spend its lobbying efforts on the domestic support price, rather than on the general level of the exchange rate, which would have caused conflicts with other interest groups. In the 1990s, however, the availability of compensatory mechanisms declined and, in the midst of a substantial real appreciation, coffee growers became much more vocal about exchange rate policy. The manufacturing sector exhibited similar behavior: during the ISI period the industrialists' association sought protection through subsidies and trade barriers, but became very vocal on exchange rate policy issues as these measures were dismantled in the 1990s.

The changing policy preferences of interest groups are tackled empirically in the cross-national study, as well as in the Peru chapter. Both studies use dummy variables to indicate periods of trade liberalization and to explore how this affected the impact of the manufacturing sector on exchange rate policy. In the cross-national study, a larger manufacturing sector is associated with the adoption of pro-competitiveness regimes, such as flexible regimes or backward-looking crawling pegs. However, these effects are much smaller during the ISI period compared to the period of liberalized trade. During the ISI period in Peru, a larger share of manufacturing was actually associated with a more appreciated rate and with the adoption of fixed or pre-announced crawling peg regimes. During the liberalization period, however, the effect of the manufacturing sector became significantly weaker. Therefore, although the manufacturing share variable has opposite effects under ISI in the two studies, in both the advent of trade liberalization affects the incentives of the manufacturing sector in the same way.

Other sectoral variables included in the studies are the share of agriculture and mining in GDP, as well as the share of exports over GDP. The presumption, in this last case, is that as the share of exports becomes larger, the group within an economy that would benefit from a depreciated exchange rate becomes larger and stronger. It would then presumably be in a better position to lobby in favor of exchange rate policies associated with a pro-competitiveness stance. While mining and agriculture did not appear to significantly affect exchange rate policy in any of the studies in which they were included, the share of exports in GDP in Chile appears to be associated with the adoption of more flexible regimes (crawling pegs and bands, rather than fixed exchange rates). In fact, the statistical analysis in the Chilean chapter implies that a 10 percentage point increase in exports as a share of GDP was associated with a reduction in the probability of a fixed exchange rate regime that was always significant, and ranged between 1.7 percent and 6 percent depending on the specification of the model. On the other hand, the likelihood of adopting a crawling peg increased between 1.9 percent and 7 percent in response to a 10 percentage point increase in export share, depending on the specification.

The presumption up until now has been that certain interest groups would exert influence on policymakers, and that their influence would be related to their share in GDP. However, there are other channels through which interest group considerations may have an effect on exchange rate policy. Exchange rate policy can be used as compensation to sectors that are hurt by other policies (such as trade liberalization). Perhaps more common, given the relatively broad effects of the exchange rate, is for governments to compensate specific sectors hit by exchange rate policy with countervailing measures. There are several examples of these compensation mechanisms in the country chapters.

The chapter on Chile develops the compensation issue most fully. In fact, the issue of compensation policies involving exchange rates is a recurrent theme, whether depreciated exchange rates were used to compensate producers for the loss of protection, or whether subsidies were used to compensate dollar debtors for exchange rate changes. Regarding the relationship between trade and exchange rate policies, the chapter suggests that exchange rate regimes tended to be more flexible (which in the case of Chile means crawling pegs and bands, regimes associated with more depreciated real exchange rates) when the economy was more open, providing evidence in favor of the compensation hypothesis. The empirical evidence in this case, complemented by commentary from policymakers, leaves no doubt about the link between trade and exchange rate policies in Chile.

The Peru study suggests that export subsidies significantly reduced pressures for a depreciated exchange rate, thus providing more evidence regarding the importance of compensation mechanisms. More generally, the link between trade and exchange rate policies underlies the policy mix observed in most countries during the ISI period: appreciated exchange rates, which allowed for the import of cheap intermediate and capital goods products, coupled with high levels of protection for final goods.

The use of other policy measures to compensate for changes in exchange rate policy has been widespread in the countries studied, and has taken a variety of forms. After the exchange rate in Chile was floated in August 1982, a preferential exchange rate system was put in place, which was valid for payment of interest and principal of all existing debts denominated in foreign currency. Brazil in 1979 and Argentina in 1981 introduced variations of the same compensatory scheme following large devaluations. Other forms of compensation included the access of large conglomerates to newly privatized assets, and the introduction of special trade regimes such as that of the auto industry in Argentina following the adoption of the country's currency board.

Political Institutions

Several chapters in this book investigate the role of the political regime in exchange rate policy. Some studies explore whether the behavior of exchange rate policies under democratic governments differs from that under dictatorships, while others look at the role of partisanship, the existence of political competition, and divided government as potential determinants of exchange rate policy.

The cross-national study finds evidence that dictatorships were associated with fixed exchange rate regimes. The regressions include a time trend, so this result cannot simply be attributed to the coinciding trends toward more flexibility and more democracy in Latin America. In the Brazilian study, the hypothesis is that democratic governments have a stronger incentive to cater to workers as opposed to tradables producers, since workers are more numerous and influence election results. Workers care about inflation and the purchasing power of their salaries. Although dictators may at times need political support, as a general rule they have fewer incentives to respond to popular demands, and thus are more likely than democratic rulers to respond to concentrated interests such as those of the tradables sector, which benefits from a depreciated exchange rate.

The evidence presented in the Brazil chapter, however, does not support this hypothesis. The authors use a Markov switching empirical model to characterize the behavior of the real exchange rate at any point in time as being in either an "overvalued" or "undervalued" state. Then they compute the effect of the political regime on the probability of remaining in each state, or switching from one state to the other. Contrary to the author's priors, dictatorship increases the probability of a switch to the overvalued state, and decreases the probability of a shift to the undervalued state, which should be the one favored by tradables producers. The authors attribute this unexpected result to the ISI pattern discussed above, in which highly protectionist trade policies during the military regime allowed tradables producers to benefit from an appreciated currency that would lower the price of capital goods and imported intermediate inputs.

The Colombian study looks at two different political-institutional variables. First, it finds that exchange rate policy has differed across political parties: the rate of nominal depreciation has been significantly higher when the Conservative party—which has a strong base of support in the coffee growing region—is in office. The difference is quite large in economic terms: the rate of quarterly nominal depreciation is nearly 4 percentage points higher under Conservative governments, although the partisan variable loses significance once the authors control for real exchange rate misalignments. Second, the chapter finds effects of the National Front, a power-sharing agreement between the two main parties that lasted from 1958 through 1974 and significantly reduced the degree of political competition. The National Front period is associated with lower rates of devaluation, suggesting that the absence of political competition reduced the incentives to pursue expansionary policies that might have compromised economic stability.

The cross-country study uses another variable related to the political regime: the proportion of government-controlled seats in the legislature. The expectation is that strong governments are more prone to adopt fixed exchange rate regimes, for they would be in a better position to implement the macroeconomic adjustments needed to sustain such a regime. The authors indeed find that strong governments are more likely to adopt fixed exchange rate regimes. The same is true for governments that face a weak and fragmented opposition.

Electoral Considerations

The evidence in both the country studies and the cross-national study on the effects of elections on exchange rate policy is generally consistent with the arguments outlined in the previous section. The study on Brazil tackles the electoral issue most carefully. The Markov switching empirical model used in the chapter seems perfectly suited to gauge the effect of elections on the pattern of exchange rates, as it distinguishes between an "overvalued" and "undervalued" state and correlates these states with economic and political trends. The chapter finds that in periods that lead to elections, the probability of remaining in an overvalued state increases, as does the probability of switching from an undervalued to an overvalued state. Specifically, the results imply that, conditional on being "undervalued," the probability that the real exchange rate will switch to the overvalued state is 17 percent during the run-up to elections in the democratic period, up from just 2.2 percent during normal times. Likewise, the probability of switching from the overvalued to the undervalued state increases from 10 percent to 19 percent during the period after elections, although in this case the difference is not statistically significant.

By averaging more than 240 elections in Latin America, the cross-national study examines the behavior of nominal and real exchange rates within a 19-month window centered on these episodes. The authors find that the rate of nominal depreciation jumps upward two to four months after elections take place. The effects are particularly strong after presidential elections: the average rate of monthly depreciation jumps from around 2.5 percent in normal times, to around 6 percent in months two through four.[11] The real exchange rate, in turn, appreciates nearly 3.5 percent in the months leading to presidential elections, and depreciates on average 6 percent during the following four months. Interestingly, these results are even stronger when government changes are considered instead of elections, suggesting that the adjustment in exchange rates tends to be delayed until the new authorities take office. The authors also show how the probability of a large real depreciation (over 25 percent) is affected by the electoral cycle. The probability falls from 3.84 percent, in the case of the whole

---

[11] The authors use geometric averages rather than arithmetic averages in order to lessen the effects of outliers.

sample, to 2.66 percent in the run-up to an election (a reduction of over 40 percent), and jumps to 9.76 percent immediately after the new government is inaugurated.

Other studies that look at the election issue are those on Peru, Colombia and Argentina. The methodology used for Peru is similar to that of the cross-national study, and the results are similar as well. These results have to be viewed with caution, however, since they are based on a small number of elections. But the pattern of real exchange rate movements around elections is very clear, showing a sharp appreciation before elections, followed by a sharp depreciation once elections have taken place. The Colombian chapter compares the devaluation rate in presidential election years (10 between 1958 and 1994) to that of nonelection years. It finds that in the months leading up to an election, the behavior of the nominal exchange rate is similar to that in the same months of a nonelection year. The rate of devaluation seems to be lower between the election and the inauguration of the new government, and higher after the new government takes office. These results, however, do not appear to be very robust: the effect of elections on devaluation disappears completely when other variables are included in the analysis.

Both Brazil and Argentina experienced several episodes that illustrate the importance of the election effect. The Brazilian chapter discusses the 1986 Cruzado Plan in Brazil, when devaluation was delayed until one week after the elections, and the 1994 Real Plan, key to Fernando Henrique Cardoso's come-from-behind victory in the October 1994 elections. The chapter on Argentina stresses the political impact of the Austral Plan, based on a fixed exchange rate, on the 1985 Congressional elections, and the desperate (and failed) attempt to control inflation with the Primavera Plan during the run-up to the 1989 presidential elections. The study also presents evidence of the importance of the rate of inflation— which, the authors show, is very closely linked to depreciation—as a determinant of the electoral result.[12]

Conclusions

The studies in this book provide strong evidence that political economy is important in determining exchange rate policies in Latin America. Much of the politics of exchange rates revolves around the tradeoff between the

---

[12] Given the small sample of elections in Argentina, however, these results should be viewed with caution.

macroeconomic credibility that a fixed rate can provide, and the price competitiveness of local producers that a flexible rate can maintain. Where concern about real appreciation dominates, such as in countries with moderate inflation and little indexing, policymakers are more likely to maintain adjustable exchange rate regimes. Hyperinflation, however, makes fixing more likely, both as concern about inflation rises and as economy-wide indexing reduces the probability of a substantial real appreciation. Where exports are particularly important, currency policy tends toward flexibility, as exporters are particularly anxious to maintain relative prices favorable to them.

Special interests also appear to affect currency policy, particularly when the manufacturing sector promotes more flexible currency regimes to maintain the competitiveness of locally produced tradables. This is, not surprisingly, especially true in relatively open economies; and in fact it seems that in the closed economies of the ISI period this consideration was weaker or absent. Stronger governments are, generally speaking, more likely to choose and sustain fixed exchange rate regimes, as the macroeconomic adjustments involved are typically difficult for governments with weak political bases of support.

Elections, too, affect currency policy, especially inasmuch as a real appreciation can deliver an electorally popular reduction in inflation and increase in purchasing power. In line with this, governments show a strong tendency to allow or engineer a real appreciation in the run-up to elections, which is then reversed after the government changes hands.

The studies in this book, and others like them, indicate the centrality of political economy considerations to the determination of exchange rate policy. To be sure, the current state of understanding of the political economy of exchange rates is rudimentary. There is a great need for more rigorous and comprehensive theoretical and empirical studies of the problem, both in Latin America and beyond. Nonetheless, on the basis of the analysis and evidence presented here, it is clear that the evolution of Latin American currency policies cannot be understood without a firm grasp of the underlying political and political economy conditions in the countries of the region.

References

Bernhard, W., and D. Leblang. 1999. Democratic Institutions and Exchange-Rate Commitments. *International Organization* 53(1): 71-97.

Calvo, G., and C. Végh. 1990. *Credibility and the Dynamics of Stabilization Policy: A Basic Framework.* IMF Working Paper WP/90/110. International Monetary Fund, Washington, DC.

Clark, W., and U. Reichert. 1998. International and Domestic Constraints on Political Business Cycles in OECD Economies. *International Organization* 52(1).

Collins, S. 1996. On Becoming More Flexible: Exchange Rate Regimes in Latin America and the Caribbean. *Journal of Development Economics* 51: 117-38.

Edison, H., and M. Melvin. 1990. The Determinants and Implications of the Choice of an Exchange Rate System. In W. Haraf and T. Willett (eds.), *Monetary Policy for a Volatile Global Economy.* Washington, DC: American Enterprise Institute.

Edwards, S. 1996. *The Determinants of the Choice between Fixed and Flexible Exchange Rate Regimes.* NBER Working Paper 5576. National Bureau of Economic Research, Cambridge, MA.

Eichengreen, B. 1995. The Endogeneity of Exchange Rate Regimes. In P. Kenen (ed.), *Understanding Interdependence: The Macroeconomics of the Open Economy.* Princeton: Princeton University Press.

Frieden, J. 1994. Exchange Rate Politics: Contemporary Lessons from American History. *Review of International Political Economy* 1(1): 81-103.

Hausmann, R., U. Panizza, and E. Stein. 2000. *Why Do Countries Float the Way They Float?* Inter-American Development Bank Research Department Working Paper 418, Washington, DC.

Hefeker, C. 1996. The Political Choice and Collapse of Fixed Exchange Rates. *Journal of Institutional and Theoretical Economics* 152: 360-79.

Kiguel, M., and N. Liviatan. 1991. The Business Cycle Associated with Exchange Rate-Based Stabilizations. *World Bank Economic Review* 6 (2): 279-305.

Klein, M., and N. Marion. 1997. Explaining the Exchange-Rate Pegs. *Journal of Development Economics.* 54: 387-404.

Lohmann, S., and S. O'Halloran. 1994. Divided Government and U.S. Trade Policy: Theory and Evidence. *International Organization* 48(4): 595-632.

Persson, T., and G. Tabellini. 2000. *Political Economics and Economic Policy.* Cambridge, MA: MIT Press.

Rogowski, R. 1987. Trade and the Variety of Democratic Institutions. *International Organization* 41(2): 203-24.

Sachs, J. 1985. External Debt and Macroeconomic Performance in Latin America and East Asia. *Brookings Papers on Economic Activity* 2.

Stein, E.H., and Streb, J.M. 1999. *Elections and the Timing of Devaluations.* Inter-American Development Bank Research Department Working Paper 396, Washington, DC.

_____. 1998. Political Stabilization Cycles in High Inflation Economies. *Journal of Development Economics* 56(1): 159-80.

CHAPTER TWO

Politics and Exchange Rates: A Cross-Country Approach

Jeffry Frieden, Piero Ghezzi and Ernesto Stein[1]

Before the collapse of the Bretton Woods system in 1973, an overwhelming majority of countries, including 90 percent of those in Latin America, had fixed exchange rate regimes. Since then, however, Latin America has seen a wide variety of exchange rate regimes and policies. Different countries, at different times, have adopted exchange rate regimes for reasons ranging from controlling inflation to reducing exchange rate volatility or improving competitiveness. Table 2.1 illustrates the shift away from fixed regimes in Latin American countries.

    This chapter explores the impact of political economy factors on exchange rate policy in Latin America. It studies what determines the choice of exchange rate regime, with particular emphasis on political, institutional and interest group factors. The presumption is that differences in institutional and political settings, as well as in economic structure, can affect the choice of regime and, more generally, exchange rate policy. In addition to these structural elements, the chapter examines whether such political events as elections and changes in government affect the pattern of nominal and real exchange rates.

    There is evidence that political economy factors are indeed important in determining an exchange rate regime. Governments with strong support in the legislature tend to choose fixed regimes, as do governments that face a fragmented opposition. This is consistent with the idea that sustaining a fixed rate may require a politically difficult adjustment. Economies with an important manufacturing sector are more prone to adopt either floating re-

[1] Jeffry Frieden is Professor of Government at Harvard University. Piero Ghezzi is an economist at the Deutsche Bank. Ernesto Stein is Senior Economist with the IDB Research Department.

Table 2.1. Use of Exchange Arrangements by Period

Type of arrangement	1960-73		1974-81		1982-88		1989-94	
	No. of obsv.	%	No. of obsv.	%	No. of obsv.	%	No. of obsv.	%
Fixed to single currency	322	88.5	159	76.4	110	60.4	56	35.9
Fixed to basket					4	2.2		
Fixed w/frequent adjustments	18	4.9	12	5.8	4	2.2	3	1.9
Forward-looking crawling peg			9	4.3	4	2.2	10	6.4
Forward-looking crawling band							6	3.8
Backward-looking crawling peg	12	3.3	22	10.6	46	25.3	12	7.7
Backward-looking crawling band							7	4.5
Dirty floating	8	2.2	6	2.9	5	2.7	22	14.1
Free floating	4	1.1			9	4.9	40	25.6
Total	364	100.0	208	100.0	182	100.0	156	100.0

gimes or backward-looking crawling pegs, both of which tend to deliver more competitive real exchange rates. The influence of the manufacturing sector on the exchange rate regime appears to have been more important in periods when trade was liberalized, since this was when the sector had to face competition from foreign producers. Finally, there is strong evidence that elections and government changes affect the path of nominal and real exchange rates. Devaluations tend to be delayed in the run-up to elections, and only occur immediately after the new government takes office.

Political Economy Determinants of the Choice of Regime

Traditionally, explanations of exchange rate policy were based on the optimal currency area and related approaches.[2] Scholars focused on how different exchange rate regimes might be desirable for countries with different economic characteristics, and investigated the impact of these characteris-

---

[2] See Mundell (1961), McKinnon (1962), and Kenen (1969). A modern survey is Tavlas (1994).

tics on policy choice.[3] Findings indicated a tendency for small and open economies facing few external price shocks to fix rather than float. But the evidence typically was weak and contradictory.

More recently, attention has shifted to the potential credibility effects of exchange rate policy. Specifically, it was argued that governments could gain anti-inflationary credibility by fixing to a nominal anchor currency.[4] This constitutes an easily observable target, and deviating from it may impose greater costs on policymakers than deviating from a monetary target. In addition, some authors have argued that a fixed exchange rate disciplines the government because any fiscal excess might end in a currency collapse.[5] While there is little systematic empirical evidence on this score, it has no doubt played a role in many Latin American experiences in the 1990s.

A weakness of these approaches is that they tend to assume a benevolent social welfare-maximizing government. This is problematic for two reasons. First, there is no consensus on welfare criteria for exchange rate regime choice, so that even such a benevolent government might face strongly conflicting advice from experts. Second, and perhaps more important, the assumption of such a benevolent government seems hard to justify on theoretical or empirical grounds. There is little reason to believe that currency policy is made any differently—that is, any less politically—than other economic policies.

In this light, a new generation of investigations of exchange rate policy explicitly incorporates political economy variables. Some studies on developed countries, especially in Europe, have looked at the impact of institutional, electoral and interest group factors on currency policy.[6] However, studies of OECD economies, most prominently of European monetary integration, may have limited applicability to the developing world. In addition, the literature is far from a consensus on the sorts of political and political economy variables expected to affect currency policy.

Some recent studies have included developing countries in the analysis of the political economy of exchange rate policy. Collins (1996) and Edwards (1996) use probit analysis to study the determinants of exchange rate regime. They build their empirical models around a framework in which the political cost associated with devaluation under fixed exchange rates plays a major role.

---

[3] See Edison and Melvin (1990).
[4] See Giavazzi and Pagano (1988) and Weber (1991).
[5] See Aghevli, Kahn and Montiel (1991). Tornell and Velasco (1995) argue against this logic, pointing out that under fixed exchange rates politicians with a high discount rate will be more prone to fiscal excesses, as the inflationary cost of such excesses is delayed.
[6] See Bernhard and Leblang (1999), Blomberg and Hess (1997), Eichengreen (1995), Frieden (1994, 1998), and Hefeker (1997).

Depreciation under more flexible regimes is less visible and, it is assumed, does not carry the same stigma. Both studies find that factors that increase the need for frequent adjustment (or in the case of Edwards, which increase the political cost of readjustment) reduce the likelihood that a country will fix. Collins does not directly use political economy variables in her analysis, but Edwards introduces variables that measure the degree of political instability and the strength of government. He finds that weaker governments and unstable political environments reduce the likelihood that a peg will be adopted.

This chapter examines a wide range of economic, political economy and political variables that might affect exchange rate policy. It contributes to the literature in several ways. First, it uses a richer and more realistic classification of exchange rate regimes than the usual fixed/flexible dichotomy. Second, it closely examines the impact of interest group variables, a factor overlooked in much previous work.[7] Third, it looks at a large number of Latin American and Caribbean countries over a relatively long period of time (between 1960 and 1994).[8] Finally, it uses new data on political institutions, based on the composition of legislatures.

Exchange Rate Arrangements

Countries do not choose exchange rate regimes for the regime per se. Different regimes produce different outcomes, and countries choose them according to the outcomes they desire. In choosing their exchange rate arrangement, policymakers must therefore make tradeoffs among these values: credibility, flexibility and stability. Implicit in the discussion that follows is the assumption that governments do have the ability to affect the level of the real exchange rate, at least in the short and medium term, through the use of exchange rate policy. This assumption is supported by the findings of the literature on purchasing power parity, which shows that deviations from purchasing power parity (PPP) are very slow to die out.[9]

---

[7] Frieden (1994, 1998) and Hefeker (1997) are exceptions.

[8] The 26 countries included in the study are Argentina, the Bahamas, Barbados, Belize, Bolivia, Brazil, Chile, Colombia, Costa Rica, Dominican Republic, Ecuador, El Salvador, Guatemala, Guyana, Haiti, Honduras, Jamaica, Mexico, Nicaragua, Panama, Paraguay, Peru, Suriname, Trinidad and Tobago, Uruguay and Venezuela.

[9] Studies for developed countries show that deviations from PPP have a half-life of between three and five years (see Rogoff, 1996). For developing countries, the evidence shows that misalignments tend to die out more rapidly. However, movements in the nominal exchange rate are still very important to determine changes in the real exchange rate. Kiguel and Ghei (1993) and Goldfajn and Valdés (1999) show that large real depreciations tend to go together with large nominal depreciations.

Governments might choose to adopt fixed exchange rates in the hope of gaining *credibility* in their fight against inflation. The use of a fixed exchange rate as a commitment technology to control inflation has become common, and it clearly responds to the needs of some governments some of the time. At the same time, fixing the exchange rate may provide *stability* of both nominal and real exchange rates, which are relative prices of great importance to local economic agents. This is especially the case in very open economies, where exchange rate volatility may have substantial costs in and of itself (especially in the absence of well-developed forward markets).[10] Fixed exchange rates, however, may compromise the third value, *flexibility*, which can have consequences for both internal and external balance. On the domestic front, fixed exchange rates limit the ability to use monetary policy to react to real shocks. This loss of flexibility, according to the theory of optimal currency areas, should be more problematic if shocks in the country that pegs are uncorrelated to those in the country to which the currency is pegged.[11]

Regarding external balance, a drawback of fixed exchange rates is that an inflation differential between the pegging country and the anchor generates an appreciation of the real exchange rate that, in the absence of compensating productivity gains, hurts the tradables sector and might generate a balance of payments crisis. Flexibility is indeed potentially valuable to a government that is unwilling to forego the use of nominal depreciations for policy purposes. Perhaps the most common such purpose among developing countries is to restore or ensure the competitiveness of its tradables producers. Sachs (1985) associates the greater success of East Asia relative to Latin America during the debt crisis of the early 1980s with the propensity of the former to maintain "more realistic" (i.e., weaker) exchange rates than the latter, thus encouraging the production of exports. Interestingly, he attributes this policy difference to interest group effects.

The benefits and costs of fixed exchange rates depend on the characteristics of the country in question. For example, concern about both credibility and competitiveness should be affected by existing levels of inflation, albeit in different ways. A country with extremely high inflation, desperate to stabilize, might be more likely to use a fixed exchange rate as a nominal anchor for

---

[10] In contrast, in high inflation countries where fixed regimes tend to require frequent readjustments, pegging the exchange rate may exacerbate, rather than reduce, the volatility of nominal and real exchange rates. See Hausmann et al. (1999).

[11] Recent studies such as Hausmann et al. (1999) and Calvo and Reinhart (2000) suggest, however, that flexible exchange rate countries in Latin America, as well as in other emerging markets, have not really allowed the exchange rate to fluctuate much. Thus, they have not really made use of the flexibility to conduct anticyclical monetary policy.

expectations—that is, for credibility purposes. On the other hand, the higher the rate of inflation, the more a fixed rate will impose competitive pressures on tradables producers and, more generally, pressures on the balance of payments.

Given the history of high inflation in Latin America, this tradeoff between credibility and competitiveness is especially important.[12] And the degree to which policymakers opt to sacrifice competitiveness for credibility, or vice versa, will presumably be a function of a variety of political economy variables. These might include the existence of other mechanisms to enhance credibility, popular pressures to reduce inflation, and the political influence of tradables producers.

In most of Latin America, the credibility-competitiveness tradeoff is central to the political economy of exchange rate policy. For this reason, it is the main tradeoff considered in defining the left-hand side variable to be used in this empirical analysis. At the same time, the desire for nominal and real exchange rate stability may sometimes matter. The classification of regimes used is flexible enough to allow organizing the regime variable along the stability vs. flexibility dimension, if desired.

Most studies of the determinants of exchange regimes, including Collins (1996) and Edwards (1996), use the International Monetary Fund's classification of exchange rate regimes, *Exchange Arrangements and Exchange Restrictions,* to create their dependent variable. Although the IMF classification has undergone some changes over time, its most recent version classifies regimes in the following categories: pegged (to a single currency or basket of currencies); limited flexibility (for cases such as ERM); adjusted according to indicators; other managed float; or free float.

Both Collins and Edwards group the arrangements into two regimes: fixed, and more flexible. Everything other than "pegged" is lumped together under the "more flexible" label.[13] This classification has some unfortunate consequences. For example, Mexico before the Tequila Crisis is classified as "more flexible." So are the *tablitas* of the late 1970s in the Southern Cone countries. Yet, within the inflation-competitiveness tradeoff that underlies these authors' works, these cases are clearly attempts to lower inflation or keep it at bay, even at the cost of accepting a larger misalignment from the target exchange rate.[14]

---

[12] Calvo, Reinhart and Végh (1995) have derived the tradeoff between the real exchange rate and the inflation objectives in the context of an intertemporal optimization model. See also Lizondo (1991, 1993) and Montiel and Ostry (1991, 1993).

[13] Edwards also tries including the limited flexibility cases together with the fixed, with no change in his results.

[14] In the tablitas, the path of the nominal exchange rate was preannounced, and the rate of devaluation decelerated, in an effort to have domestic inflation converge with that of the anchor.

Cottarelli and Giannini (1998) have recently expanded on the IMF classification, including a special category for forward-looking crawling pegs such as the *tablitas*. This appears to be a step in the right direction. The classification below goes a step further, taking advantage of the fact that, while the IMF classification is not disaggregated enough for the present purpose, the descriptions that appear in *Exchange Arrangements and Exchange Restrictions* are detailed enough to allow a reclassification. Distinctions are made between the following regimes:[15]

1. Pegged to single currency
2. Pegged to basket of currencies
3. Pegged with frequent adjustments (sustained less than six months)
4. Forward-looking crawling pegs (such as the tablitas)
5. Forward-looking crawling bands[16]
6. Backward-looking crawling pegs
7. Backward-looking crawling bands
8. Managed floating
9. Free floating

This classification makes it possible to capture various dimensions related to the exchange rate regime by grouping the different categories in different ways. For the credibility versus competitiveness dimension emphasized in this chapter, these nine categories are placed in the following four groups: fixed (includes pegged to single currency, pegged to basket of currencies, and pegged with frequent adjustments); forward-looking crawling pegs and bands; backward-looking crawling pegs and bands; and flexible (including free and managed floating).[17] Lumping the two floating regimes together is justified since, in emerging markets, even countries classified as independently floating have engaged in a substantial amount of intervention.[18]

Determining how these groups should be ordered on the credibility vs. competitiveness dimension requires looking first at some of the outcomes associated with each of them. The first row of Table 2.2 presents the mean of the real exchange rate for each of these four groups.[19]

---

[15] The regimes were classified month by month. Whenever there were changes, a country's regime in a given year is the one that was in place for a larger portion of that year.

[16] The term "forward-looking" is used for those regimes in which the path of the exchange rate is either preannounced, as in the *tablitas*, or targeted according to desired or expected inflation.

[17] Given the difficulties in classifying the pegged-with-frequent-readjustments regime into one of the four groupings, in some exercises the observations under this regime will be excluded in order to check the robustness of the results.

[18] Calvo and Reinhart (2000) have called this behavior "fear of floating."

[19] The real effective exchange rates calculated by Goldfajn and Valdés (1999) were used.

Table 2.2. Real Exchange Rates and Inflation by Regime

Regime	Fixed	Forward-looking	Backward-looking	Floating
Average real exchange rate	97.4	90.3	109.0	106.0
Average annual depreciation	-1.55%	-6.31%	0.98%	1.39%
Average annual rate of inflation	17.2%	54.4%	50.3%	42.8%

Note: Higher values of real exchange rate indicate more depreciated rates.

To make the comparison meaningful, the real exchange rate in each country was normalized to average 100 throughout the period. The second row presents the average rate of change of the real exchange rate under each group, and the third row presents the average annualized rate of inflation.

Table 2.2 suggests possible orderings of the different groups along the credibility-competitiveness dimension. The fixed and forward-looking regimes have produced, on average, both appreciated and appreciating real exchange rates. The forward-looking pegs and bands are the regimes associated with the most appreciated rate (an average real exchange rate of 90.3), followed by the fixed regimes, with an average of 97.4. Likewise, the forward-looking regimes produce, on average, an annual appreciation of more than 6.3 percent, compared to 1.6 percent in the case of the fixed regimes. The fixed regime, in turn, is associated with the lowest average inflation. This should not be surprising, as the forward-looking regime is usually implemented only when inflation is high enough that a peg would not be sustained.

These two regimes are clearly at the credibility (or anti-inflationary) end of the spectrum. It is not obvious, however, how they should be ordered. On the one hand, the fact that the forward-looking regimes are the ones that tend to deliver the most appreciated and appreciating real exchange rates should not come as a surprise. Countries fix their exchange rates for a variety of reasons, only one of which is to provide a credible and visible target to fight inflation. For example, small and very open economies with low inflation and geographically concentrated trade, such as most Caribbean countries, may choose to fix in order to stabilize exchange rates. In these cases, a fixed exchange rate need not cost the country that adopts it a loss of competitiveness. Forward-looking crawling pegs such as the *tablitas*, however, are unmistakably meant to bring inflation under control, and since the exchange rate is used as a nominal anchor for inflation, this inflation objective comes at the expense of an appreciation of the real exchange rate and loss of international competitiveness. On the other hand, after controlling for the rate of inflation, fixing should deliver lower inflation and faster loss in competitiveness compared to a preannounced crawl. For this reason, this chapter's empirical tests will place the fixed exchange rate first in the ordering, followed by the forward-looking regimes. However, the tests will also check whether the results obtained depend critically on this choice.

At the other extreme of the tradeoff are backward-looking regimes. These are the regimes associated with the most depreciated rate, 109.0, compared to 106.0 for the flexible regimes. The greater rate of depreciation under flexible regimes may occur because these regimes are sometimes implemented immediately after balance of payments crises following an appreciated exchange rate. Backward-looking regimes, on the other hand, are usually put in place when the exchange rate is already depreciated in order to keep its level competitive. A backward-looking crawling peg, adjusting according to the inflation differential, appears to be a more active policy for maintaining competitiveness than flexible regimes.

The appropriate technique when working with multinomial discrete dependent variables, when one has reasons to expect a certain ordering of the groups, is ordered logit or probit. Following the above discussion, most of the empirical tests will make use of a left hand side variable, REGIME, which takes the following values:

0   Fixed (to single currency, basket, or frequent adjustments)
1   Forward-looking crawl and bands
2   Floating (managed or independent)
3   Backward-looking crawl and band.

As discussed above, however, robustness checks are performed to see whether these results change under different specifications of the left hand side variable, such as switching the order of the first two groups, or excluding from the sample the observations associated with fixed regimes with frequent adjustments.

Potential Determinants of Exchange Rate Regimes

Macroeconomic, External and Structural Variables

Inflation generally has an important effect on an exchange rate regime. High inflation makes a peg unsustainable, and even moderate inflation will require frequent readjustments of the peg. Inflation increases the political cost of abandoning a peg and decreases the likelihood of choosing a fixed regime. High inflation should not discourage, however, the adoption of forward-looking crawling pegs, such as *tablitas*. On the contrary, high inflation increases the credibility gains provided by nominal anchors, and forward-looking pegs can provide this nominal anchor function without making the regime unsustainable.

The empirical analysis uses the log of inflation, as the effects are not expected to be linear, and the variable is lagged one period to avert potential endogeneity problems, as the regime can have an effect on contemporaneous inflation.[20] In addition to the log of inflation, a dummy variable (HYPER) is used, which takes a value of 1 when the inflation rate is greater than 1,000 percent. This variable captures the fact that it may be easier to stabilize prices by fixing the exchange rate starting from hyperinflation, as compared with moderate or high inflation. Under hyperinflation, the nominal exchange rate becomes a natural reference for prices, and this makes it easier to stop the inertial component of inflation by pegging the exchange rate. It is expected that, controlling for inflation, hyperinflation will increase the likelihood of adopting a peg.

Another factor that affects the sustainability of fixed exchange rate regimes is the availability of foreign reserves. Lack of reserves increases the probability of adjusting or abandoning the peg, and thus the probability of incurring the political cost of doing so. Rather than the more traditional measure of reserves in terms of months of imports, (RESM2), the ratio of central bank reserves over money supply (M2) is used.[21] Since the effects of reserves are likely to be non-linear, an alternative dummy variable is used (RESERVESD) that takes a value of 1 when the ratio of reserves to M2 is below a critical threshold.[22] A high value of reserves is expected to be associated with fixed regimes, and reserves below the threshold to be associated with more flexible arrangements. Due to possible endogeneity problems, both variables are lagged in the regressions.

---

[20] More precisely, the present tests use the log (1+inflation/100).

[21] Data on reserves and M2 come from the IMF's *International Financial Statistics*.

[22] This threshold is defined as the mean of the ratio minus the standard deviation.

The desirability of fixed exchange rate regimes may also depend on other policies in place. For example, controls on capital flows may increase the sustainability of fixed exchange rates, since it is less likely that inconsistencies between fiscal or monetary policy and exchange rate policy will result in capital outflows and the collapse of the regime. A related point is that capital controls make it possible for countries to fix the exchange rate without sacrificing their monetary policy. For these reasons, fixed exchange rate regimes are expected to be more prevalent in periods when countries have capital controls.

Two different measures of capital controls were used in the econometric tests. The first is a dummy that indicates the existence of restrictions on capital account transactions. The second is a variable that adds together four dummy variables, each representing the existence of 1) restrictions on capital account transactions; 2) restrictions on current account transactions; 3) multiple exchange rates; and 4) surrender of export proceeds. The original source for the capital controls data is the IMF's *Exchange Arrangements and Exchange Restrictions*.[23] As will be discussed in more detail below, this dataset has serious shortcomings, in that it provides information only on the existence of controls, rather than on the severity of the controls. Since 1996, the IMF has been publishing much more detailed data on capital account restrictions, which takes into account a large variety of dimensions. Unfortunately, this dataset is not available for the period under study.

For several reasons, it is expected that more open economies will tend to adopt fixed exchange rates. First, the more open the economy, the larger the potential cost of exchange rate volatility. Second, in more open economies, domestic monetary shocks are more easily channeled abroad, so there is less need for an autonomous monetary policy. Third, in more open economies, the law of one price is more likely to operate. In this context of more flexible prices, one of the advantages of floating exchange rates—that they allow changes in real exchange rates when prices are sticky—fades away. Fourth, commitment to fixed exchange rates may become more credible in open economies since, in a context of flexible prices, governments will be less able to engineer a real devaluation through a nominal devaluation. In other words, devaluations become less effective as a means of achieving internal or external balance, and so the temptation to devalue becomes weaker. The empirical analysis includes an indicator of openness, measured as imports plus exports as a share of GDP, and it is expected to have a negative sign.[24]

---

[23] The authors are grateful to Gian Maria Milesi Ferreti for making this data available in electronic form.

[24] The data comes from the Economic and Social Database of the Inter-American Development Bank.

It is further expected that countries that are subject to significant external shocks will be more likely to adopt more flexible regimes. To measure the importance of external shocks the tests use the coefficient of variation of the terms of trade for the whole period (TOT VOLATILITY). The lack of monthly terms of trade data prevented construction of a variable for terms of trade volatility that can change in response to changes over an extended period of time in a country's structure of imports and exports. The effects of the terms of trade shocks should be more severe for more open economies. For this reason, the measure of terms of trade volatility interacted with openness is also considered.[25]

Collins (1996) introduced a time trend into her empirical analysis to capture what she called the "climate of ideas" regarding the appropriate exchange rate regimes for small open economies. A possible drawback of this measure is that it assumes a linear trend in the climate of ideas. As an alternative, this chapter presents a different variable, VIEWS, which measures the percentage of countries in the world under fixed exchange rate regimes. The data for the construction of this variable comes from Goldfajn and Valdés (1999). However, the correlation between the VIEWS variable and the time trend turned out to be extremely high (-0.96). For this reason, the empirical analysis that follows presents only the results using the time trend.

Institutional Variables

An institutional variable that could have an effect on the exchange rate regime is the degree of central bank independence. However, it is not clear in which direction central bank independence should affect the regime. In countries where the central bank is in charge of exchange rate policy, an independent central bank that pursues price stability may be more prone to tie its own hands by adopting a fixed exchange rate regime. On the other hand, central bank independence may be seen as an alternative to a peg as a means to provide credibility.[26] As a measure of central bank indepen-

---

[25] Notice that the variation within countries of this interactive term comes solely from variations in openness. The volatility of terms of trade was measured for the whole period in each country. This would only be a problem for those countries that significantly altered the composition of their trade during the period under consideration.

[26] Even if one did find that central bank independence is associated with fixed regimes, one should be cautious in the interpretation of these results. Both variables could in fact be explained by a third factor, which is not easy to capture in a model: society's aversion to inflation. Posen (1995) has made exactly this point in questioning the importance of central bank independence as a determinant of the rate of inflation.

dence, this chapter uses the index of legal independence developed by Cukierman (1992), which includes criteria such as appointment, dismissal and terms of office of the governor, central bank objectives, and the limitations on the bank's ability to lend to the public sector. One problem in using this variable is that it is available only for half of the countries in the sample.

Interest Group Variables

This chapter also explores the impact of sectoral interest groups, an issue that has been overlooked in previous studies. This neglect is probably due to the difficulty associated with understanding the preferences of different interest groups, and finding good variables to capture the influence that these groups may have on policymakers. In addition, it is often believed that exchange rate policy has broad effects on the population, rather than specific effects on different groups. In contrast, trade policy has long been recognized as having important distributional effects. Even though the role of interest groups may be stronger in trade policy, the hypothesis here—which is supported by evidence in the chapters on Peru and Colombia—is that different groups have very different preferences regarding exchange rate policy, and that these preferences can play a role in the choice of regime. In addition, as countries advance in the process of trade liberalization, this role in choosing the exchange rate regime becomes more fundamental. While an array of subsidies and specific tariffs are available to compensate those who are hurt by the exchange rate policy in place, special interest groups tend to concentrate their demands on these specific measures. However, as liberalization makes these compensatory mechanisms less available, these groups become vocal about exchange rate policy.

It stands to reason that tradables producers should favor a regime that avoids a real appreciation. This should be true both of producers of goods for export, whose (domestic currency) earnings are higher the weaker the exchange rate, and of import-competers. However, there are many potential complications to this simple expectation. One has to do with the price of inputs: firms that use a high proportion of tradables in general, and imports in particular, get less benefit from a depreciation. Many mining firms, for example, use extremely high shares of imported inputs and may be indifferent to the exchange rate. Similarly, some firms or sectors may care less about the exchange rate to the extent that they have international market power and/or the demand for their product is inelastic. The most important (and perhaps only) Latin American example is that of coffee growers during the period when the International

Coffee Agreement was in force. For them, the principal decision variable was the world price of coffee.

Perhaps the most important peculiarity in trying to examine sectoral interests in Latin American currency policy is the role of trade policy, and especially the very high levels of trade protection prevailing in most of the region until the middle 1980s. Where trade barriers to finished manufactured goods were prohibitive, as they were in much of the region from the 1940s until the 1980s, many manufacturers were essentially in nontradable production. They were relatively indifferent to the impact of the exchange rate on their output prices, as they were sheltered by trade barriers. Some of them even preferred a strong (appreciated) real exchange rate, which made imported inputs—machinery, intermediates, raw materials, spare parts and borrowing—cheaper in local currency terms.

The empirical tests include three different variables representing different tradables sectors: agriculture, manufacturing and mining. In light of the discussion above, one would expect the agricultural sector to favor pro-competitiveness regimes (i.e., enter the regressions with a positive sign); the mining sector to be indifferent; and the manufacturing sector to support more flexible regimes when trade is liberalized and to be indifferent when operating in highly protected markets. For lack of a better indicator of the lobbying power of each group, it is simply assumed that each sector's influence on policymakers is proportional to its share in the country's GDP. Due to concerns about endogeneity (for example, there may be a shift to nontradables production under an appreciated exchange rate), these variables (AGRIL, MININGL and MANUFL) are lagged one period.

A separate set of regressions explores changes in preferences as trade becomes liberalized. A dummy variable (LOWTARIFF) is constructed to pick up cases of liberalized trade. The construction of this variable, though, confronted the problem of the lack of good databases on tariffs and other barriers with the coverage needed in terms of countries and years. It was possible to gather data from different sources on average tariffs for 21 of the 26 countries in the sample. However, in most cases data starts only in 1985, and in the best cases in 1980.[27] The criterion used in this instance was to assign a value of 1 to cases where the average tariff was lower than 20 percent. The choice of this threshold took into account the fact that during the import-substitution industrialization period, tariffs for final goods were

---

[27] Data on average tariffs was provided by Alan Winters of the World Bank Trade Division and by Antoni Estevadeordal of the Integration Division of the Inter-American Development Bank.

much higher than those for intermediate inputs and capital goods. An average tariff of 20 percent generally implies a higher tariff for final goods, and an even higher effective rate of protection. For those years where data were not available, the series was completed using information on dates of trade reform in Edwards (1994), and on the basis of the authors' knowledge of the countries. It is expected that LOWTARIFF will have a positive sign, indicating that pressures for a competitive exchange rate are greater when barriers to trade are small.

If the manufacturing sector's changes regarding the exchange rate regime in fact depended on the degree of protection, the share of manufactures in GDP would be expected to have a larger impact when trade is liberalized. This hypothesis is tested by interacting the LOWTARIFF dummy with a measure of the importance of manufacturing, expecting the coefficient for the interactive term to be positive—i.e., in more liberal, low trade barrier periods, manufacturers would support exchange rate policies associated with greater attention to competitiveness—and the coefficient for MANUFL to be insignificant, indicating indifference about the regime during highly protected periods.

It would have been desirable to include a variable that captured the degree of liability dollarization in the economy. Presumably, individuals and firms with dollar liabilities would be more supportive of fixed exchange rate regimes, since devaluations may hurt them considerably. Unfortunately, it was not possible to find a good measure of dollar liabilities.[28]

Political Variables

Two variables were constructed using data on the composition of the legislature obtained from Nohlen (1993): the share of government seats in the legislature (GOVSEATS), and the effective number of parties in the legislature (EFPART).[29] GOVSEATS is expected to have a negative sign for two

---

[28] The tests included proxying dollar liabilities with the ratio of foreign liabilities of deposit money banks (lines 26c+26cl of the IFS) over quasi-money (line 35 of the IFS). This was expected to be a reasonable measure of the share of deposits denominated in foreign currency, which in turn could be a good proxy for dollar liabilities. However, in some countries this ratio was often greater than 1. In any case, the variable was not significant when included in the regressions.

[29] One problem with GOVSEATS is that there is not always complete information available regarding the coalitions in Congress. Where coalitions were known, the share corresponding to them was counted, as was that of the party of the president. This continuous variable is preferable to simply recording whether the government has a majority in the legislature, since it captures the substantial difference between respective shares of either 5 or 35 in terms of the government's ability to pass key legislation, particularly when the opposition is fairly fragmented. A majority variable was also used in the regressions, with fairly similar results.

reasons, both associated with the political cost of devaluing or abandoning a *tablita*. First, a higher share of seats means that the government faces less political competition, so a readjustment may be less costly. In addition, a stronger government may be in a better position to implement the necessary measures to prevent an exchange rate adjustment. This last idea is consistent with the findings of the literature on the political economy of fiscal policy, which suggests that stronger governments are associated with lower deficits.[30]

The effective number of parties is generally used to measure the fragmentation of the party system.[31] There is no clear prior of how this variable on its own would affect exchange rate policy, except for the fact that where fragmentation is greater, the government will probably have a smaller share of seats in the legislature.[32] As an indicator of the strength of government, the share of government seats is obviously much better. However, the effective number of parties has a simple interpretation once the share of government seats is accounted for: it measures the fragmentation of the opposition. Therefore, the effective number of parties in the legislature is expected to have an effect similar to that of the share of government seats. A weaker and more fragmented opposition diminishes the political cost of a devaluation and at the same time makes it easier for the government to achieve a winning coalition in support of the adjustment programs necessary to sustain a peg. The effective number of parties is expected to be more important whenever the government does not control a majority of seats. For this reason, EFPART is interacted with MINORITY, a dummy that takes a value of 1 when GOVSEATS<50%, in order to be able to test this conjecture.

Also included is a measure of political instability (POLINS), based on the number of government changes per year, as well as the occurrence of coups. The POLINS variable is a dummy that takes a value of 1 if a country has gone through three or more government changes in the last five years, or if it has gone through two or more government changes in the last three years.[33] It also takes a value of 1 in years in which there

---

[30] See Grilli, Masciandaro and Tabellini (1991) and Roubini and Sachs (1989).

[31] The effective number of parties is defined as EFPART $= 1/\sum_i s_i^2$, where s_i is the proportion of representatives party $_i$ has in the lower (or single) house.

[32] These two variables are in fact highly and negatively correlated.

[33] As an exception, countries are coded as politically stable if they are in the fourth year of a government, even if they have had three government changes in the past five years. For example, if a country had three government changes in 1970, and then had the same government for four years, it would be coded as politically unstable from 1970 through 1972, but stable in 1973.

were successful coups, and in the first year following a successful coup.[34] More unstable political systems have been associated with larger government deficits, which would suggest a positive coefficient, indicating that more unstable systems will make it more difficult for the government to sustain a peg. On the other hand, governments in unstable situations tend to have a higher discount rate and therefore may not care as much about the long-term sustainability of the policies they follow. This may make it more likely for them to choose fixed regimes (see Edwards, 1996).

Finally, a dummy is included for dictatorship (DICT) based on the variable "democracy" from the Polity III database.[35] The expected sign of this variable is not clear. On the one hand, dictatorships could be more prone to choose fixed regimes, as the political cost of devaluing should be smaller for de facto governments. In addition, they tend to be strong governments and may find it easier to impose adjustment measures needed to sustain a fix. On the other hand, dictatorships tend to be comparatively more attuned to interest groups, from whom they derive rents, and less to the population at large, as they do not need to buy their votes.

Table 2.3 presents descriptive statistics for each of the explanatory variables. Table 2.4 presents the means of these variables for each of the four groups of exchange rate regimes, as previously defined.

Empirical Results

The results of the ordered logit regressions are presented in Tables 2.5 through 2.7. Table 2.5 begins by using only macroeconomic/external/structural variables as regressors. Institutional, interest group and political variables are then introduced. The regressions in Table 2.6 explore the impact of trade liberalization in more detail. Finally, Table 2.7 presents some sensitivity analysis.

---

[34] Data on government changes and coups was taken from Nohlen's *Enciclopedia Electoral Latinoamericana* (1992), and complemented for recent years by Zárate's database on political leaders, http://www.terra.es/personal2/monolith. Although other databases on government changes and coups exist, they did not have the desired coverage and were plagued by inaccuracies.

[35] The Polity III democracy variable is an index that takes values from 0 to 10, and captures the competitiveness of political participation, the openness and competitiveness of executive recruitment, and the existence of constraints on the power of the executive. Here, the dummy DICT is used, which takes a value of 1 when the index of democracy is 3 or below.

Table 2.3. Summary Statistics of Explanatory Variables

Variable	No. of obsv.	Mean	Standard deviation	Minimum	Maximum
Log inflation	812	0.248	0.537	-0.1216	4.775
Hyper	837	0.016	0.128	0	1
Open	836	0.637	0.405	0.083	2.498
Views	910	0.715	0.230	0.391	0.992
Capital controls 1	721	0.717	0.450	0	1
Capital controls 2	720	2.512	1.293	0	4
Reserves/m2	860	0.242	0.205	0.00042	1.552
Reserves dummy	860	0.059	0.236	0	1
TOT volatility	805	0.133	0.080	0.030	0.418
Manufl	815	0.183	0.057	0.069	0.321
Agrl	793	0.168	0.093	0.018	0.469
Minl	734	0.062	0.072	0.00047	0.331
Low tariff	645	0.184	0.388	0	1
Polins	907	0.196	0.397	0	1
Dict	745	0.474	0.500	0	1
Efpart	646	2.454	1.296	1	8.68
Govseats	647	0.597	0.197	0.039	1

The main results of Table 2.5 can be summarized as follows:

Macroeconomic/external/structural factors: The log of inflation (lagged) is never significant as a determinant of the exchange rate regime, probably reflecting two conflicting effects: while high inflation makes credibility more desirable, it reduces the sustainability of fixed exchange rates. The hyperinflation dummy is significant in all of the regressions and has a negative sign. This is consistent with the view that it is easier to get out of hyperinflation by providing a nominal anchor than it is to stabilize prices in this way under moderate or high inflation, as during hyperinflation the nominal exchange rate becomes a natural reference point for prices. The coefficient for openness was also negative and significant in all the regressions, indicating that more open economies, as expected, are more likely to adopt fixed exchange regimes.

Surprisingly, the coefficient for the reserves/M2 ratio was marginally significant but had a positive sign. Thus, the prior that countries with low reserve ratios would be less prone to fix due to sustainability issues was not confirmed by the data. This result was highly robust to a variety of definitions for the reserves variable. For example, the contemporaneous reserves ratio was used in place of the lagged one, as well as a

Table 2.4. Summary Statistics: Means of Explanatory Variables under Different Exchange Rate Regimes

Variable	Fixed	Forward-looking	Flexible	Backward-looking
Log inflation	0.162	0.639	0.535	0.436
Hyper	0.0095	0.069	0.043	0.023
Open	0.699	0.476	0.550	0.380
Views	0.772	0.494	0.506	0.577
Capital controls 1	0.693	0.620	0.631	0.940
Capital controls 2	2.354	2.310	2.190	3.656
Reserves/m2	0.225	0.220	0.271	0.333
Reserves dummy	0.065	0.000	0.045	0.051
TOT volatility	0.135	0.168	0.141	0.103
Manufl	0.172	0.219	0.199	0.225
Agrl	0.176	0.118	0.149	0.153
Minl	0.067	0.066	0.052	0.042
Low tariff	0.060	0.517	0.586	0.272
Polins	0.227	0.000	0.159	0.070
Dict	0.534	0.482	0.215	0.391
Efpart	2.304	3.754	3.324	2.285
Govseats	0.633	0.448	0.447	0.557

dummy that takes a value of 1 when the ratio of reserves to M2 is below a certain threshold, defined as the sample mean of the ratio minus the standard deviation. Both cases produced similar results. The explanation for this apparent puzzle is that emerging countries tend to keep large stocks of reserves, even when formally floating their exchange rates.[36]

Perhaps even more puzzling is the effect of the volatility of the terms of trade. Countries subject to strong external shocks were expected to prefer more flexible regimes, yet the coefficient came out negative and significant. There are, however, some concerns about the measurement of this volatility. The variable used adopts the same value for the whole period in each country, ignoring the fact that many countries have substantially altered the composition of exports and imports during the sample period. Similar results were obtained by using the interaction of the coefficient of variation of terms of trade and openness in place of volatility.

---

[36] This behavior, which has been documented by Calvo and Reinhart (2000) and by Hausmann, Panizza and Stein (2000), has prompted Calvo to say that emerging countries that float do so "with a lifejacket."

Table 2.5. Ordered Logit Regressions for REGIME with Economic, Institutional, Sectoral and Political Factors

	(1)	(2)	(3)	(4)	(5)	(6)
Log inflation	0.079	0.022	0.13	-0.052	-0.11	-0.12
	(0.44)	(0.08)	(0.63)	(-0.26)	(-0.48)	(-0.52)
Hyper	-1.47	-2.59	-1.78	-1.57	-1.79	-1.80
	(-2.22)	(-2.50)	(-2.56)	(-2.24)	(-2.38)	(-2.39)
Open	-2.43	-6.68	-2.37	-2.76	-3.49	-3.44
	(-5.29)	(-6.37)	(-4.90)	(-5.42)	(-5.95)	(-5.84)
Reserves/m2	0.73					
	(1.78)					
TOT volatility	-4.06					
	(-1.97)					
Capital controls1	0.21					
	(0.92)					
CBI		1.67				
		(0.77)				
Manufl			10.96	8.28	11.95	12.42
			(3.87)	(3.65)	(4.20)	(4.30)
Agrl			0.0057			
			(0.004)			
Minl			1.28			
			(0.61)			
Polins				-1.10		-0.92
				(-3.39)		(-1.97)
Govseats					-2.58	-3.06
					(-2.77)	(-3.04)
Efpart					-0.29	-0.098
					(-2.31)	(-0.57)
Efpart * Minority						-0.19
						(-1.61)
Dict				-0.49	-1.07	
				(-2.15)	(-2.29)	
Trend	Yes	Yes	Yes	Yes	Yes	Yes
N	616	323	679	670	562	562

Notes: A positive sign means that the variable increases the probability of adopting "pro-competitiveness" regimes. z-statistics in parentheses.

The dummy for the restrictions on capital account transactions, included in the first regression of Table 2.5, was not significant, while the composite capital controls variable (not shown) was positive and significant. This result is also surprising, as fixed exchange rate regimes were expected to be more likely when restrictions on the capital account were present. This result is very likely due to the important shortcomings of the capital controls dataset. As discussed above, this dataset provides information on the existence of controls, rather than the severity or the nature of the controls. Careful examination of the dataset revealed that, contrary to what was expected, capital controls in the world, according to this measure, have not had a declining trend, and, in the case of Latin America, they have increased over time. This casts serious doubts on the quality of the capital controls data. In fact, since 1996 the IMF has published much more detailed data on capital account restrictions, which take into account a large variety of dimensions. Unfortunately, this dataset is not available for the period under study.[37] In addition to the variables discussed above, all regressions in Table 2.5 include a time dummy, which was positive and highly significant.

Institutional factors: The coefficient for central bank independence, measured by the legal index of independence (which is included in regression 2 in Table 2.5) had a positive sign, suggesting that CBI is to some extent a substitute for a fixed exchange rate as a way to provide credibility. The coefficient, however, was not significant.

Interest group factors: Column 3 presents the regression where all three tradables sectors are included. As expected, the share of mining in GDP was not significant, since mining generally is a highly capital-intensive activity with a large proportion of imported inputs. Contrary to the priors, the share of agriculture in GDP did not have a significant effect on the choice of regime either. One possible explanation is that the share in GDP is an imperfect indicator of the lobbying power of this sector, more so than in the other sectors studied. This could be due to the important heterogeneity found across countries in terms of the composition of the agricultural sector. While in some countries this sector is composed mainly of very small farms, whose owners are not organized as a group, in others the sector is highly concentrated, and the landown-

---

[37] Miniane (2000) has extended the new IMF methodology backwards, and his more disaggregated capital control indices now cover the period 1983-98. Unfortunately, the coverage of Latin American countries in his sample is somewhat limited. Although his results are preliminary, his indices show a clear downward trend in capital account restrictions, a result that is consistent with the priors.

ers are a strong class with important influence on government policy. The immobile character of land may be another factor that limits the leverage of this sector. The coefficient corresponding to the share of manufacturing in GDP, in contrast, was positive and significant, a result that is robust to a variety of specifications. Thus, economies with a larger share of manufacturing tended to choose more flexible, pro-competitiveness regimes. As will be discussed in more detail below, this result is even stronger during periods of liberalized trade.

Political factors: These are introduced in regressions 4 through 6 in Table 2.5. Column 4 introduces the political instability dummy, as well as the dictatorship dummy. The dictatorship dummy has a negative and significant coefficient, suggesting that authoritarian governments tend to rely more heavily on regimes that cater to the anti-inflation objective, even after controlling for the rate of inflation.[38] It is important to note that a time trend is included in the regression, so this result is not simply explained by the coinciding trends toward more democracy and more backward-looking and flexible exchange rate regimes. Political instability also seems to increase the likelihood of adopting fixed exchange rate regimes.[39]

Column 5 introduces the share of government seats in the legislature, as well as the effective number of parties. Both variables have negative and significant coefficients. This confirms the priors that strong governments tend to fix, as do governments with a weak opposition. Our interpretation is that government strength relative to the opposition diminishes the political cost associated with devaluation, and at the same time makes the need for a devaluation less likely, as it is easier for the government to achieve a winning coalition in support of the necessary adjustment programs.

Column 6 provides further support for this interpretation. In addition to the effective number of parties, this regression included an interactive term of the effective number of parties, with a slope dummy which takes a value of 1 when the government does not have majority in Congress, and 0 otherwise. Although the coefficients for the number of parties and the interactive term are not significant by themselves, a

---

[38] Similar results were obtained when the Polity III democracy index was used instead of the dictatorship dummy.

[39] This result contrasts to that in Edwards (1996), who finds that political instability reduces the likelihood of adopting pegs. In his work, Edwards used political instability measures (such as government changes and government transfers) for the 1970s to explain the exchange rate regimes of the 1980s and early 1990s. This variable more accurately captures the existence of the type of political instability that would matter for the adoption of an exchange rate regime.

test of the hypothesis that the sum of the coefficients is 0 is rejected at the 5 percent significance level, indicating that EFPART was significant when the government did not have a majority of seats in the legislature, but not otherwise. This suggests that the weakness of the opposition is particularly important when the government does not have a majority of legislative seats, but is not crucial when it does.

It should be noted that the dictatorship variable is not included together with the variables based on the composition of the legislature. The reason is that in a very significant portion of the observations classified as dictatorships (index of democracy smaller than or equal to three), there is no data for the composition of the legislatures because in most cases there *is* no legislature.[40]

Role of Trade Liberalization

Table 2.6 explores the role of trade liberalization in the choice of exchange rate regime. Column 1 adds the trade liberalization dummy to the specification shown in column 5 of the preceding table.[41] The coefficient for this dummy is positive and significant. This is consistent with the hypothesis that pressures for a competitive exchange rate, and for a regime that delivers it, are smaller during periods when trade barriers are very high. This result is also consistent with anecdotal evidence from other countries.[42] The third column incorporates, in addition to the low tariff dummy, an interaction term of low tariffs and the share of manufacturing in GDP. Neither of the coefficients is significant. Columns 2 and 4 present regressions similar to those in columns 1 and 3 but exclude the time trend, which is very highly correlated with the trade liberalization dummy.[43] When the time trend is excluded, both the liberalization dummy and the interactive term become significant. Therefore, the result that trade liberalization matters for the choice of regime is even stronger when the time trend is excluded from the regressions.

---

[40] When all four political variables were included together, the dictatorship variable lost significance, and the political instability variable became only marginally significant. None of the other results changed.

[41] The specification that includes the dictatorship dummy and not the political variables based on the composition of the legislature was used, since the combination of these last variables and the trade liberalization dummy together reduce the size of the sample to less than half of the total observations.

[42] See the chapter on Colombia.

[43] The correlation coefficient between these two variables is 0.58. It is likely that at least part of the time effect is explained by the move toward trade liberalization in the region.

Table 2.6. Impact of Trade Liberalization
(Ordered logit regressions. Dependent variable: REGIME)

	(1)	(2)	(3)	(4)
Log inflation	-0.079	0.25	-0.043	0.31
	(-0.41)	(1.35)	(0.22)	(1.68)
Hyper	-1.30	-1.04	-1.37	-1.16
	(-1.89)	(-1.50)	(-1.96)	(-1.65)
Open	-2.83	-1.83	-2.83	-1.88
	(-5.36)	(-3.99)	(-5.36)	(-4.05)
Manufl	5.27	5.29	4.93	4.65
	(2.08)	(2.23)	(1.93)	(1.94)
Manufl*Low tariff			1.55	3.89
			(0.72)	(1.82)
Low tariff	0.52	1.75	0.29	1.13
	(1.97)	(8.14)	(0.69)	(2.75)
Polins	-1.11	-1.28	-1.13	-1.29
	(-3.17)	(-3.77)	(-3.22)	(-3.81)
Dict	-0.47	-0.81	-0.47	-1.81
	(-2.00)	(-3.70)	(-1.99)	(-3.67)
Trend	Yes	No	Yes	No
N	552	552	551	551

Note: z-statistics in parentheses.

Sensitivity Analysis

Table 2.7 explores whether the main results are robust to different definitions of the left-hand side variable, as well as to different sample periods. Column 1 simply reproduces regression 5 in Table 2.5. The second column excludes observations prior to 1973 so as to see whether the results change if the Bretton Woods years are excluded. During those years, more than 90 percent of the observations correspond to the fixed exchange rate regime (see Table 2.1). All the variables included, with the exception of the log of inflation, are significant. The next subsection will use this regression in order to interpret the economic significance of the explanatory variables. Columns 3 and 4 test the robustness to small changes in the specification of the regime variable. Column 3 excludes the observations in which the arrangement was fixed but with frequent adjustments. The reason is that it is not obvious in which grouping one should include this arrangement. Results are very similar to those in column 1, with the single exception of political instability, which loses significance.

Table 2.7. Sensitivity Analysis (Ordered logit regressions. Dependent variable: different definitions of regime)

	(1) REGIME	(2) REGIME (1973-1994)	(3) REGIME2 (Excluding adjustable pegs)	(4) REGIME3 (forward-looking before fixed)
Log inflation	0.11 (-0.48)	-0.009 (-0.04)	-0.19 (-0.83)	0.16 (0.82)
Hyper	-1.79 (-2.38)	-1.98 (-2.54)	-1.47 (-1.86)	-1.86 (-2.32)
Open	-3.49 (-5.95)	-3.46 (-5.63)	-3.56 (-6.08)	-1.17 (-3.69)
Manufl	11.96 (4.20)	11.12 (3.50)	13.51 (4.62)	8.54 (3.64)
Polins	-0.91 (-1.98)	-1.38 (-2.59)	-0.75 (-1.59)	-0.30 (-0.90)
Govseats	-2.58 (-2.77)	-1.88 (-1.87)	-3.06 (-3.23)	-2.01 (-2.64)
Efpart	-0.30 (-2.31)	-0.26 (-1.99)	-0.37 (-2.53)	-0.23 (-2.10)
Trend	Yes	Yes	Yes	Yes
N	562	380	538	562

Note: z-statistics in parentheses.

Column 4 inverts the order of the dependent variable. As discussed above, there are arguments in favor of placing the fixed variable at the beginning of the order, as done throughout the chapter. But there are also arguments that would suggest placing the preannounced crawling pegs and bands at the beginning of the order. In particular, countries may fix for different reasons, but they only adopt preannounced crawls in order to reduce the rate of inflation, even at the expense of competitiveness. For this reason, column 4 orders the regimes in the following way: 1) forward-looking (or preannounced) crawling pegs and bands; 2) fixed; 3) flexible; and 4) backward-looking crawling pegs and bands.[44] As in the previous regression, the only change is that political instability loses significance.

---

[44] It is worth noting that, since the dependent variable is ordinal rather than cardinal, this does not imply important changes, given the scarcity of observations in the forward-looking grouping. There are only 29 observations in this grouping out of a total of 910.

In summary, Table 2.7 suggests that the results are quite robust to changes in the specification of the model.

Economic Interpretation of the Results

While the tables presented above show the statistical significance of the variables of interest, they do not express the economic significance of these variables. In order to explore their economic significance under the ordered logit model, more calculations are needed. This contrasts with OLS models, in which the impact of the different explanatory variables can be directly seen from the size of the coefficients. This section provides the economic interpretation for one of the regressions shown above: the second column of Table 2.7, which excludes the Bretton Woods years, a period when there is very little variation regarding the exchange rate regime.

The exercise carried out is the following: for each non-dummy variable, the change in the probability of each regime is calculated when the variable of interest increases by one standard deviation, centered on the mean, and all the other variables remain at their means. For the dummy variables, the change in the probabilities is calculated when the dummy goes from 0 to 1.[45] The results of the calculations are presented in Table 2.8.

The first column in the table presents the changes in the probability of each regime when the log inflation variable changes by one standard deviation around its mean.[46] This change of one standard deviation around the mean is equivalent to an increase in inflation from around 2 percent to 90 percent. Consistent with the results of the regressions, the effect of this variable on the probability of the different regimes is minimal. In contrast, hyperinflation has a large effect on the probabilities. Having inflation greater than 1,000 percent increases the probability of adopting a fixed exchange rate regime by nearly 21 percentage points. Openness also has important effects. A change in openness from 47 to 86 percent (representing a one standard deviation increase, centered on the mean) increases the probability of adopting a fixed exchange rate regime by 25 percentage points.

The effect of the share of manufacturing in GDP is quite substantial as well. A 5.5 percentage point increase in the share of manufacturing, centered on its mean, reduces the probability of a fixed regime by 11 percentage points. This means that each percentage point increase in the share

---

[45] While the marginal effects are often used to interpret the effects of explanatory variables in the logit models, Long (1997) argues in favor of looking at the impact of discrete changes instead, given that the effects are non-linear.

[46] The mean and standard deviations correspond to the 1973-94 period.

Table 2.8. Economic Interpretation: Change in the Probability of the Different Exchange Rate Regimes in Response to Changes in Explanatory Variables (Using regression 2, Table 2.7)

	Log inflation	hyper	open	manufl	polins	govseats	efpart
Mean of variable	0.336363	0.0254	0.66505	0.1857	0.1503	0.595	2.4429
Change in variable[1]	0.629907	1	0.3968	0.0553	1	0.2009	1.3122
Δp(fixed)	0.0012	0.2076	0.2503	-0.1129	0.1928	0.0695	0.0632
Δp(forward-looking)	-0.0002	-0.0487	-0.0437	0.0209	-0.0416	-0.0129	-0.0118
Δp(flexible)	-0.0006	-0.1016	-0.1200	0.0547	-0.0942	-0.0337	-0.0307
Δp(backward-looking)	-0.0004	-0.0574	-0.0866	0.0373	-0.0571	-0.0228	-0.0207

[1]The magnitude of the change in the explanatory variable is one standard deviation around the mean, in the case of the non-dummy variables, and 1 in the case of dummy variables.

of manufacturing in GDP reduces the probability of fixing by around two percentage points. As will be seen below, the effect of the share of manufacturing has changed substantially across time, in line with the predictions above regarding the impact of trade liberalization. Political instability increases the probability of fixing by 19 percentage points, while an increase of one standard deviation in the share of government seats in the legislature, and the effective number of parties, increase the probability of a fixed regime by 7 and 6 percentage points, respectively.

Since these effects are non-linear, and vary depending on the value of the explanatory variables at which they are measured, it is worthwhile to look at some of them in more detail. Particular attention will be paid to the effects of the manufacturing share, the share of government seats in the legislature, and the effective number of parties. It is worthwhile to further explore the differential impact that the share of manufacturing can have under highly protected trade policy and liberalized trade conditions. The probabilities of each regime are therefore presented as a function of the share of manufacturing for 1975 and 1992. In 1975, all countries for which data were available were highly protectionist. In 1992, almost all countries in the sample had liberalized their trade flows substantially. Comparing Figures 2.1 and 2.2, which show the cumulative

Figure 2.1. Effect of Share in Manufacturing on Regime Choice, 1975

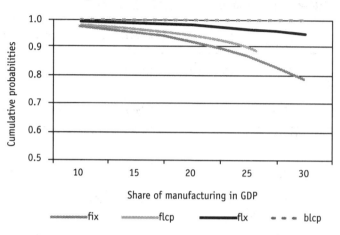

Share of manufacturing in GDP

fix   flcp   flx   ••• blcp

Figure 2.2. Effect of Share in Manufacturing on Regime Choice, 1992

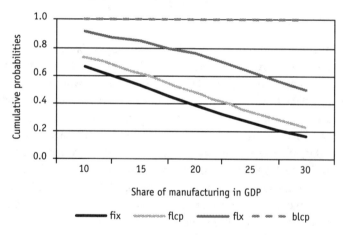

Share of manufacturing in GDP

fix   flcp   flx   ••• blcp

probabilities for the different regimes, it is easy to see that the effects of the manufacturing share on regime choice are much larger during periods of liberalization. For example, a change in the share of manufacturing from 15 percent to 25 percent in 1975 would have been associated with a reduction in the probability of choosing a fixed regime of around 8.5 percentage points. In contrast, in 1992, a similar change would have led to a reduction in the probability of adopting a fixed regime of nearly 25.8

Figure 2.3. Effect of Share of Government Seats on Regime Choice

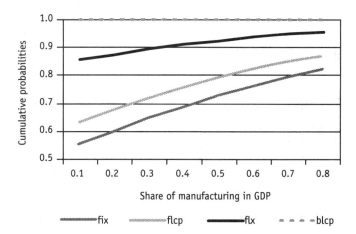

Share of manufacturing in GDP

percentage points. Similarly, the probability of adopting a backward-looking crawl would have increased by 2 and 21 percentage points in 1975 and 1992, respectively.

The effect of changes in the share of government seats on the probability of the different regimes is shown in Figure 2.3. The probability of a fixed regime increases with the share of government seats. Furthermore, while there are non-linearities in the effects, these do not seem to be that important. For example, an increase of one standard deviation (equivalent to 20 percentage points) in the share of government seats starting from 10 percent increases the probability of a fixed regime by 9 percentage points, while a similar increase starting from 60 percent raises the probability of a fixed regime by 6.2 percentage points.

Figures 2.4 and 2.5 show the effects of the number of parties on the choice of regime. As discussed above, the strength of the opposition could be an important variable when the government does not control the legislature, since it may be easier to form coalitions when different small groups are competing for the perks that may be involved in forming an alliance with the government. However, this variable is not expected to be as important when the government already has control of the legislature. This hypothesis has already been explored in the first set of regressions, but in that case no information was obtained about the magnitude of the effects. Figure 2.4 shows the impact of the effective number of parties when the share of government seats in the legislature is 30 percent, while Figure 2.5 shows the same when the share of government

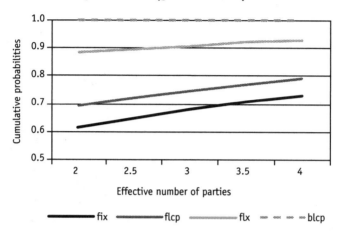

Figure 2.4. Effect of Effective Number of Parties on Regime Choice (govseats=0.30)

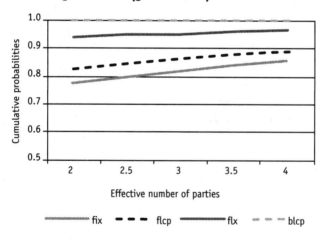

Figure 2.5. Effect of Effective Number of Parties on Regime Choice (govseats=0.7)

seats is 70 percent. Comparing both figures reveals that the effects are larger when the government does not control the legislature. In this case, for example, an increase from two to three parties results in an increase in the probability of a fixed regime of 6 percentage points. By comparison, when the government controls 70 percent of the seats, a similar increase in EFPART results in an increase in the probability of a fixed regime of 4.3 percentage points. This complements the results of the last regression in

Table 2.5, which suggested that the effective number of parties is not significantly different from 0 when the government controls the legislature, but is significant when it does not.

Elections, Changes in Government, and the Timing of Devaluations[47]

In addition to the more structural variables that can affect the choice of regime, the timing of shifts in exchange rate policy may also be affected by the timing of political events such as elections and changes in government. If there is in fact a political cost associated with devaluation, as suggested by Cooper (1971), at no time should that cost be more salient than before elections. The run-up to an election is the time when the gap between the politician's discount rate and that of the public is at its peak. Governments may be willing to let the economy incur large costs in the long term (here the long term starts immediately after the election, or, at most, after the change in government) in exchange for (real or apparent) benefits in the short run. In contrast, at no time should the political cost of devaluation be smaller than immediately after the transfer of government, as the incoming government can blame the outgoing one for making the devaluation necessary.

This has led to many episodes of electorally motivated delays in devaluations, including the Cruzado Plan in Brazil in 1986, the failed Primavera Plan in Argentina in 1989, and the 1994 Mexican Peso crisis. Under the Cruzado Plan, the exchange rate peg gave rise to mounting current account deficits. But "in the best Brazilian political tradition," according to Cardoso (1991), corrective actions were put on hold until right after the legislative elections. The main element of the Primavera Plan in Argentina was the reduction of the rate of crawl in an attempt to moderate inflation in the run-up to the 1989 presidential elections (Heymann, 1991). However, a speculative attack led to a sharp devaluation that ended the stabilization attempt before the elections, with disastrous electoral results for the ruling party. Regarding the Mexican experience in 1994, Obstfeld and Rogoff (1995) have noted that the skepticism over exchange rate commitments prevailing at the time was compounded by the government's previous track record of devaluing in presidential election years.[48]

---

[47] This section draws on Stein and Streb (1999).

Why are devaluations politically costly? First, devaluations can have a negative effect on real income, particularly in the short term, through a variety of channels. On the one hand, they increase the demand for domestic output by increasing the price of foreign goods relative to domestic goods. This is the substitution effect, which is expansionary. On the other hand, they reduce real wealth, provided that some of it is in domestic currency. This is a contractionary income effect. In addition, devaluations shift income from wage earners with a high propensity to spend to profit recipients with a low propensity to spend. As this shift involves many losers and few winners, it can be particularly costly around elections.[49] For a long time, it has been argued that in the case of developing countries, devaluations are contractionary (see Díaz Alejandro, 1963, and Krugman and Taylor, 1978), which means that the income effect is larger than the substitution effect. The most recent empirical evidence is not conclusive, but it suggests that the effect is likely to be contractionary in the short term but more neutral in the long term.[50] Before elections, naturally, the predominant focus is on what happens in the short term.

Stein and Streb (1998, 1999) identify another channel through which devaluations can be politically costly in the context of a rational political budget cycle model in the Rogoff (1990) tradition. Voters dislike devaluation (which, in the context of the one-sector model used by the authors, coincides with the rate of inflation) because it acts as a tax on money balances. Governments face a tradeoff between devaluation today and tomorrow, and, with incomplete information, they exploit this tradeoff for electoral purposes, using a low rate of devaluation before elections as a signal of their competence, thus increasing their chances of reelection. Hence, the pattern of devaluations around elections is part of a political budget cycle, a feature that has been overlooked in conventional stories of political budget cycles that concentrate on a closed economy.[51] The model in Stein and Streb (1999) has very clear-cut empirical implications: governments do not always have incentives to manipulate exchange rates around elections.

---

[48] Until 1994, the exact timing in Mexico had been after elections, but before the change in government. In this way, the outgoing president would spare his successor (who was actually named by the incumbent) the political cost of devaluing. This pattern changed in 1994, when the devaluation occurred after the change in government.

[49] There are, of course, other important channels through which a devaluation affects real income. For a comprehensive account, see Agenor and Montiel (1996).

[50] The counterpart of this is the expansionary effects associated with exchange rate-based stabilization in the short run, characterized by the real appreciation of the currency (see Kiguel and Liviathan, 1993). This is one reason why stabilization programs put in place shortly before elections tend to be based on the use of the exchange rate as a nominal anchor (Stein and Streb, 1998).

[51] See Rogoff (1990), Rogoff and Sibert (1988) and Persson and Tabellini (1990). An exception to the focus on the closed economy is Clark (1998).

But when they do, it is always in the same direction: postponement of devaluations until after elections.

Even if one were to rule out manipulative theories, an alternative source of exchange rate movements in electoral years is uncertainty regarding the election results. Not only is it uncertain who the winner will be, but there is also uncertainty regarding the policies each candidate will follow. In this case, however, the pattern of the exchange rate around elections is not as clear. Part of the devaluation could occur before the elections take place, reflecting increased uncertainty, and the chances of the different candidates. After the elections, the exchange rate would appreciate or depreciate, depending on who the winner was and which economic policies were followed. In expected value, one should not anticipate a devaluation immediately after elections through this channel.

What does the existing evidence say? There are a few more systematic empirical studies that look at the relationship between elections, changes in government, and the timing of devaluations. This incipient literature appears to support the hypothesis that devaluations tend to be delayed until after elections or government changes. A recent study of fiscal policy in Latin America by Gavin and Perotti (1997) examines the determinants of shifts in exchange rate regimes from fixed to flexible. They find that the likelihood of such a shift increases significantly right after an election. Klein and Marion (1994) study the duration of exchange rate pegs to the U.S. dollar for a sample of 17 Latin American countries over 1956-91. In contrast with Gavin and Perotti, who focus only on regime shifts, these authors consider step devaluations as the end of one spell and the beginning of another. They find that the likelihood a peg will be abandoned increases immediately after an executive transfer. Edwards (1993) studies the timing of 39 large devaluations (15 percent or more) in democratic regimes, and finds that they tend to occur early on in the term in office. Edwards suggests that governments tend to follow the classic rule of "devalue immediately and blame it on your predecessors."

The purpose of this chapter is to extend the empirical literature regarding the pattern of nominal and real exchange rates around political events such as elections and changes in government. The data on elections and changes in government is based on Nohlen (1992) and on the Lijphart Elections Archive.[52]

---

[52] See http://dodgson.ucsd.edu/lij/

Figure 2.6. Nominal Exchange Rate Depreciation around Elections (Presidential and Parliamentary) - 242 Episodes

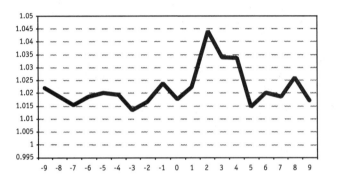

The Evidence

The methodology used is a very simple one. It involves studying the pattern of nominal and real exchange rates around major political events (elections and government changes) by averaging the behavior of the relevant exchange rate variables around these events, covering all the episodes of each type. It is easiest to describe the method by using an example such as the pattern of nominal exchange rate changes around elections. First, all election episodes in the database are pulled together (a total of 242, counting both presidential and parliamentary elections). The behavior of nominal exchange rates is considered by looking at a 19-month window centered on elections. For each episode, month 0 corresponds to the month of the election, month -1 the month prior to the election, and so on. The rate of nominal depreciation across all episodes is then averaged for each of the 19 months in the window (-9 through 9). The average nominal rate of depreciation, month by month, is presented in Figure 2.6.

The pattern in the figure is striking and provides strong support for the hypothesis that devaluations are delayed until after elections. In months 2, 3 and 4 after an election, the average rate of nominal depreciation is 2 percentage points higher than it is for other months, and the average rate of depreciation is more than doubled. The larger effect occurs two months after the election. (It should be stressed that geometric rather than arithmetic averages were used in order to lessen the effects of outliers.[53])

---

[53] The figure calculated with arithmetic averages was even more striking.

Figure 2.7. Nominal Exchange Rate Depreciation around Elections (Presidential) - 131 Episodes

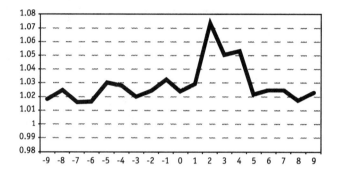

The pattern is even stronger when only presidential elections are considered, as shown in Figure 2.7. In this case, the average rate of nominal depreciation in month 2 reaches 7 percent, around 4.5 percentage points higher than in other months. The behavior of the nominal exchange rate around parliamentary (non-presidential) elections, in contrast, did not show any interesting pattern.

Are devaluations delayed until after elections, or after government changes? The previous pictures do not provide a clear answer, since different countries at different times have different lags between the dates of elections and those of government changes. It is clear from Figure 2.8 that the most relevant event is the change in government. In this case, all the effect is concentrated in month 1, when the depreciation is some 5.5 percentage points higher than in other months. The fact that devaluations occur two to four months after elections reflects the fact that the lag between the election and the change in government in most cases is between one and three months. This suggests that, while in some cases such as Mexico pre-1994, the outgoing government implemented the devaluation, in most cases the incumbent does not want to endure the political cost of the devaluation, even once the election has taken place. An interesting topic for future research is whether the pattern differs for the cases where one government is followed by another government of the same party.

Figure 2.9 restricts the episodes to constitutional government changes. The effect is even stronger: the average devaluation one month after elections is now greater than 10 percent, and around 7 percentage points higher than in other months. In contrast, Figure 2.10 shows that that the effects in the case of non-constitutional changes in government

Figure 2.8. Nominal Exchange Rate Depreciation around Governmental Changes - 187 Episodes

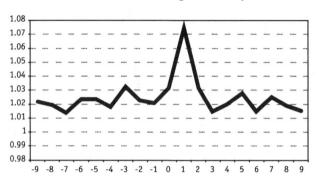

Figure 2. 9. Nominal Exchange Rate Depreciation around Constitutional Changes - 118 Episodes

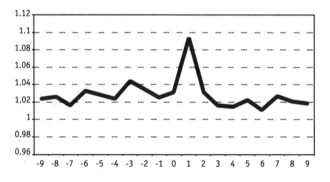

Figure 2.10. Nominal Exhange Rate Depreciation around Nonconstitutional Changes - 69 Episodes

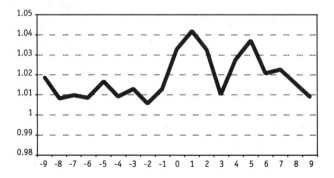

Figure 2.11. Real Exchange Rate around Elections (Presidential) - 106 Episodes

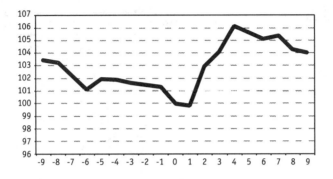

Figure 2.12. Real Exchange Rate around Constitutional Changes - 86 Episodes

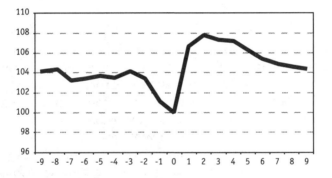

are much smaller. In this case the depreciation starts in month 0, which would suggest that, at least in some cases, the changes in government are endogenous to exchange rate crises. This is a matter which, again, is left for future research.

The real exchange rate shows a similar pattern. In this case, to make the level of the exchange rate comparable across countries, the real exchange rate in each country is normalized so that the (geometric) average would be 100. For the purposes of the figures, the month-by-month averages are normalized so that they would be 100 at time 0 (the date of the election or the change in government). Figure 2.11 shows the pattern of the real exchange rate around presidential elections. There is a gradual 3 percent appreciation in the months preceding an election, followed by a much steeper depreciation after elections have taken place. As with the nominal

Table 2.9. Probabilities of Changes in Real Exchange Rate between t and t+6

Size of real depreciation	All cases	Recently inaugurated constitutional govt.	Impending presidential elections
<-25% (app)	1.18	1.63	2.18
-25% to -20%	1.27	2.09	0.24
-20% to -15%	2.28	2.09	4.36
-15% to -10%	4.57	5.81	6.05
-10% to -5%	12.86	9.53	15.74
-5% to 5%	60.89	56.51	53.51
5% to 10%	7.47	6.74	7.75
10% to 15%	2.84	3.72	3.63
15% to 20%	1.82	2.09	2.91
20% to 25%	0.98	0.00	0.97
>25%	3.84	9.76	2.66
No. of observations	7,247	430	413

exchange rate, the real depreciation, which totals 6 percent, occurs in months 2 through 4. From month 5 onwards, the real exchange rate returns to the pattern of gradual appreciation. As with the nominal exchange rate, the pattern is even more clear around constitutional government changes (see Figure 2.12), when most of the depreciation (almost 7 percent) occurs in month 1, and the appreciation resumes in month 3.

The preceding figures show a very clear picture of the average behavior of nominal and real exchange rates around major political events. However, it is interesting as well to know something about the distribution of the behavior of the exchange rate around these events. In order to see this, we look at the probability at any given time that the real exchange rate will appreciate or depreciate by certain pre-specified amounts during the following six months. These probabilities are presented in the first column of Table 2.9. The last figure in the column indicates that, at any point in time, the probability of a real depreciation of 25 percent or more within six months is 3.84 percent.

A subsequent question is how these probabilities change around major political events. More specifically, what are these probabilities if there is a constitutional government change sometime between t+1 and t+5? A government change in the middle would be expected to increase the probability of a large real depreciation. The probabilities, which appear in column 2 of the table, confirm the priors. The probability of a large real depreciation of at least 25 percent is now close to 10 percent. Thus, the change in government increases the probability of a large devaluation by a factor of 2.5.

How do these probabilities change when there is a presidential election immediately after t+6 (or more precisely, if the election occurs between t+7 and t+10)? The resulting probabilities are listed in column 3. An impending presidential election, as expected, reduces the probability of a large real depreciation by more than 30 percent. The most interesting comparison, however, is between columns 2 and 3 in the table. Compared to the "impending presidential election" situation, the "recently inaugurated constitutional government" case is 3.7 times more likely to have produced a large real depreciation (of 25 percent or more). In contrast, the "impending election" scenario is 2.4 times more likely to have produced a real appreciation (larger than 5 percent).

Conclusions

This chapter has explored the political economy determinants of exchange rate policy in Latin America, finding that political economy factors have in fact played a role in shaping exchange rate policy. In particular, there is evidence that governments with strong support in the legislature tend to choose fixed regimes, as do governments that face a fragmented opposition. This is in line with the idea that sustaining a fixed rate may require politically difficult fiscal adjustment, and that strong governments are in a better position to engineer such an adjustment. At the same time, these findings may be capturing the fact that governments with strong support in Congress suffer a smaller political cost in case of devaluation.

Economies with an important manufacturing sector are more prone to adopt either floating regimes or backward-looking crawling pegs, both of which tend to deliver more competitive exchange rates. The influence of the manufacturing sector on the exchange regime appears more important in periods when trade was liberalized, so that this sector had to face the competition of foreign producers. This result is complemented by similar findings in the country studies in this book on Peru and Colombia.

Finally, there is strong evidence that major political events such as elections and government changes affect the path of nominal and real exchange rates. More specifically, devaluations tend to be delayed in the run-up to elections, and only occur immediately after the new government takes office.

References

Agenor, P. and Montiel, P. 1996. *Development Macroeconomics.* Princeton: Princeton University Press.

Aghevli, B., M. Khan, and P. Montiel. 1991. *Exchange Rate Policy in Developing Countries: Some Analytical Issues.* IMF Occasional Paper No. 78. International Monetary Fund, Washington, DC.

Bernhard, W., and D. Leblang. 1999. Democratic Institutions and Exchange-Rate Commitments. *International Organization* 53(1): 71-97.

Blomberg, S.B., and G.D. Hess. 1997. Politics and Exchange Rate Forecasts. *Journal of International Economics* 43: 189-205.

Calvo, G.A., and C.M. Reinhart. 2000. Fear of Floating. University of Maryland, College Park, MD. Mimeo.

Calvo, G., C. Reinhart, and C. Végh. 1995. Targeting the Real Exchange Rate: Theory and Evidence. *Journal of Development Economics* 47: 97-133.

Cardoso, E. 1991. From Inertial to Megainflation: Brazil in the 1980s. In M. Bruto et al. (eds.), *Lessons of Economic Stabilization and its Aftermath.* Cambridge, MA: MIT Press.

Clark, W., and U. Reichert. 1998. International and Domestic Constraints on Political Business Cycles in OECD Economies. *International Organization* 52(1).

Collins, S. 1996. On Becoming More Flexible: Exchange Rate Regimes in Latin America and the Caribbean. *Journal of Development Economics* 51: 117-38.

Cooper, R. 1971. *Currency Devaluations in Developing Countries.* Essays on International Finance 86. Princeton University, Princeton, NJ.

Cottarelli, C., and C. Giannini. 1998. *Credibility Without Rules? Monetary Frameworks in the Post-Bretton Woods Era.* IMF Occasional Papers 154. International Monetary Fund, Washington, DC.

Cukierman, A. 1992. *Central Bank Strategy, Credibility and Independence: Theory and Evidence.* Cambridge, MA: MIT Press.

Díaz Alejandro, C.F. 1963. A Note on the Impact of Devaluation and the Redistributive Effect. *Journal of Political Economy* 71: 577-80.

Edison, H., and M. Melvin. 1990. The Determinants and Implications of the Choice of an Exchange Rate System. In W. Haraf and T. Willett (eds.), *Monetary Policy for a Volatile Global Economy.* Washington, DC: American Enterprise Institute.

Edwards, S. 1996. *The Determinants of the Choice of Between Fixed and Flexible Exchange Rate Regimes.* NBER Working Paper 5576. National Bureau of Economic Research, Cambridge, MA.

_____. 1994. The Political Economy of Inflation and Stabilization in Developing Countries. *Economic Development and Cultural Change* 42(2).

Eichengreen, B. 1995. The Endogeneity of Exchange Rate Regimes. In P. Kenen (ed.), *Understanding Interdependence: The Macroeconomics of the Open Economy*. Princeton, NJ: Princeton University Press.

Frieden, J. 1998. The Political Economy of European Exchange Rates: An Empirical Assessment. Harvard University. Mimeo.

_____. 1994. Exchange Rate Politics: Contemporary Lessons from American History. *Review of International Political Economy* 1(1): 81-103.

Gavin, M., and R. Perotti. 1997. Fiscal Policy in Latin America. In B.S. Bernanke and J. Rotemberg (eds.), *NBER Macroeconomics Annual*. Cambridge, MA: MIT Press.

Giavazzi, F., and M. Pagano. 1988. The Advantage of Tying One's Hands: EMS Discipline and Central Bank Credibility. *European Economic Review* 32(2): 1055-75.

Goldfajn, I., and R. Valdés. 1999. The Aftermath of Appreciations. *Quarterly Journal of Economics* 114(1): 229-62.

Green, W. 1997. *Econometric Analysis*. Upper Saddle River, NJ: Prentice Hall.

Grilli, V., D. Masciandaro, and G. Tabellini. 1991. Institutions and Policies. *Economic Policy* 6: 341-91.

Hausmann, R., M. Gavin, C. Pagés, and E. Stein. 1999. Financial Turmoil and Choice of Exchange Rate Regime. Inter-American Development Bank Research Department Working Paper 400, Washington, DC.

Hausmann, R., U. Panizza, and E. Stein. 2000. *Why Do Countries Float the Way They Float?* Inter-American Development Bank Research Department Working Paper 418, Washington, DC.

Hefeker, C. 1997. *Interest Groups and Monetary Integration*. Boulder, CO: Westview Press.

Heymann, D. 1991. From Sharp Disinflation to Hyperinflation, Twice: The Argentina Experience. In M. Bruno et al. (eds.), *Lessons of Economic Stabilization and its Aftermath*. Cambridge, MA: MIT Press.

Kenen, P.B. 1969. The Optimum Currency Area: An Eclectic View. In R.A. Mundell and A. Swoboda (eds.), *Problems of the International Economy*. Chicago: University of Chicago Press.

Kiguel, M., and N. Ghei. 1993. *Devaluations in Low-Income Countries*. Policy Research Working Paper 1224. World Bank, Washington, DC.

Klein, M., and N. Marion. 1997. Explaining the Duration of Exchange-Rate Pegs. *Journal of Development Economics* 54: 387-404.

Krugman, P., and L. Taylor. 1978 Contractionary Effects of Devaluation. *Journal of International Economics* 8: 445-56.

Lijphart, A. Lijphart Elections Archive. http://dodgson.ucsd.edu/lij/

Lizondo, J.S. 1993. *Real Exchange Rate Targeting under Imperfect Asset Substitutability*. IMF Staff Papers 40: 829-51.

_____. 1991. Real Exchange Rate Targets, Nominal Exchange Rate Policies and Inflation. *Revista de Analisis Económico* 6: 5-22.

Long, J.S. 1997. Regression Model for Categorical and Limited Dependent Variables. Advanced Quantitative Techniques in the Social Sciences, No. 7. Sage Publications, Thousand Oaks, CA.

McKinnon, R.I. 1962. Optimum Currency Areas. *American Economic Review* 53: 717-25.

Miniane, J. 2000. New Measures of Capital Account Restrictions. Unpublished.

Montiel, P.J., and J. Ostry. 1992. *Real Exchange Rate Targeting under Capital Controls: Can Money Provide a Nominal Anchor?* IMF Staff Papers 39: 58-78.

_____. 1991. *Macroeconomic Implications of Real Exchange Rate Targeting in Developing Countries*. IMF Staff Papers 38: 872-900.

Mundell, R.A. 1961. A Theory of Optimum Currency Areas. *American Economic Review* 51: 657-64.

Nohlen, D. 1993. *Enciclopedia Electoral Latinoamericana y del Caribe*. San José, Costa Rica: Instituto Interamericano de Derechos Humanos.

Obstfeld, M., and K. Rogoff. 1995. The Mirage of Fixed Exchange Rates. *Journal of Economic Perspectives* 9: 73-96.

Persson, T., and G. Tabellini. 1990. *Macroeconomic Policy: Credibility and Politics*. London: Harwood Academic Publishers.

Posen, A. 1995. *Central Bank Independence and Disinflationary Credibility: A Missing Link?* Federal Reserve Bank of New York Staff Reports, No. 1 (May).

Rogoff, K. 1990. Equilibrium Political Budget Cycles. *American Economic Review* 80: 21-36.

Rogoff, K., and N. Sibert. 1988. Elections and Macroeconomic Policy Cycles. *Review of Economic Studies* 55(1): 1-16.

Roubini, N. 1991. Economic and Political Determinants of Budget Deficits in Developing Countries. *Journal of International Money and Finance* 10: S49-S72.

Roubini, N., and J. Sachs. 1989. Political and Economic Determinants of the Budget Deficits in the Industrial Democracies. *European Economic Review* 33: 903-38.

Sachs, J. 1985. *External Debt and Macroeconomic Performance in Latin America and East Asia*. Brookings Papers on Economic Activity: 2.

Stein, E., and J.M. Streb. 1999. Elections and the Timing of Devaluations. Inter-American Development Bank Research Department Working Paper 396, Washington, DC.

———. 1998. Political Stabilization Cycles in High Inflation. *Journal of Development Economics* 56(1): 159-80.

Tavlas, G. 1994. The Theory of Monetary Integration. *Open Economies Review* 5(2).

Tornell, A., and A. Velasco. *Fixed versus Flexible Exchange Rates: Which Provides More Fiscal Discipline?* NBER Working Paper 5108. National Bureau of Economic Research, Cambridge, MA.

Weber, A. 1991. Reputation and Credibility in the European Monetary System. *Economic Policy* 12.

Zárate, R. Zárate's Political Collections. http://www.terra.es/personal2/monolith.

CHAPTER THREE

From Redistribution to Stability: The Evolution of Exchange Rate Policies in Argentina, 1950-98

Eugenio Díaz-Bonilla and Hector E. Schamis[1]

Argentina used a variety of exchange rate regimes between 1950 and 1988, from a floating to a fixed exchange rate in a dollar standard currency board. The evolution of nominal parity and the real exchange rate have differed significantly as well.[2] Those regimes have coexisted with different development strategies, ranging from import-substitution industrialization to more open regimes, that included multiple combinations of monetary, fiscal, financial, labor and sectoral policies, generating significant changes in the incentives for social coalition building. On the political side, different exchange rate policies combined with diverse political and institutional settings in both democratic and authoritarian regimes.

The Argentine experience has thus produced a rich set of historical cases and observations for testing hypotheses. In addition to issues of economic consistency and the credibility of exchange rate policies,[3] there is the question of the conditions under which political sustainability comes into play, namely, how distributive considerations retain great significance even

[1] Eugenio Díaz-Bonilla is a researcher with the Fundación Andina and the International Food Policy Research Institute. Hector E. Schamis is a researcher at the Fundación Andina and a professor at Cornell University.
[2] The *nominal exchange rate* is defined in domestic currency per unit of foreign currency (basically the U.S. dollar). Therefore the terms *devaluation, depreciation* or *weak currency* (revaluation, appreciation or strong currency) mean an increase (decrease) in the amount of domestic money paid for one unit of foreign currency. The *real exchange rate (RER)* is defined as the ratio of the price of tradables to nontradables. Therefore the terms devaluation or depreciation of the RER (revaluation or appreciation) mean an increase (decrease) in that ratio.
[3] See Kiguel (1994), Calvo and Végh (1999), Corbo and de Melo (1985), Drazen and Helpman (1986), Buiter (1986) and Tornell and Velasco (1995).

in the presence of economy-wide policies.[4] Questions arise as to why policies that may generate imbalances are implemented in the first place, and why, once there is disequilibrium, some policies are chosen instead of other alternatives that are equally available. The small but growing amount of literature on the political economy of exchange rates, however, remains largely limited to the industrialized world.[5] A focus on a medium-sized, developing economy such as Argentina—characterized by weak fiscal accounts, shallow capital markets, vulnerable banking systems, and feeble regulatory institutions in the context of inconsistent development strategies— may well raise new questions in this field of research.

A point of departure for a discussion of exchange rate policies is the dual role of the exchange rate: the nominal aspects related to the short-run management of aggregate demand, and the real aspects affecting aggregate supply in the longer run. This dual role is reflected in the two approaches that have usually been considered in defining the proper exchange rate policy. One is the real exchange rate approach, which emphasizes the distinction between tradable and nontradable goods, and the effect of the exchange rate on external competitiveness and the trade balance (Balassa, 1977, 1985). The other is the nominal anchor approach, which highlights the role of the exchange rate in the inflationary process and its relationship with monetary aggregates, interest rates, capital flows, and the functioning of the financial system. This dual role is at the core of many inconsistencies in macroeconomic programs (see Corden, 1990 and Williamson, 1991), but it also highlights the distributional consequences of different exchange rate policies.

For instance, producers of tradables generally prefer a devalued exchange rate (depending on the import content of their products), while producers of nontradables may benefit from a strong currency. Debtors in domestic currency may be helped by devaluations that increase inflation and reduce the real cost of servicing their debt; this situation is reversed, however, if, as in many Latin American countries in the recent past, debtors' liabilities are in foreign currency. In terms of the exchange rate regime, financiers and foreign investors would favor exchange rate stability and credible nominal anchors. Producers and workers, in turn, may prefer a more flexible exchange rate if this allows the economy to absorb external shocks with less disruption of real activity.

---

[4] See Díaz-Bonilla (1989), Frieden (1991), Laban and Sturzenegger (1994a and 1994b), and Schamis (1999).
[5] For example, see Odell (1982), Gowa (1983), Destler and Henning (1989), Frieden (1994), and Kirshner (1995).

The dual role of the exchange rate must be seen in the context of what Maier (1987) has called the "historical political economy" of Argentina in the postwar period. Di Tella (1987) observes a cycle with two phases in Argentina's exchange rate policies: the "repressed stage," when some key prices are controlled to tame inflation, and a subsequent "loosening stage," when those controls collapse and inflation jumps to new levels. The repressed stages are usually associated with fixed exchange rates or managed crawling pegs, which, because of inconsistencies with other macroeconomic policies and distortions in relative prices, generate disequilibria that are not sustainable. When that happens, the exchange rate regime changes abruptly (usually along with the minister of finance). The loosening stage, in turn, is a period of far higher inflation, when exchange rate regimes switch to different types of floating and, in several instances, multiple exchange rates (see Figures 3.1, 3.2 and 3.3).

While Di Tella's cycles provide a way of describing Argentina's economic history, there is no thorough explanation of the factors that generated those cycles. Moreover, the dynamics of the cycles themselves were already changing: by the 1980s, in fact, they had become shorter and more violent, and finally reached hyper-inflationary levels in 1989-90. However, since 1991, when Congress passed the Convertibility Law, pegging the peso one-to-one to the dollar, the cycles seem to have stopped. Argentina's performance has been in line with exchange rate-based stabilization programs characterized by an initial increase in domestic absorption, a progressive decline in inflation, and the deterioration of the real exchange rate and external accounts. The "loosening" stage, however, has not taken place.[6]

An attempt to explain, first, why the cycles have become shorter and more violent and, second, why they have subsequently receded, implicitly borrows the argument of cycles of repression and loosening. This analysis can be modified and extended, though, by considering the interaction of the exchange rate regime, broader macroeconomic and development strategies, and political and institutional settings. In contrast with Di Tella's discussion, three types of repression-loosening cycles can be observed (see Figures 3.1, 3.2 and 3.3). The first type corre-

---

[6] The boom-bust nature of exchange rate-based stabilization programs is well documented. While they usually begin with a consumption boom, they normally end up with a recession. Therefore for countries suffering from high inflation, it is a matter of recession now or recession later (see Kiguel and Liviatan, 1992, and Hoffmaister and Végh, 1996). A thorough review of this literature can be found in Calvo and Végh (1999).

Figure 3.1. Exchange Rate

(Average, natural logs)

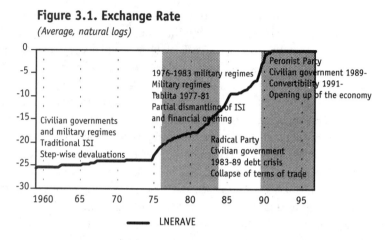

——— LNERAVE

Figure 3.2. Exchange Rate under Import Substitution Industralization

(Average, logs)

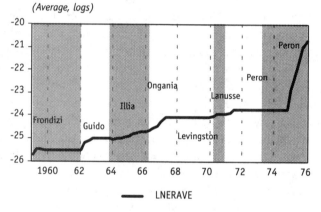

——— LNERAVE

sponds to the politics of redistribution under classic import-substitution industrialization (ISI). This phase shows periodic, step-wise adjustments in the nominal exchange rate (see Figure 3.2). Those discrete adjustments appear to be related to the redistribution struggle in which the agrarian surplus was directed toward manufacturing, with controls in the capital account. This period extends from the 1950s to the mid-1970s, ending with the military coup of March 1976.

The second phase opens with the 1976 military regime but continues through the civilian government of the *Unión Cívica Radical* (1983-89) under the Alfonsín administration and the first 18 to 20 months of the Menem administration elected in 1989. This second phase is character-

**Figure 3.3. Exchange Rate from High
Inflation to Stability**
(Average, logs)

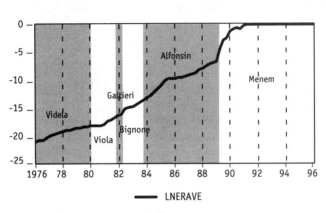

LNERAVE

ized by increasingly large devaluations and accelerating inflation, which reached hyperinflationary proportions in 1989-90. The large jump in inflation reflects how the politics of redistribution began to be played at the level of a fiscally constrained public sector. Neither the military regimes (1976-83) nor the Alfonsín administration (1984-89) were willing or able to control the distributive struggle that was affecting the public budget (and economic management of the civilian government was further affected by very negative international economic conditions). With the elimination of controls in the capital account, this setting led to exchange rate crises linked to persistent fiscal imbalances, along the lines described by Krugman (1979) and extended by Calvo (1996).

In the third period, since the early 1990s, the politics of redistribution turned into the politics of (hyper)inflation, in response to which a broad coalition favoring stability emerged. This political support allowed the implementation of an important institutional innovation: the currency board created by the Convertibility Plan during the Menem administration, which established a fixed exchange rate for the peso (at a one-to-one parity with the dollar). This institutional innovation eliminated all discretionary power in the management of the exchange rate while substantially limiting the use of passive monetary policies to accommodate distributional conflicts. Those conflicts also appeared to have become more muted, in part because supporting international conditions and domestic growth created better overall economic conditions that helped reduce the negative impact of some of the new policies on specific groups. As a result, and in contrast to the previous two periods,

Figure 3.4. REREX and World Agricultural Prices

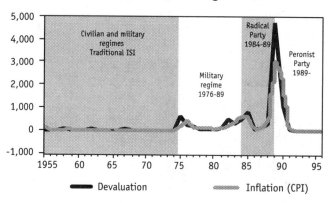

Figure 3.5. Devaluation and Inflation
(Annual percentage, average)

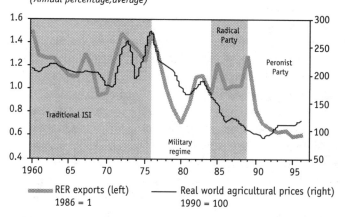

the third period is remarkably stable in exchange rate and price levels (see Figures 3.1, 3.3 and 3.4).

In contrast to the previous discussion of the nominal exchange rate, Figure 3.5 shows the real exchange rate for exports (REREX),[7] along with the world real price of agricultural products, the main component of Argentina's total exports. In general, it appears that the behavior of the real exchange rate in Argentina, when not affected by world conditions, is the byproduct of policies linked to the management of inflation, where the exchange rate is usually utilized as a monetary anchor. Thus, the discussion below concentrates on the behavior of the nominal exchange rate.

Historical Perspective

The Politics of Redistribution during ISI

Despite great political instability, this period shows remarkable continuity in terms of applying the general policies associated with an ISI strategy. Three democratically elected governments, three military regimes, and one civilian (but military-controlled) administration maintained closed trade regimes and controls on capital movements (see Tables 3.1 and 3.2). In a context of great instability, with alternating civilian and military governments, this phase also included periods of armed conflict between factions of the military, as in 1962-63. The Peronist Party, ousted from office in 1955, was banned from participating in elections during the next two decades, making the political process all the more unstable.

The exchange rate moved incrementally (see Figure 3.2), with more or less stable periods followed by upward adjustments. Table 3.2 shows the different exchange rate regimes and policies since the end of the 1950s. The step-wise adjustments in the nominal exchange rate were associated with the internal economic limits of the inward-oriented industrialization strategy and its built-in distributional conflict. The strategy was based on the redistribution of the agrarian surplus, generated by the fertile Pampas, toward industrialization and an expanding state sector. This benefited workers and the urban middle classes. Consequently, political

---

[7] REREX is defined as PREX*(1-TE)/PD; i.e., the price deflator of exports (PREX) from national accounts, adjusted by export taxes (TE) divided by the price deflator of the domestic non-traded good (PD), calculated from national accounts. Similarly, RERIM (not shown in the figure) is equal to PRIM*(1+TM)/PD, where PRIM is the price deflator of imports from national accounts, adjusted by import taxes (TM). See Devarajan, Lewis and Robinson (1993) for a general discussion on this issue.

Table 3.1. Presidents and Ministers of the Economy

Arturo Frondizi, May 1958	Donato del Carril, May 1958 Alvaro Alsogaray, June 1959 Roberto Alemann, April 1961
José M. Guido, March 1962	Coll Benegas, January 1962 Jorge Wehbe, March 1962 Federico Pinedo, April 1962 A. Alsogaray, May 1962 E. Mendez Delfino, December 1962 J.M. Martínez de Hoz, May 1963
Arturo Illía, October 1963	Eugenio Blanco, December 1963 Juan C. Pugliese, August 1964
Juan C. Onganía, June 1966	Jorge Salimei, June 1966 A. Krieger Vasena, January 1967 J.M. Dagnino Pastore, June 1969
Roberto Levingston, June 1970	C. Moyano Llerena, June 1970 Aldo Ferrer, October 1970
Alejandro Lanusse, March 1971	Juan Quilici, June 1971 Cayetano Licciardo, October 1971 Jorge Wehbe, October 1972
Hector Cámpora, May 1973 Raul Lastiri, July 1973 Juan D. Perón, October 1973 Isabel Perón, July 1974	Jose Gelbard, May 1973 Alfredo Gomez Morales, October 1974 Celestino Rodrigo, June 1975 Pedro Bonanni, July 1975 Antonio Cafiero, August 1975 Emilio Mondelli, February 1976
Jorge Videla, March 1976	J. Martínez de Hoz, March 1976
Roberto Viola, March 1981	Lorenzo Sigaut, March 1981
Leopoldo Galtieri, November 1981	Roberto Alemann, December 1981
Reynaldo Bignone, July 1982	J. Dagnino Pastore, July 1982 J. Wehbe, August 1982
Raul Alfonsín, December 1983	Bernardo Grinspun, December 1983 Juan Sourrouille, February 1985 J.C. Pugliese, March 1989 J. Rodriguez, May 1989
Carlos Menem, July 1989	Miguel Angel Roig, July 1989 Nestor Rapanelli, July 1989 Erman Gonzalez, December 1989 Domingo Cavallo, January 1991 Roque Fernandez, July 1996

Table 3.2.   Exchange Rate Regimes

A.   **ISI PERIOD**

-Important devaluation in 1959.
-1960-61 dirty float.
-In 1961, fixed exchange regime.
-1962 first quarter: important devaluation.
-First quarter 1962-first quarter 1967: flexible exchange rate under different governments.
-First quarter 1967-first half 1970: strong initial devaluation and then fixed exchange rate.
-Mid-1970-first quarter 1973: multiple exchange rates with a changing mix of commercial and financial rates for different transactions.
-Second quarter 1973-last quarter 1974: fixed exchange rate.
-Strong devaluation in the last quarter of 1974.
-Another strong devaluation in the second quarter of 1975 (el "Rodrigazo") (transition towards the inflationary period).

B.   **INFLATIONARY PERIOD**

-March 1976-December 1978: passive crawling peg.
-December 1978-first quarter of 1981: pre-announced sliding peg (tablita; system collapsed in 1981.
-First quarter 1981-June 1985: floating exchange rate/adjusted passively to inflation, until Austral Plan of June 1985.
-June 1985-first quarter of 1991: four different attempts at fixing or controlling to some degree the exchange rate (Austral and Primavera plans during the Alfonsín administration and the programs implemented by Rapanelli and Erman Gonzalez during the Menem administration), all ending in episodes of sharp devaluations and very high inflation.

C.   **STABILITY**

-March 1991 to date: the Convertibility Plan, which pegged the peso to the dollar one-to-one, and transformed the central bank into a quasi currency board.

support for ISI was based on a mostly urban alliance between industrialists, wage earners, and public sector contractors and employees.

The exchange rate regime usually involved fixed (but adjustable) rates designed to maintain low inflation and support industrialization. The import substitution strategy could at least initially be pursued with fixed exchange rates because high trade protection shielded domestic industry from external competition, even in the face of the usual appreciation of the real exchange rate. In addition, a fixed parity helped steady the price of imported inputs and capital goods needed for ISI. As noted by Braun and Joy (1967) and Díaz-Alejandro (1963), given that

Argentina's exports are mainly food products (or "wage goods" in Ricardian terminology) a devaluation would put pressure on industrial wages.[8] Therefore, for industrialists and urban workers, a fixed exchange rate was perceived as the preferred alternative. Furthermore, the private sector was linked to the state as suppliers, and public sector enterprises were likewise inward-oriented and did not need an externally competitive RER for their operation.

The export-oriented agricultural sector, in contrast, preferred a competitive exchange rate. The periodic overvaluation of the real exchange rate caused by the fixed nominal parity and the general bias of economic policy toward the protection of industry acted as an important disincentive for agriculture.[9]

The economic limits of the ISI strategy periodically emerged, leading to balance of payment crises and sharp devaluations. The stop-go nature of ISI, and, therefore, the cycles of repression and loosening in the exchange rate regime, resulted largely from the economic model's inherent limitations. The acceleration of the economy usually led to fewer exports (because a larger percentage of the wage goods were consumed domestically due to growing incomes) and more imported inputs and capital goods (demanded by expanding industries), generating balance of payment crises when official external reserves reached very low levels. At times, the limits inherent in the development strategy were exacerbated by external shocks, leading to crises even though the economy was not expanding rapidly. In any case, given a context of capital controls, exchange rate crises during most of this period developed relatively slowly, following the decline in reserves caused by the gradual deterioration of the trade balance, and reinforced by the over-invoicing of imports and the under-invoicing of exports.

But there was also a political limit, imposed by the distributive dispute between industrialists and workers over domestic income. During democratic, and particularly Peronist, governments, the influence of labor usually increased, leading to higher wages (see Figures 3.6 and 3.7). That increase in salaries most often took place in the context of accommodating

---

[8] This is a clear difference from other Latin American countries. For instance, in Colombia and Brazil agricultural exports were not "wage goods" and thus there was no tradeoff between keeping a competitive exchange rate and industrialization.

[9] See Díaz-Alejandro (1970), Little, Scitovsky and Scott (1970) and Balassa et al. (1971). Relatively high prices for cereals and beef during the 1950s (as a result of the Korean War) and during the 1970s (linked to worldwide expansionary Keynesian policies and the oil crisis) alleviated the impact of an overvalued currency (see Figure 3.5). It should also be noted that there were different agricultural groups in Argentina during the 1960s and 1970s more oriented toward the domestic market (sugar, fruits and vegetables, as well as some subtropical products such as cotton, tobacco, and yerba mate). Economic incentives for these producers were not that different from those for the urban-industrial complex.

Figure 3.6. Real Wage and Unemployment

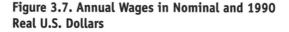

    ꞏꞏꞏꞏꞏꞏ Unemployment (%)   ▬▬ Real wage (upper estimate)

Figure 3.7. Annual Wages in Nominal and 1990 Real U.S. Dollars

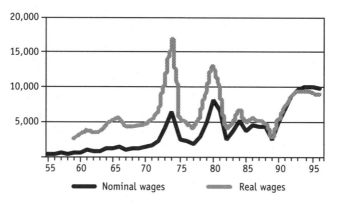

        ▬▬ Nominal wages   ▬▬ Real wages

monetary policies, which fueled inflation and created the conditions for recurrent balance of payment crises. When the inherent limits of the development strategy converged with growing wage pressures from labor unions and expanded distributional conflict over economic resources, important industrial sectors and parts of the middle classes with private sector employment abandoned the original ISI coalition and sided with agrarian interests and the military in the coming coup against the civilian government. High levels of inflation, international reserves insufficient to sustain normal levels of imports and service the external debt, social unrest, and the need to "reestablish order" were the reasons generally cited to justify the military coup against a civilian government accused of being too corrupt or too weak to control the economic and social crisis.

The return of Peronism to power in 1973 closed a political cycle of almost two decades since its proscription after the 1955 military coup. In economic terms, the 1973 program represented the culmination of the ISI development strategy. It established a fixed exchange rate while instituting price controls, increasing wages and salaries, and implementing different expansionary fiscal and monetary policies to foster industry, employment and growth.

By mid-1974, though, Argentina's economic and political condition had begun to deteriorate. After the death of Juan Peron in July 1974, his wife Isabel, the elected Vice-President, took his place. The exchange rate peg continued during the third quarter of 1974. By 1975, however, the terms of trade had declined significantly (see Figure 3.8) and the economy entered a recession. The government tried to rekindle economic growth through stimulative fiscal and monetary policies, but this only fueled inflation, which made the real exchange rate decline even further. The deterioration of the external account forced sharp exchange rate adjustments in the last quarter of 1974, and, particularly, during the second quarter of 1975. This last episode, known as "el Rodrigazo" (after the then Minister of the Economy, Celestino Rodrigo), was the first in a series of maxi-devaluations that began to affect the behavior of economic agents.

Against a backdrop of deteriorating economic conditions, great political uncertainty and escalating violence by guerrilla groups, paramilitary operators, and the armed forces, Isabel Peron was toppled by a military coup in March 1976. From then on, industry's share of GDP declined and real wages fell. This apparently reinforced the impression among the workers and the lower middle class that the Peronist Party was associated with high salaries and a sense of political recognition, while the opposite occurred when that party was ousted by the military. On the other hand, for agrarian and financial groups, and the business community in general, the perception was one of economic mismanagement and a clear decline in their share of national income. The military coup of 1976 basically reflected these concerns.

Inflation, Indebtedness and the Shifting Development Paradigm: The Military Regime, 1976-83

After taking power in March 1976, the military regime followed economic policies broadly in line with previous governments of the armed forces. It was pro-agriculture, anti-labor and suspicious of industrialists who had been allied with the Peronists. The military government was ruthless in repressing

Figure 3.8. Terms of Trade
(1986=100)

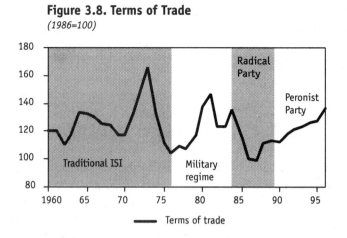

— Terms of trade

workers and political dissidents, and it also partially dismantled consumer-oriented industries, primarily because the military leaders and their civilian allies traced the origins of Argentina's crises to the political distortions associated with the ISI strategy. In their view, previous governments allowed inefficient domestic industrial firms to develop hand-in-hand with government-protected unions, leading to ever-increasing demands on national resources, and even to proposals, as in Chile, to establish complete state control of productive resources (see Canitrot, 1980; Schamis, 1991).[10] The economic policies of the 1976 military regime consequently affected the manufacturing sector on three different fronts: open trade, currency appreciation, and high interest rates. Over 1976-81, the industrial sector as a whole lost about 10 points of participation in GDP, the urban-based ISI coalition was significantly weakened, and agrarian and financial groups recovered the centrality they had lost as a consequence of the 1930s crisis.

The military government's approach was made clear with its initial economic package of April 1976, which included devaluation of the peso, trade liberalization measures, elimination of the nationalization of deposits (a system of 100 percent reserves for the banking system and credit allocation and control by the central bank, instituted during the Peronist government), and elimination of price controls. The existing system of negotiations between representatives of business and unions to determine wages and

---

[10] At the beginning of the 1970s, all three countries in the Southern Cone (Argentina, Chile and Uruguay) had military governments, an indication of the serious political crises prevailing at the time.

salaries was abolished. The unions were placed under the control of the Ministry of Labor, and the government set wages. Increased prices for agricultural products and freer prices for other goods on the one hand, and controlled wages on the other, led to a decline of real wages, which in 1976-77 stood at 60 percent of the level reached in 1974-75, while the ratio of agricultural to nonagricultural goods increased 20 percent.

The financial system, which had been tightly controlled under the Peronist government's system of "nationalization of deposits," benefited as well from the new policies. By mid-1977, the government had implemented a financial reform that deregulated the banking industry. Subsidized credit, central to the whole ISI experiment, came to an end. The financial system expanded substantially during those years, but this growth included a significant number of fragile financial intermediaries that were unable to withstand the shocks that came in the period that followed. In addition, increased uncertainty over rising inflation led to growing dollarization (Claassen and De la Cruz Martinez, 1994).

Although the economic environment created by the military regime proved harsh for much of the inward-oriented manufacturing sector, generous tax incentives were used by the armed forces to support some heavy industries linked to the military complex. This support was rationalized, in part, by concerns over possible conflicts with Chile and Brazil, and later with the United Kingdom over the Malvinas Islands, that would require an industrial base for military purposes. Security concerns were also partially behind a program of fiscal incentives for industries in poor and underpopulated provinces, reflecting the armed forces' concerns regarding the security of the borders in those areas. Besides the distorted development pattern caused by this approach, the system of industrial incentives represented a heavy burden on the national budget (World Bank, 1988).

Outlays linked directly or indirectly to military operations and programs contributed to fiscal imbalances (see Figure 3.9), and those large fiscal deficits were behind levels of inflation for the whole period that remained well above the historical averages (surpassed only by the inflationary explosions of 1975-76, as shown in Figure 3.4). In addition, because inflation remained high, the Olivera-Tanzi effect (i.e., the losses in revenues in non-indexed tax systems due to lags in collection when prices are increasing rapidly) worked against the possibility of placing fiscal accounts under control.

High inflation was a permanent problem for the economic team of the military government. Besides the economic inefficiencies and waste of resources generated by high inflation, it was also eroding whatever legitimacy the regime may have had before the public, as the need to control inflation had been one of the main rationales for justifying the 1976 coup.

Figure 3.9. Fiscal Deficits as a Percentage of GDP

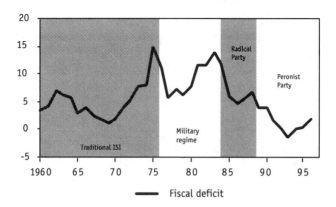

By the end of 1978, inflation continued unabated at about 150 percent per year, and the economy was in recession. The failure to achieve the main objective of non-inflationary growth that the military government had set for itself fueled the search for new approaches. This came in the form of the economic package of December 1978.

The 1978 Program

This program aimed to break inflationary expectations and reduce uncertainties through the pre-announcement of three main variables controlled by the government: the devaluation rate (the schedule was known as the *tablita*), the prices of goods and services provided by public enterprises, and minimum wages. Of those pre-announced variables, the exchange rate came to receive the greatest attention and had the strongest impact on the economy until the scheme was abandoned in 1981. The exchange rate was pre-established in advance for eight-month periods. When that period was about to expire, the rate for the subsequent period was established according to the desired inflation goal for the next period. Domestic inflation was supposed to converge with international inflation, adjusted by the preset ratio of devaluation.

Another component of the program was the modification of controls on international capital flows established by the financial reform of mid-1977 to fend off destabilizing capital inflows. The 1978 program lifted those controls in the hope that domestic interest rates, which were deemed too high, would come down to lower levels defined by world interest rates, adjusted by country risk and the rate of devaluation. In addition to the

Figure 3.10. Ratio of Broad Money to International Reserves and Devaluation

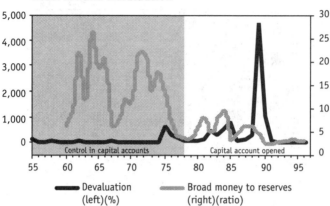

Devaluation (left)(%)   Broad money to reserves (right)(ratio)

expected economic benefits, the liberalization of capital accounts also opened more business opportunities for a growing financial system.

This important change can be seen in the different relationship between broad money and international reserves before and after 1978 (see Figure 3.10). While capital controls allowed the government to main-tain ratios of 10-25 units of domestic currency per unit of international reserves, the opening up of the capital account apparently enabled markets to impose a very specific ratio (about 3 to 1) between these two variables, as exchange rate crises occurred every time the ratio increased over that value.

The 1978 program also reduced the financing of provinces and public enterprises through the national budget. The gap was covered by increased domestic and international borrowing on the part of the public sector at all levels. By 1981, total external debt had undergone an almost threefold increase since 1978, from $13.3 billion to $35.7 billion (see Figure 3.10). The liberalization of foreign borrowing created the temporary illusion of a fiscal bonanza, and the military saw an opportunity to launch grand projects (e.g., nuclear plants and missiles) and modernize its equipment. Over time, defense expenditures—including public enterprises in the heavy industry sectors linked to the military complex—grew disproportionately vis-à-vis other items.

The pre-announced rate of devaluation was set at levels below the rate of inflation, and the process of exchange rate appreciation already un-derway accelerated substantially after 1978. In 1979, the current account turned negative after three years of positive figures (although the trade

Figure 3.11. External Debt and World Interest Rates

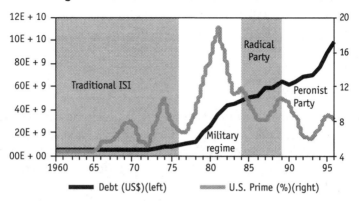

Debt (US$)(left)   U.S. Prime (%)(right)

balance still showed a surplus). In 1980 and 1981, however, the trade balance also became negative.

The balance of payments crisis was deep enough to cast doubts on the sustainability of the predetermined exchange rate. Additional private capital inflows almost came to a halt on expectations of future devaluations far above the predetermined *tablita*. Capital inflows were also slowed by increasing interest rates in the United States (which rose from 15 percent in 1980 to almost 19 percent in 1981). In February 1981, the government devalued the peso by 10 percent, followed by devaluations of over 20 percent in April and June under a new military regime.

These devaluations hit firms with dollar debts hard, exacerbated existing problems in the real economy, and led to the collapse of several important banks and financial institutions. Government attempts to rescue the banking sector, moreover, produced a large quasi-fiscal deficit. Inflation, which had declined to close to 100 percent annually over 1979-80, jumped back up to about 170 percent in 1981. Before and after those changes, the government borrowed in international markets to defend the value of the local currency, and when this was no longer possible, it absorbed, under pressure from international banks and local groups, an important share of the private external debt. The public sector was thus saddled with a substantial debt burden (see Figure 3.11).

The Malvinas War in 1982—which took place under yet another military ruler, the third during the military regime—added to the fiscal problems and general uncertainty. Between 1981 and 1983, fiscal deficits ranged between 12 percent and 14 percent (figures not far from the record of almost 15 percent set in 1975 by the Peronist government, one of the arguments for the military coup of 1976). When international markets dried up for public borrowers after the Mexican crisis of August 1982, the economy sank into recession with high levels of inflation.

Analysis

From the standpoint of economic analysis, the pattern of exchange rate crises is easily explained by the inconsistency between the exchange rate regime, utilized as a nominal anchor to tame inflation, and the persistent fiscal deficit with a liberalized capital account.[11] But from a political economy perspective, the main question is why such inconsistent policies were pursued and the failure of previous attempts disregarded. These policies can be better understood as the result of conflicting forces and interests. First, there was the political need to control inflation, which had been, along with restoring order, one of the main justifications for military intervention in 1976. Next, the armed forces wanted to maintain and develop an industrial base for defense, which converged with the interests of some protected industries, particularly heavy industry. These actions added to fiscal deficits and economic inefficiencies. Finally, the financial community preferred an open capital account and a stable exchange rate. The economic program was unable to balance these diverging objectives and eventually collapsed. The military regime's legacy included weak fiscal accounts, mounting external debt, a distorted development pattern, and a fragile financial system, which created important constraints on the ability of subsequent civilian governments to engage in economic management, including exchange rate policy.

Return to Democracy

After defeating the Peronist candidate by a solid margin in a free election, the Alfonsín government took office amidst great expectations. Alfonsín was able to paint the Peronist Party as the continuation of the despised military and handed the Peronists their first electoral defeat ever. The Alfonsín administration's initial economic policies appear to have been based on two premises. First, wages needed an upward correction, and second, the expectation of better treatment from creditor

---

[11] The question of what went wrong with the stabilization and liberalization programs of the Southern Cone is discussed by Edwards (1984), Balassa (1985), Corbo and de Melo (1987), and the special issues of *World Development* edited by Corbo and de Melo (1985) and *Economic Development and Cultural Change* edited by Edwards and Teitel (1986).

countries regarding Argentina's external debt. This debt had been contracted by the military (in part to finance the armed crisis with Chile and the Malvinas War), and there seemed to be some doubts as to its real amount and even its legitimacy (particularly the private debt that had been absorbed by the public sector with Dagnino Pastore as Minister of the Economy and Domingo Cavallo as President of the Central Bank).

Wages, which had already recovered somewhat in 1983 under the military regime, were raised further by the Radical administration in 1984, almost reaching their 1974 peak in real terms (see Figure 3.6). Although the fiscal deficit was somewhat reduced, it still stood in double figures. The economic team also tried to maintain a competitive exchange rate, an approach that some of its members had successfully applied, though in a very different economic environment, during the previous Radical government of the 1960s. These expansionary policies led to an acceleration of inflation, which reached over 600 percent in 1984 and 1985. As a result, the Minister of the Economy was replaced in early 1985.

In June 1985, the new economic authorities unveiled the Austral Plan, which included a fixed exchange rate, along with fiscal and monetary adjustments to control inflation. The deficit was brought down from about 12 percent in 1984 to the 5 to 6 percent range over the next three years (see Figure 3.9). Inflation also declined to below 90 percent per year in 1986, the first time it declined to double digits since 1980 (see Figure 3.4). Although the advances in fiscal and monetary discipline and inflation reduction were significant in comparison to previous years, they did not go far enough in controlling macroeconomic imbalances. Eventually, the exchange rate had to be readjusted after three quarters from the initial peg, and it was then changed periodically until the Primavera Plan in August 1988, when there was a brief attempt to fix the exchange rate again.

At the beginning, the Austral Plan had an important political impact on the 1985 Congressional elections. The traditional effect of stabilization plans that use the exchange rate as anchors, leading to a consumption boom and sharp declines in inflation, kicked in just in time (see Calvo and Végh, 1999). Improved economic conditions contributed significantly to the Radical Party's victory in 1985, consolidating its position in Congress. However, this economic and political effect proved short-lived. First, the exchange rate-based stabilization plan moved from the "boom" to the "bust" phase. Second, commodity prices collapsed worldwide in 1986 (see Figure 3.4). These circumstances, combined with the fact that the Alfonsín administration had not obtained the hoped-for relief from the external debt,[12] kept both external accounts and the public budget under

pressure. Third, influenced by its electoral victory, the Alfonsín administration began to flirt with the idea of creating a "Third Historical Movement"[13] to absorb part of the Peronist Party into a new and dominant
political coalition.

On the economic front, these attempts to capture part of the
Peronist Party's electoral base led to greater difficulty in controlling fiscal
and monetary variables (to the extent that it became more difficult to
adjust salaries or privatize public enterprises). On the political side, the
Peronist Party stepped up its opposition, particularly through the largely
Peronist workers unions, which staged a record 580 strikes in 1986.

By 1987, economic conditions had deteriorated markedly. Congressional and provincial elections in that year resulted in a major defeat
for the Radical Party, a turning point in its ability to govern. The Primavera
Plan in August 1988, which also had an important political component
related to the 1989 presidential elections (see Stein and Streb, 1998),
was the last attempt to try to control macroeconomic variables. But the
Alfonsín government appeared unwilling (because of its view of what
the adequate development strategy should be) or unable (given its political weakness after the defeat in the 1987 elections) to take a drastic
approach to solving the tug-of-war over fiscal resources.

In the past, the Peronist Party had resolved distributional conflict by simply printing money, and the military regime by contracting
external debt. The Radical administration, with reduced access to external borrowing and high inflation that constrained monetary creation,
resorted to piling up short-term domestic debt. The objective was to buy
time to keep the exchange rate and prices under control until the presidential elections of 1989. Domestic debt jumped from around 7 percent of GDP in 1986 to about 15 percent in the first half of 1989 (IMF,
1990). Because of the accumulation of the internal debt and higher
international interest rates, public sector interest payments in constant
pesos more than doubled between 1984 and 1989 (IMF, 1998).

The Primavera Program collapsed, leading to hyperinflation by
mid-1989. The Alfonsín administration was leaving office, and the Radical Party's candidate had been defeated in the May 1989 presidential
election by Carlos Menem, the Peronist candidate. The transition between
the outgoing and the incoming administrations, the first between two

---

[12] The possibility of reducing the burden of the external debt had to wait until the Brady Plan was
launched in 1989 (when the Alfonsín administration was already nearing the end of its term).
[13] The first two being those led by Hipilito Yrigoyen (also a memeber of the Radical party) at
the beginning of the century and Juan Peron in the late 1940s.

civilian, democratically elected governments from different parties since the 1920s, was marred by great uncertainty. The accumulated imbalances of the Radical government, along with doubts about the economic policies of the new government, led in 1989 to hyperinflation,[14] street riots, and assaults on supermarkets. Chaotic social conditions forced President Alfonsín to transfer government well before the originally scheduled change of administration.

Analysis

As in the case of the military regime, it is easy to pinpoint the problems of the economic strategy. The initial approach of targeting the real exchange rate and increasing salaries led inevitably to high inflation. Later, trying to control inflation by fixing the exchange rate with persistent fiscal deficits and accumulation of short-term domestic debt created the conditions for explosive exchange rate crises and hyperinflation. Again, the key question is why those policies were followed at all. The answer is apparently that the Alfonsín administration was never able to resolve the conflict between trying to strengthen the political position of the Radical Party (which required capturing part of the Peronist vote) and implementing the difficult economic decisions aimed at controlling fiscal accounts (which would have most certainly alienated some of the same groups). Only after the hyperinflationary experience did there emerge the foundations for a broad-based coalition in support of needed economic changes.

From Hyperinflation to Stability: The Politics of the Fixed Exchange Rate Regime

Although the Menem administration's initial programs led to economic turbulence,[15] they laid the foundation for the period of stability that began in 1991. Different governments since the mid-1970s had tried half-heartedly to open up the economy, control fiscal deficits, privatize public enterprises and deregulate markets. But these objectives were pursued more firmly

---

[14] The quarterly rate of devaluation was 816 percent in the second quarter under the Alfonsín administration and almost 370 percent in the third quarter under the Menem administration.
[15] The recurrent problem of short-lived programs to fix the exchange rate that ended in an inflationary explosion, continued during the first 18 months of the Menem administration. In addition to enduring the hyperinflation of 1989, the Argentine economy under President Menem had two other similar episodes: full hyperinflation in 1990 (quarterly inflation of 334 percent and a devaluation of 267 percent), and very high inflation in the first quarter of 1991 (quarterly inflation of 39 percent and a devaluation of 60 percent).

starting in 1989, and by 1991 the Menem government began to fully implement policies in support of these goals.

The cornerstone of the anti-inflationary program was the exchange
rate policy, as defined in the Convertibility Law passed by Congress in
March 1991. This plan pegged the peso to the dollar at a one-to-one parity
and transformed the monetary and exchange rate functions of the central
bank into a currency board.[16] The law directed the central bank to maintain
liquid international reserves to cover (almost) 100 percent of the monetary
base. As a consequence, the monetary authorities could not increase this
aggregate except when international reserves expanded through a trade
surplus or net capital inflows.[17]

Since passage of the law, the exchange rate has remained fixed for
30 quarters (as of March 1999), by far the longest period of exchange rate
stability in Argentina in half a century.[18] The fixed exchange rate survived
the so-called "tequila effect" in 1994-95 and a presidential election in 1995,
as well as the financial crises in Asia, Russia and Brazil. Di Tella's cycles of
"repression" and "loosening" appear to have ended.

The current exchange rate arrangement has become more sustainable for several economic and political reasons. The main considerations
included, first, the emergence of a broad-based coalition for stability, linked
to memories of hyperinflation. A second element has been the legal/institu-
tional framework of the Convertibility Plan. Third, there have been changes
in the evolution of distributive disputes over factor returns (capital and labor), sectoral incomes (agriculture versus industry), and fiscal resources, all
of which were key elements behind major devaluations in the past. Finally,
higher levels of economic growth, the product of better economic policies
and more supportive international conditions, reduced the salience of distributive conflicts and allowed some compensation for the losers from a
fixed exchange rate, at least initially.

---

[16] The original promoter of the idea of a currency board appears not to have been Cavallo
himself but Juan Llach, who served as Undersecretary of Economic Policy. Nothing in his
previous writings suggested that Cavallo would opt for a policy of fixed exchange rates after
having made his name writing primarily about the problems of such regimes and of overvalued exchange rates in Argentine history (see Cavallo and Mundlak, 1982; and Cavallo and
Domenech, 1988). Other proposals for a currency board included Almansi and Rodríguez
(1989).

[17] The Convertibility Law did not establish special requirements concerning broader monetary
aggregates and foreign reserves. The supply of liquidity beyond the monetary base depends
on monetary instruments that the central bank still controls, such as the possibility of changing
the reserve requirements for the banking system and the use of short-term swaps. This allowed some room for maneuver in monetary policy.

[18] The previous record of exchange rate stability went from 1940 to 1946.

Legal/Institutional Aspects

The fixed parity established in the Convertibility Law meant that changing the nominal value of the exchange rate required an act of the legislature. At the same time, the law mandated full convertibility between domestic and foreign currency. Therefore, a minister who wants to devalue faces two equally complicated options. One alternative is to ask Congress to sanction the new parity, but this runs the risk of a very fast loss of the foreign currency reserves of the central bank while the parliamentary debate takes place. The other option is to stop exchanging dollars for pesos (perhaps through a banking holiday while Congress is deliberating), but in this case the official responsible for the decision faces the possibility of legal challenges, since the Convertibility Law indicates the obligation to exchange dollars and pesos at the established parity. As a consequence, this institutional device has made it virtually impossible to devalue the currency.

But the precommitment features of the Convertibility Law went beyond the exchange rate and drastically limited the credit that the central bank could freely create for the public and private sectors. In fact, this strict monetary framework is perhaps much more important than the fixed parity itself for price stability, to the extent that it has prevented the monetization of sectoral disputes that occurred in the past. However, a mere legal/institutional argument begs the question of why this strong pre-commitment device was not used before.

The Politics of (Hyper)inflation and Dollarization

The coalition in favor of low inflation had and still enjoys broad support. Stability of the exchange rate became increasingly associated with price stability in the public mind. On the heels of two bouts of hyperinflation, there was broad consensus in 1991 to avoid yet another episode.

The post-1991 anti-devaluation coalition also included specific groups, such as those indebted in dollars, who may have experienced important economic losses when the exchange rate depreciated. Table 3.3 shows the jump in dollar-denominated debts. Credit in dollars in the banking system increased by 12.5 billion pesos (with an almost equivalent value in dollars) between 1992 and 1995, which represented about 61 percent of all banking credit. The private sector issued bonds denominated in foreign currencies for almost $9 billion between 1991 and 1995, three-quarters of which had maturities of five years or less. The public sector increased its foreign debt by some $25.8 billion in the same period. In addition, there were important flows of foreign direct investment, and participation of foreign investors in Argentina's stock exchange increased significantly.

Table 3.3. Dollarization and External Debt

	1991	1992	1993	1994	1995	1996	1997
1.Banking system (stock at end period)							
-Dollar deposits (millions of pesos)	6,583	10,842	17,532	23,555	23,590	28,405	33,475[a]
-Dollar deposits (% M3)	32.9	33.6	36.6	41.9	43.7	43.9	43.3[a]
-Credit in dollars (stock in millions of pesos)							
-Private sector	9,198	15,488	20,945	27,382	28,523	31,684	37,992
-Public sector	...	4,010	3,270	3,429	3,544	4,432	5,230
-Total	...	19,498	24,215	30,811	32,067	36,116	43,222
-Credit in dollars (% credit)	50.6	54.2	53.1	58.9	61.2	62.7	64.3
2.Foreign direct investment							
-Flows (millions of US$)	...	4,044	2,556	3,066	4,179	...	...
-Accumulated investment	...	14,829	16,476	20,401	24,630	...	...
3.Bond issues, private							
-Flows (millions of US$)	265	1,230	3,902	2,580	952	2,539	...
4.Public debt (Stock in billions of US$)							
-Local currency	1.2	0.7	5.9	7.3	6.7	10.7	...
-Foreign currency	57.2	58.4	61.9	72.2	83.0	89.0	...
-External debt	57.2	57.4	60.3	69.6	68.2	72.5	...
-Internal debt	0.0	1.0	1.6	2.6	14.8	16.5	...
-Total	58.4	59.1	67.8	79.5	89.7	99.7	109.4

[a] End of third quarter.

This debt expansion touched large sectors of the population. Middle- and even lower middle-income families had access to consumption loans, many of them in dollar terms, generating a constituency that was grateful to the government for expanding consumption possibilities and very fearful of a devaluation. Equally concerned were private sector firms that accumulated debts in foreign currency (including the banking system), different domestic economic groups (which in association with foreign investors bought state-owned enterprises), and construction companies. On the asset side, foreign direct and portfolio investors were also concerned about the stability of the exchange rate.

Finally, the government, as a major debtor in foreign currency, would have been very negatively affected by a devaluation, which could have most certainly triggered a fiscal crisis through multiple mechanisms. First, the recession that has usually accompanied devaluations would have reduced tax receipts. Second, the increase in pesos of Argentina's payments of the external public debt would not have been compensated by income in dollars, as in the cases of Mexico's oil-linked public revenues or Chile's copper exports. Third, the deterioration of the fiscal situation would have put downward pressure on public bonds, affecting the privatized social security system and the banking system (which had those assets in their portfolios). Any attempt to alleviate those problems would have compounded fiscal difficulties.

All in all, the dollarization of debts created a strong constituency for exchange rate stability. However, widespread dollarization at the beginning of the 1980s did not prevent the devaluations and economic morass linked to the debt crisis. Clear differences between both episodes, in addition perhaps to the magnitude of dollar indebtedness, have already been discussed: the impact of hyperinflation on the economic behavior of Argentines and the institutional basis of convertibility, with its strong precommitment through a legislative act. But other elements also contributed to exchange rate stability during the 1990s.

Key elements behind major devaluations in the past had been the distributive disputes over factor returns (capital and labor), sectoral incomes (agriculture versus industry), and fiscal resources, which were monetized through the passive adjustment of monetary policies. The Convertibility Plan established a more disciplined monetary framework, which limited the possibility of monetization of those distributive struggles. Perhaps more importantly, such distributive struggles also appeared to have become more circumscribed in the 1990s, in part helped by higher rates of economic growth and better international conditions. Fiscal adjustment advanced more than in the previous decade (although less than what would have been necessary to ensure a better performance when external capital flows dwindled in 1995) and the labor movement showed a relatively subdued response to weak wage and employment conditions. The next section explains the role played by four additional factors in explaining the stability of the fixed exchange rate: economic growth, fiscal adjustment, weaker labor response, and better international conditions.

Sectoral Policy Reform, Productivity and Growth

Although fixing the exchange rate reflected the concerns of a broad spectrum of Argentine society, the ensuing overvaluation of the real exchange rate negatively affected different productive sectors. The economic program included specific policies that moderated the impact of such overvaluation. The agricultural sector was helped by the elimination of export taxes (a longstanding request of rural groups) and by the liberalization of several markets for products, inputs and auxiliary services that were previously regulated (helping to improve the price/cost equation for the sector).

Industrial producers, although affected by the drastic reduction of import tariffs implemented since 1991, received some help from different selective policies, including reimbursement of indirect taxes to exporters, expedited antidumping procedures, and special promotion regimes in some industries, such as automobiles.

More generally, all productive sectors benefited, at least initially, from the consumption boom usually associated with the establishment of fixed exchange regimes. When consumption growth began to slow, the creation of MERCOSUR—following the impact of the 1994 Real Plan in Brazil in changing the usual Argentine trade deficit with its neighbor into a trade surplus—stimulated economic activity and generated further gains in outward orientation and productivity. It can be argued that the increase in productivity due to additional investments, the decline in several components of the internal costs linked to deregulation and enhanced competition, and greater market opportunities in MERCOSUR were important supply-side reasons that contributed to high levels of economic growth over 1991-94, helped the economy through the difficult period of 1995-96, and led to a significant rebound in 1997 (see Figure 3.12).

However, not all this acceleration in economic activity was based on sustainable supply-side measures (including inflows of long-term capital), but rather was aided in good measure by reversible capital inflows and over-stimulative monetary and fiscal policies. This generated the conditions for a downturn in 1995, when international conditions changed after the 1994 Mexican devaluation (see IMF, 1995, and Díaz-Bonilla, 1996). Going against the policy prescription of trying to moderate the expansionary im-

Figure 3.12. Gross Domestic Product

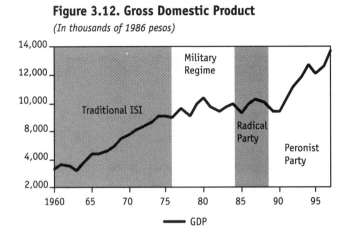

(In thousands of 1986 pesos)

pact of capital flows with tighter monetary and fiscal policies (see Calvo, Leiderman and Reinhart, 1996, and Schadler et al., 1993), Argentina in fact strengthened the influence of its economic policies through a process of rapid credit creation and increased public expenditures. This fueled the consumption boom and economic growth of 1991-94.[19]

Overall, expansive monetary and fiscal policies weakened the banking system, made the country more vulnerable to the 1994-95 external shocks, and, combined with a fixed exchange rate regime and trade liberalization, had a strong negative impact on sectors producing tradable goods. This amplified the impact of reduced trade barriers and led to the bankruptcy of firms that would have been competitive under a different combination of macroeconomic policies.[20] More prudent

---

[19] As already mentioned, the Convertibility Law only mandates backing of the monetary base with international reserves, but not broader definitions of money supply. Economic authorities were able to reduce reserve requirements for the banking system in 1992-93 (IMF, 1995, and Díaz-Bonilla, 1996). Capital flows and reduced reserve requirements led to a rapid expansion of credit (IMF, 1995), which deteriorated the ratio of monetary aggregates to foreign currency reserves (except for the mandatory coverage of the monetary base). Argentina's financial system began to experience difficulties well before the Mexican devaluation (see Corrigan, 1996). However, a forceful tackling of the problems was delayed (especially in the case of insolvent public banks owned by the provincial governments), probably influenced by the political need to change the Constitution in 1994 to get the presidential reelection approved. Those delays exacerbated the severity of the banking and economic crisis in 1995 (see Díaz-Bonilla, 1996).

[20] This discussion is related to two other issues. The first is the sustainability of the exchange rate peg if the value selected is "too tight" (see Williamson, 1994, on the UK and EMU). A second issue is that if an initial value that is "too tight" is combined with a drastic program of trade liberalization, the restructuring of the economy may also harm sectors that would not have been considered inefficient under more adequate levels of the initial peg. See the seminal works of Little, Scitovsky, and Scott (1970) and Balassa et al. (1971), and more recent discussion in Bruton (1989).

monetary and fiscal policies from 1991-94 could have headed off some of these problems, leaving the country stronger for the changing economic conditions in 1995.

The reasons to avoid tackling the issue of an overheated economy in 1993-94 appeared to have been both economic and political. At the economic level, some voices argued that interventions to sterilize capital flows would have been self-defeating because they would have increased interest rates, attracted even more capital, and weakened fiscal accounts. Usually this criticism was directed at monetary sterilization of money expansion through the issuing of government debt. In contrast, others, acknowledging the perils of sterilization (see Calvo, 1991) argued correctly that there were other interventions available, including fiscal tightening, increasing banking reserves and improving banking supervision (see Rodriguez, 1993; Calvo, Leiderman and Reinhart, 1996; Schadler, et al., 1993).

The political argument was that the expansion was needed to maintain the momentum for reforms.[21] The economic team, coming from outside the Peronist Party, did not initially enjoy widespread political support within the government. But its standing was strengthened by the expansion of consumption and overall positive economic conditions. In this period of economic buoyancy, it was easier to implement drastic privatization of public sector enterprises, reduction in trade protection, and other difficult measures. Also, the economy's strong performance during those years produced handsome electoral returns for the Menem administration, which won the Congressional midterm elections in 1991 and 1993 and the presidential election in 1995.

Fiscal Adjustment

Fiscal deficits of about 6 percent of GDP in 1988 were reduced to about 3.8 percent in 1989-90 and 1.6 percent in 1991, and declined to almost negligible levels in 1992-93. Fiscal consolidation was helped by better tax administration and the Olivera-Tanzi effect working in reverse (once inflation declined dramatically). On the expenditure side, different factors contributed to getting public accounts under control: privatizations, the reduction of subsidies to domestic industrial groups, further adjustments in military expenditures, the decline in world interest rates, and the international debt settlement of 1992 under the Brady

---

[21] At least two high officials of the economic team at that time argued that much in conversations with one of the authors of this chapter.

Plan. Public accounts improved significantly compared to the situation in the 1980s, and this proved enough to forestall the occurrence of an exchange rate crisis a la Krugman.

However, the government did not take advantage of the favorable initial economic conditions to place fiscal accounts on a more solid footing to diminish the impact of future external shocks to Argentina. During the key political year of 1994, when the Constitution was changed to allow presidential reelection in 1995, the fiscal accounts turned into a deficit.[22] In addition, important distributive issues affecting the public budget are still pending, as witnessed by recent debates in Argentina on tax, labor and education reforms. Different social demands increasingly put forward by the electorate may well require additional expenditures. The form of the social coalition supporting the current exchange rate regime will undoubtedly be influenced by how these fiscal redistribution issues develop in the future.

The Response of the Labor Movement

There were several facets to the decline of labor unions in Argentina's economic and political arenas. One was the restructuring and downsizing of the industrial sector that began in the 1970s. At the political level, the progressive weakness of labor unions within the Peronist Party after so many years of predominance can be traced to the defeat in the presidential election of 1983, the first time the Peronist Party had ever lost a general election. The rejection of the Peronist candidates was widely attributed to the Argentine electorate's growing distaste for old-guard union bosses, a dominant force in the Peronist Party, who alienated voters with strong-arm tactics and violent slogans. After another electoral drubbing in the 1985 Congressional elections, a new current emerged within the Peronist Party. This process generated an important renewal of its leadership, reducing significantly the political clout of unions and increasing the presence of middle-class urban leaders. Under the new leadership, the Peronist Party won the 1987 midterm elections, consolidating the presence of nonunion cadres in its political structure.

In the presidential primaries within the Peronist Party for the 1989 general election, displaced union leaders supported Carlos Saul Menem in helping defeat Antonio Cafiero, the leader of the 1987 renewal movement. Once Menem prevailed in the presidential election, however, the new presi-

---

[22] IMF estimates show a positive fiscal impulse of about 1.5 percent of GDP in 1994 (IMF, 1998), which can be considered a manifestation in Argentina of the traditional political cycle linked to important elections.

dent brought wholesale change to the political leadership of the party, further weakening the influence of unions in the new Peronist government.

In the first main confrontation with unions in the case of the privatization of the *Empresa Nacional de Telecomunicaciones* (the public telephone company), the Menem administration, supported by a strong current of public opinion against the notoriously bad service of the telephone company, first politically isolated and then fired striking employees. This sent a clear signal to different public sector unions that the economic restructuring of the public sector was moving forward and that there were tangible costs in opposing it. On the other hand, labor unions were allowed to participate (or to increase their previous participation) in several profitable activities related to health services, management of pension funds, and even privatizations, opening new economic opportunities for the most business-oriented unions (Murillo, 1997).

This pattern of selective rewards and punishments was successfully utilized to carry out the substantial restructuring of Argentina's public sector. In particular, the Menem administration kept open for a long time the possibility of wholesale reform of labor laws, including reductions in the legal powers and functions of unions, as a bargaining tool in the nuanced relationship between the government and the labor movement.

By 1996, levels of unemployment not experienced for half a century coexisted with real wages that, even in the upper estimates, were below the averages for the two decades between the mid-1960s and mid-1980s (see Figure 3.6).[23, 24] The consequent soft labor market also contributed to muting the response of workers.[25]

In summary, the mute response of the labor movement to the drastic economic changes implemented by the Menem administration can

---

[23] There is some uncertainty regarding data on wages. Official figures were compiled until 1992 and then discontinued. For 1993 there is no official data. Then in mid-1994, the Ministry of the Economy began publishing the salaries of workers included in the Integrated System of Retirement and Pensions (about 29 percent of the workforce in 1996), which can be considered a high upper bound for the average wage in the economy. Figure 3.6 includes the middle point of three alternative estimates by the authors based on data from the *Fundación Mediterránea, Carta Económica* and the 1994-97 figures from the Integrated System.

[24] The comparison must be understood in relative terms. A lower real wage in the 1990s compared to the 1960s, for example, only means that nominal wages in the current decade are buying less of the standard basket of goods and services represented in the Consumer Price Index than nominal wages in the 1960s.

[25] The usual perception that Argentine wages are high rests depends on how one measures them in U.S. dollars (see Figure 3.7 for wages in real 1990 dollars). The combination of salaries high in dollars and low in pesos is still affecting the performance of the Argentine economy, an issue related to defining the adequate exchange rate in the context of the overall economic program.

be attributed to the decline of industrial employment; the erosion of the political clout of unions within the Peronist Party after the 1983 and 1985 electoral defeats; public opposition to inefficient public firms; the cleavage between more entrepreneurial unions (trying to take advantage of the new business opportunities to provide different services to their affiliates) and those oriented to the traditional defense of workers' rights; and more difficult employment conditions after 1994. The struggle over factor returns that played havoc with previous fixed exchange rate regimes did not achieve the same intensity this time.

International Conditions

While several previous episodes of exchange rate instability had been associated with external shocks, the Convertibility Plan coincided with improved international economic conditions. First, in 1989 the newly elected Bush administration decided to change the prevailing approach to debt, opening the possibility of debt reductions. Argentina eventually obtained debt relief in 1992 through the Brady Plan. Second, the slowing of the U.S. economy at the beginning of the 1990s led the Federal Reserve to adopt a more expansionary monetary policy, which contributed to lower interest rates in 1991-92 (see Figure 3.11). This changed international environment, along with a better framework of macroeconomic policies in several Latin American countries, generated the return of capital to the region just as the Convertibility Plan was being implemented.[26] In addition, the terms of trade, which had collapsed in 1986-87, began a slow but firm recovery that accelerated towards the mid-1990s and lasted until 1998 (see Figure 3.8).

The exchange rate regime was tested when sentiment in world capital markets changed after Mexico's devaluation in 1994. The fiscal, financial and growth imbalances accumulated during 1991-94 left Argentina too weak to withstand the comparatively mild external shock and the economy entered a recession in 1995.[27]

However, international organizations and developed countries, particularly the United States, were more willing to provide financial support to Argentina than in the past. First, Argentina was considered an example in implementing policies of "hard money and free markets"

---

[26] See Calvo, Leiderman and Reinhart (1992, 1993) for a discussion of the causes of capital inflows to Latin America.

[27] See Díaz-Bonilla (1996) for a comparison of the 1982 and 1994 external shocks to Argentina. While in 1982 the entire Latin American region fell into recession, the 1995 episode was mainly circumscribed to Mexico and Argentina, suggesting that internal conditions rather than the external shock were the main reasons for the ensuing economic recession.

(as the policies of the Washington Consensus were summarized), and could not be allowed to falter after the problems experienced by Mexico (another country popularly considered to have followed such recommendations).[28] Second, there had been an important change in the international posture of Argentina, such as its participation in the Gulf War and its contribution to United Nations peacekeeping operations. These changes improved the international image of a country that not long before had been at war with one of NATO's main allies over the Malvinas Islands.

As a result, capital flight that had occurred after the 1994 Mexican devaluation was offset in great measure by an important financial package put together by the International Monetary Fund, the Inter-American Development Bank and the World Bank, with strong backing from the U.S. government. This had not happened during the 1980s debt crisis.

Analysis

Argentina's experience with hyperinflation in 1989-90 led to the emergence of a broad-based coalition in favor of stability, which, because expectations of devaluations and inflation had become far more synchronized than before, gave strong backing to the implementation of the strict fixed exchange rate system of the Convertibility Law. This institutional innovation practically eliminated discretion in the management of the exchange rate while substantially limiting the use of passive monetary policies to accommodate distributional conflicts. Those distributional conflicts also appeared to have diminished in intensity, in part because of the way the Menem administration handled traditional power centers such as the military and the labor unions. Finally, supportive international conditions along with domestic growth facilitated the economic adjustment of some of the affected groups.

Although the desire for economic stability still runs strong in Argentina, and is focused primarily on the exchange rate regime, the contours of the stability coalition may change in the future if domestic economic conditions, already affected by events such as the Asian, Russian and Brazilian financial crises, weaken further, and if distributive issues resurface.

---

[28] In fact, Mexico had also implemented unsustainable monetary and financial policies in 1994, linked to its own political cycle. See the economic analysis in Calvo and Mendoza (1996).

Quantitative Analysis

During the ISI period, exchange rate policies reflected the dual distributive conflict between agriculture and industry, and between capital and labor. Devaluations were controversial but controlled events that improved the price of agricultural goods and cut real wages. Later, however, in the context of an open capital account with large fiscal deficits, a weak financial system, and spreading dollarization, devaluations began to have increasingly negative systemic effects on inflation and growth, which eventually overshadowed traditional distributional issues. Inflation, which was a problem even for non-elected military governments, became even more relevant to the political process once democracy returned in 1983. By then, devaluations and expectations of inflation had become largely synchronized, and manipulating inflation by controlling the exchange rate produced positive political results for the incumbent, as was the case of the Austral Plan in 1985 and with the Menem administration up until 1997. The other side of the coin was the political price paid by the Radical Party, especially after the hyperinflationary experience of 1989.

While the previous sections presented a mostly qualitative historical analysis of those hypotheses and explanations, the arguments are explored quantitatively in the sections that follow.

Distributional Issues

One of the key distributional issues in the history of Argentina's exchange rate policy is the impact of devaluations on real wages. Granger-causality tests (see Table 3.4) provide a first approximation. For the period from 1955-97, the null hypothesis that real wages and the exchange rate do not Granger-cause each other is not rejected. For the shorter period from 1955-76, however, when traditional ISI prevailed, the null of no Granger causation in both directions is strongly rejected. This appears in line with the hypothesis that during the ISI period the distributional conflict involved the interaction of devaluation and real wages, while later the mechanism appears to have changed.

This issue is further analyzed by utilizing an unrestricted Vector Autoregressive Model (VAR) to study the impulse-response functions.[29] The

---

[29] The length of the VAR models was established considering the Schwartz criteria (due to the importance of the degrees of freedom) and the behavior of the residuals. The residuals were checked to ensure normality, homoskedasticity and lack of autocorrelation. The impulse-response functions were calculated with 100 Monte Carlo repetitions. A general discussion of estimation and inference in VARs can be found in Canova (1995). See also Sims, Stock and Watson (1990).

Table 3.4. Granger-Causality Tests: Real Wages and the Nominal Exchange Rate

Pairwise Granger Causality Tests
Sample: 1955 1997; Lags: 2

Null Hypothesis:	Obs	F-Statistic	Probability
REAL WAGE does not Granger Cause EXCHANGE RATE	40	0.18141	0.83487
EXCHANGE RATE does not Granger Cause REAL WAGE		0.59682	0.55607

Sample: 1955 1976; Lags: 2

Null Hypothesis:	Obs	F-Statistic	Probability
REAL WAGE does not Granger Cause EXCHANGE RATE	20	7.08484	0.00682
EXCHANGE RATE does not Granger Cause REAL WAGE		12.9346	0.00054

Sample: 1977 1997; Lags: 2

Null Hypothesis:	Obs	F-Statistic	Probability
REAL WAGE does not Granger Cause EXCHANGE RATE	20	0.15172	0.86053 EX
CHANGE RATE does not Granger Cause REAL WAGE		0.91526	0.42165

VAR is run with the exchange rate, GDP and real wages (using that ordering for identification of the shocks).[30] Argentina's terms of trade are considered as an exogenous variable. For the whole period, the impulse-response functions suggest that a devaluation results mainly in a fall of GDP in the first two periods (where the confidence bands show statistical significance), with negligible declines in real wages (see Figure 3.13, first column of graphics). Also, increases in real wages appear to lead to devaluations (third column).

The hypothesis of the contractionary effect of devaluations (see Krugman and Taylor, 1978), which seems to be borne by the impulse-response functions, may be the result of the supply-side shock affecting intermediate imports and/or the demand shock resulting from nominal assets (mainly money supply) that are cut in real terms by the devaluation and/or a banking crisis, leading to sharp declines in deposits and credit, which would affect both aggregate supply and demand.

---

[30] The three-equation VAR can be derived from a setting where aggregate supply depends on capital stock, employment and intermediate inputs, and aggregate demand has a domestic component (that depends on income and assets), and net exports (that depends on the exchange rate and terms of trade). Also, labor demand depends on real wages and the level of activity for a given stock of capital; labor supply depends on real wages; and the demand for intermediate inputs (which have an important component of imports) depends on the exchange rate and world prices. With aggregate demand equal to aggregate supply, a clearing labor market, and capital stock and assets fixed in each temporary equilibrium, the VAR utilized here follows.

Figure 3.13. VAR Nominal Exchange Rate, GDP and Real Wages, 1955-97

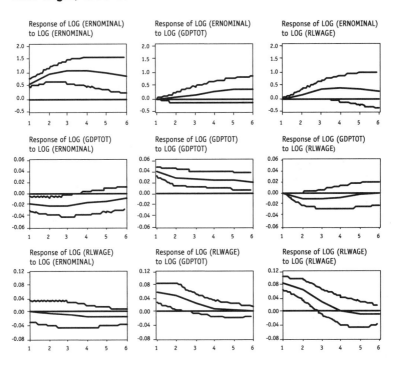

However, if the VAR model is estimated separately over the period before and after the 1978 opening of the capital account (see Figures 3.14A and B), there are two important differences. First, the negative impact of devaluation on real wages is stronger and statistically better defined in the period from 1955-77. Second, the recessionary impact on the GDP is larger and significant in the years after 1978, compared to a smaller and statistically insignificant effect during the traditional ISI period.

It appears that during ISI, devaluations could be utilized to cut real wages, and that, after the initial negative impact, the economy began to grow again. But after 1978, the responses to devaluations were deeper and there were longer declines in economic activity, with real wages changing far less than before. Real wages fell more (i.e., workers were "surprised") in the 1960s and 1970s than in the next two decades, when workers seem to have been able to get their nominal wages adjusted up after a devaluation. This reduced the positive supply-side impact that upward adjustments of the nominal exchange rate may have had on external competitiveness, leaving only the negative impact of devaluations on GDP growth through other

Figure 3.14A. VAR: Nominal Exchange Rate, GDP and Real Wages, 1955-77

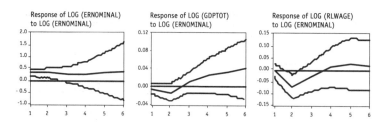

Figure 3.14B. VAR: Nominal Exchange Rate, GDP and Real Wages, 1978-97

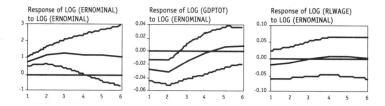

channels, such as the increase in costs of imported intermediate inputs and the decline in real money supply.

Other distributional impact of the devaluations is associated with the price of agricultural vis-à-vis nonagricultural goods. The Granger causality tests (see Table 3.5) suggest that the main influence on the ratio of agricultural to nonagricultural prices comes from world prices. However, there is a clear difference between the ISI period, when the ratio of agricultural to non-agricultural prices is Granger-caused by world prices, and the period after the mid-1970s, when the influence of the exchange rate on that ratio increases.

The impulse-response functions show that the domestic price ratio for the whole period basically followed world real prices (see Figure 3.15).[31] However, from the mid-1970s onwards the VAR model suggests a

---

[31] Construction of the VAR considers that the domestic price of agricultural goods depends on the exchange rate, world agricultural prices, and commercial policies. The domestic price of nonagricultural goods is a linear combination of the domestic price of industrial goods (which in turn depends on world industrial prices, the exchange rate and commercial policies) and the domestic price of services. If commercial and other policies do not change, the ratio of domestic agricultural to nonagricultural prices depends on the real world price of agricultural goods (which is deflated by manufacturing unit values) and the nominal exchange rate. The ordering for the VAR is world prices, nominal exchange rate and domestic prices.

Table 3.5. Granger-Causality Tests: Devaluation and Relative Prices

Pairwise Granger Causality Tests
Sample: 1950-97
Lags: 2

Null Hypothesis:	Obs	F-Statistic	Probability
EXCHANGE RATE does not Granger Cause WORLD REAL AGRICULTURAL PRICES	35	0.32409	0.72568
WORLD REAL AGRICULTURAL PRICES do not Granger Cause EXCHANGE RATE		3.42192	0.04585
RELATIVE PRICES AGRIC/NONAGRIC do not Granger Cause WORLD REAL AGRIC PRICES	35	1.00529	0.37793
WORLD REAL AGRIC PRICES do not Granger Cause RELATIVE PRICES AGRIC/NONAGRIC		3.34404	0.04886
RELATIVE PRICES AGRIC/NONAGRIC do not Granger Cause EXCHANGE RATE	35	0.04252	0.95843
EXCHANGE RATE does not Granger Cause RELATIVE PRICES AGRIC/NONAGRIC		0.90735	0.41438

Pairwise Granger Causality Tests
Sample: 1950-78
Lags: 2

Null Hypothesis:	Obs	F-Statistic	Probability
EXCHANGE RATE does not Granger Cause WORLD REAL AGRICULTURAL PRICES	17	9.60543	0.00323
WORLD REAL AGRICULTURAL PRICES do not Granger Cause EXCHANGE RATE		3.57696	0.06047
RELATIVE PRICES AGRIC/NONAGRIC do not Granger Cause WORLD REAL AGRIC PRICES	17	1.35804	0.29399
WORLD REAL AGRIC PRICES do not Granger Cause RELATIVE PRICES AGRIC/NONAGRIC		8.59318	0.00483
RELATIVE PRICES AGRIC/NONAGRIC do not Granger Cause EXCHANGE RATE	17	0.10239	0.90346
EXCHANGE RATE does not Granger Cause RELATIVE PRICES AGRIC/NONAGRIC		1.83466	0.20174

Pairwise Granger Causality Tests
Sample: 1978-97
Lags: 2

Null Hypothesis:	Obs	F-Statistic	Probability
EXCHANGE RATE does not Granger Cause WORLD REAL AGRICULTURAL PRICES	19	0.67229	0.52627
WORLD REAL AGRICULTURAL PRICES do not Granger Cause EXCHANGE RATE		1.44112	0.26970
RELATIVE PRICES AGRIC/NONAGRICU do not Granger Cause WORLD REAL AGRIC PRICES	19	0.47353	0.63242
WORLD REAL AGRIC PRICES do not Granger Cause RELATIVE PRICES AGRIC/NONAGRIC		1.47752	0.26170
RELATIVE PRICES AGRIC/NONAGRIC do not Granger Cause EXCHANGE RATE	19	3.60038	0.05476
EXCHANGE RATE does not Granger Cause RELATIVE PRICES AGRIC/NONAGRIC		4.99030	0.02311

greater role for devaluations (see Figure 3.16). A possible interpretation is that during the ISI period, when high real agricultural prices prevailed in world markets, the exchange rate had to be adjusted only when crises erupted. However, once world agricultural real prices began to fall in the 1980s, governments tried to compensate for the persistent decline through devaluations. This of course, led to higher inflation.

Also, the idea that devaluations unequivocally benefited the agricultural sector has to be seen in a broader context. Another VAR model with the exchange rate and two indices of agricultural and industrial production shows that for the whole period, a devaluation had a negative impact on industrial production, and a positive impact on agriculture only after a period of initial decline (see Figure 3.17). But again, the periods

Figure 3.15. VAR: World Agricultural Prices, Nominal Exchange Rate, and Domestic Price Ratio, Agricultural/ Nonagricultural, 1960-97

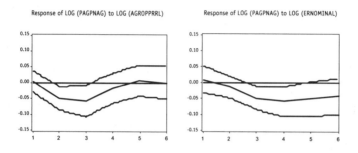

Figure 3.16. VAR: World Agricultural Prices, Nominal Exchange Rate, and Domestic Price Ratio, Agricultural/ Nonagricultural, 1977-97

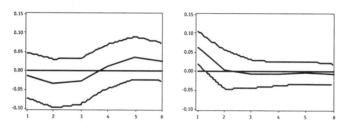

before and after the mid-1970s show different responses to a devaluation. During the ISI period, the negative impact of a devaluation on industry was smaller and eventually there was a return to growth, while the positive effect on agriculture was far stronger than for the whole period (see Figure 3.18A). In the period after 1978 (see Figure 3.18B), a devaluation negatively affected both agriculture and industry.

The conclusion is that even though a devaluation in the 1980s would have improved relative prices for agriculture, it would also have had a negative impact on agricultural growth. This may reflect larger forward and backward links of the agricultural sector with the rest of the economy, as well as the stronger negative effects of devaluation on GDP growth during the last decades compared to the ISI period. Therefore, it can be argued that the relative price effect of a devaluation, with its distributional advantage for agriculture, may have been more than offset by the income effect of a fall in production, at least for the period after 1978. The new dynamics of devaluations, with broader-

Figure 3.17. VAR: Nominal Exchange Rate, Agricultural Production and Industrial Production, 1960-97

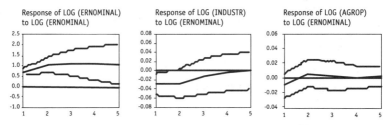

Figure 3.18A. VAR: Nominal Exchange Rate, Agricultural Production and Industrial Production, 1965-77

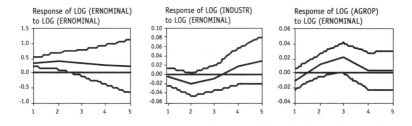

Figure 3.18B. VAR: Nominal Exchange Rate, Agricultural Production and Industrial Production, 1978-97

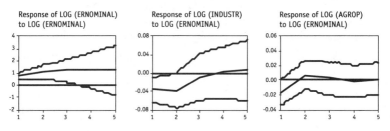

based effects, tended to dominate the issue of relative factor returns as a main concern for policymakers and the public. Part of this shift may be related to the growing role of the exchange rate as a nominal anchor for expectations.

The Politics of Inflation and Devaluation

The relationship between devaluation and inflation is analyzed here with Granger causality and cointegration tests, applying Johansen's procedure, on quarterly data from 1957 to 1997. The results appear in Tables 3.6 and 3.7.

Table 3.6. Granger-Causality: Inflation and Devaluation

Pairwise Granger Causality Tests
Sample: 1957:1 1997:4
Lags: 2

Null Hypothesis:	Obs	F-Statistic	Probability
DEVALUATION does not Granger Cause INFLATION	151	183.263	0.00000
INFLATION does not Granger Cause DEVALUATION		6.02627	0.00306

Pairwise Granger Causality Tests
Sample 1957:1 1978:4
Lags: 2

Null Hypothesis:	Obs	F-Statistic	Probability
DEVALUATION does not Granger Cause INFLATION	77	32.2001	1.0E-10
INFLATION does not Granger Cause DEVALUATION		0.60681	0.54785

Pairwise Granger Causality Tests
Sample: 1979:1 1997:4
Lags: 2

Null Hypothesis:	Obs	F-Statistic	Probability
DEVALUATION does not Granger Cause INFLATION	74	108.162	0.00000
INFLATION does not Granger Cause DEVALUATION		2.86563	0.06375

The Granger-causality tests suggest that the rates of inflation and devaluation have become more coordinated over time:[32] non-Granger causality in both directions is strongly rejected for the whole period, and also for the period after the opening of the capital account (although at a somewhat lower significance level). On the other hand, for the 1960s and 1970s only the null of devaluation not causing inflation is rejected, suggesting that in the earlier period devaluations preceded higher inflation—but not necessarily the other way around.

A different way to look at this issue is to ask whether both variables are cointegrated. Unit root tests (not shown here) indicate that the exchange rate and the consumer price index (CPI) in levels are I(2), while their rates of change are I(1). Therefore, it is appropriate to ask about the possible cointegration relationship between rates.

---

[32] Devaluation is measured as the rate of change of the nominal exchange rate in pesos per U.S. dollar, and inflation is measured as the rate of growth of the consumer price index. Both growth rates were calculated in levels and not as the difference of logarithms, since the values differed significantly for the period of hyperinflation.

Table 3.7. Cointegration Tests

Sample: 1957:1 1978:4
Included observations: 72
Test assumption: No deterministic trend in the data
Series: INFLATION DEVALUATION
Lags interval: 1 to 2, 3 to 4, 5 to 6

Eigenvalue	Likelihood ratio	5 percent critical value	1 percent critical value	Hypothesized no. of CE(s)
0.096651	9.638690	19.96	24.60	None
0.031710	2.320127	9.24	12.97	At most 1

Sample: 1979:1 1997:4
Included observations: 74
Test assumption: No deterministic trend in the data
Series: INFLATION DEVALUATION
Lags interval: 1 to 2, 3 to 4, 5 to 6

Eigenvalue	Likelihood ratio	5 Percent critical value	1 Percent critical value	Hypothesized no. of CE(s)
0.194188	22.36754	19.96	24.60	None*
0.082736	6.390604	9.24	12.97	At most 1

*(**) denotes rejection of the hypothesis at 5%(1%) significance level. L.R. test indicates 1 cointegrating equation(s) at 5% significance level.

Performing a standard Johansen test before and after the opening up of the capital account (December 1978), the null of at least one cointegrating equation cannot be rejected for the period without capital controls (see Table 3.7).[33] However, the same test for the period 1959:1-1978:4 cannot reject the null of no cointegration (i.e., zero cointegrating equations). This suggests that while the rates of inflation and devaluation moved somewhat independently from each other in the 1960s and 1970s, this was no longer the case in the 1980s and 1990s.

Inflation reacts later and less strongly to a devaluation during the 1959-78 period than after the opening of the capital account (Figures 3.18.A and 3.18.B). Following the devaluations of the mid-1970s and early 1980s, inflation, and presumably inflationary expectations as well, appear to have been more linked to the exchange rate than before.[34] Basically, the greater

---

[33] The test was run with six lags to whiten the residuals and with an intercept in the cointegrating equation, but not in the VAR. The main thrust of the results holds under other specifications.
[34] Calvo and Végh (1999) argue that the exchange rate "provides a much clearer signal to the public of the government's intentions and actual actions than a money supply target. Thus if the public's inflationary expectations are influenced to a large extent by the ability to easily track and continuously monitor the nominal anchor, the exchange rate has a natural advantage" (p. 46).

coordination between devaluation and inflation after the 1980s leads to the politics of inflation as the determinant factor for exchange rate policies.

Electoral Results

Since democracy was restored in Argentina in 1983, a relevant question in political terms has been the issues that have led voters to reward or punish incumbents. In economic terms, the most obvious issues are inflation and unemployment. Figures 3.19 and 3.20 are scatter diagrams showing the percentage vote for the incumbent in the presidential and congressional elections since the return to democracy in 1983, against (the log of) inflation and unemployment, respectively.[35] Inflation appears negatively correlated with the votes for the incumbent, while unemployment does not show any strong correlation.

Table 3.8 shows the results of a simple regression exploring the link between inflation and unemployment, on one hand, and votes for the incumbent, on the other (see, for instance, Fair, 1996, and Lewis-Beck and Rice, 1992).[36] Given the lack of degrees of freedom, the results are only suggestive, but they coincide with the bivariate diagrams in showing that inflation appears negatively correlated with the vote for the incumbent. Also, the coefficient for inflation is statistically significant, but its small size suggests that the political impact is important only at high levels of inflation. Adjusting for other influences, unemployment also appears negatively correlated with the vote of the incumbent, but is not statistically significant. However, during the last election in 1997 the issue of unemployment showed a greater salience, suggesting that the politics of unemployment may be increasing in importance vis-à-vis the politics of (hyper)inflation.

---

[35] Between 1983 and the time this chapter was written, there had been three presidential and congressional elections (1983, 1989, 1995) and the percentage vote utilized for the incumbent corresponds to the presidential candidate; the rest were only congressional elections (1985, 1987, 1991 and 1993) and the percentage vote was for the political parties as a whole. The 1983 election is not included in the diagrams as there was no incumbent, being the first democratic election after a military regime. A special election to elect representatives to change the Constitution is not included in the diagrams either. Inflation and unemployment correspond to the year average.

[36] The equation includes all elections mentioned in the previous footnote. As there was no incumbent in the 1983 election, the Peronist Party was chosen as the incumbent because it can be argued that the Radical candidate, Raul Alfonsín, was successful in portraying Peronist candidates as the continuation of the previous military regime. There are dummies for 1983 (trying to capture the special conditions of the first election after a military regime), and for presidential elections, considering that they may be different from the other elections.

Figure 3.19. Elections and Inflation

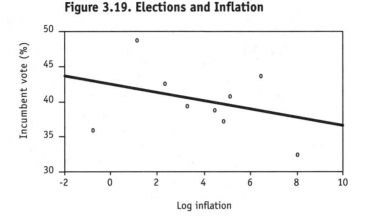

Figure 3.20. Elections and Unemployment

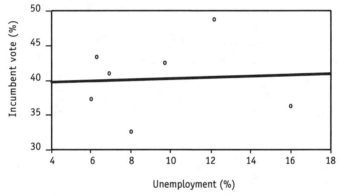

Findings

The VAR impulse-response functions show that devaluations did indeed modify sectoral returns to different social groups and productive sectors over the whole period considered. They affected real wages (which were cut during the ISI period but less so since the end of the 1970s) and the relative price of both agricultural and nonagricultural goods (which tended to improve, but were basically dominated by world prices). However, the distributional and other consequences of adjustments in nominal exchange rates produced different impacts during the ISI period with capital account controls, compared to subsequent years. Since the end of the 1970s, devaluation appears to have had less of an impact on relative prices (which appeared to be more rigid, particularly real wages) and more on overall growth. Devaluations came to negatively affect even those sectors (such as agriculture) that were supposed to benefit from upward adjustments of the nominal exchange rate.

Devaluations also generated inflation in the 1960s and 1970s, but with a lag, and the impact was smaller than that of subsequent devaluations. During the period with trade and capital controls, devaluation and inflation were not as synchronized as they became later. And to the extent that there was a linkage, it ran from devaluations to inflation. However, once the capital account was opened in the second half of the 1970s, and as the country experienced traumatic devaluations in 1975 and the beginning of the 1980s, expectations of inflation and devaluation became more closely coordinated. For the period since 1979, inflation and devaluation cointegrate, and Granger causation in both directions cannot be ruled out.

With the advent of democracy, the electorate was able to express its preferences on economic and other issues. Inflation appears to have been the main concern at high levels and, to the extent that inflation was linked to the nominal exchange rate, devaluations became a political liability. At the current configuration of inflation-unemployment levels, unemployment may be turning into a more determinant factor for the percentage vote of the incumbent. However, the statistical analysis does not suggest that the link between devaluation and inflation has been broken. Therefore, the political costs of a devaluation may be as significant as before.

Exchange Rate Policies: From the Politics of Redistribution to Inflation and Beyond

This chapter has examined the political economy of Argentina since the 1950s in order to explain exchange rate crises and policies. The point of departure has been the observation by Di Tella (1987) regarding the existence of a cycle with two phases in exchange rate policy: the "repressed stage," when some key prices (including the exchange rate) are controlled to tame inflation, and the "loosening stage," when those controls collapse and inflation jumps to new levels. This regularity, however, extended beyond the period analyzed by Di Tella, and the cycle became shorter and more violent from the mid-1980s to the beginning of 1991. During those years, the periods of fixed exchange rates lasted less time than before and the ratcheting up effect on inflation increased. However, since passage in 1991 of the Convertibility Law, which pegged the peso one-to-one to the dollar, the "loosening" stage has not taken place, even after the "tequila effect" in 1995 and the financial crises in Asia, Russia and Brazil in 1997.

Table 3.8. Vote for the Incumbent, Inflation and Unemployment

LS // Dependent Variable is VOTINCUMB
Date: 07/02/98   Time: 12:27
Sample: 1 9
Included observations: 9

Variable	Coefficient	Std. Error	t-Statistic	Prob.
INFLATION	-0.005573	0.001872	-2.976666	0.0409
UNEMPLOYMENT	-0.586350	0.463660	-1.264611	0.2747
C	46.04942	4.724196	9.747567	0.0006
DUM1	9.242833	4.140635	2.232226	0.0894
DUM3	-10.25139	5.941378	-1.725423	0.1595

R-squared	0.692087	Mean dependent var	39.93333
Adjusted R-squared	0.384174	S.D. dependent var	4.800781
S.E. of regression	3.767392	Akaike info criterion	2.952947
Sum squared resid	56.77297	Schwarz criterion	3.062516
Log likelihood	-21.05871	F-statistic	2.247672
Durbin-Watson stat	2.903164	Prob(F-statistic)	0.226044

The questions, then, are why these cycles of repression and loosening of the exchange rate have taken place in Argentina, why they have become shorter and more explosive in the second half of the 1980s, and why they seem to have disappeared since the 1991 Convertibility Plan. Briefly, it appears that in the first period, step-wise adjustments reflected the politics of redistribution in the context of ISI with capital controls, within an international environment in which Argentina generally enjoyed more favorable terms of trade than in subsequent decades. This development strategy was based on the redistribution of the still sizable agrarian surplus toward industry, which benefited urban groups and an expanding public sector. This pattern of redistribution among landowners, industrialists and workers led to recurrent, though usually gradual, strangulations in the trade balance, eventually corrected by adjustments in the exchange rate. Controls on the capital account allowed governments to manage the timing and size of the devaluations. Exchange rate crises during this period thus occurred in slow motion, fueled by the deterioration of trade accounts over time.

While the economy during this period was dominated by the stop-go nature of the ISI strategy, the political process related to the distributional struggle among landowners, industrialists and urban workers was played in a context that excluded the Peronist Party, leading to what O'Donnell (1973) labeled the "impossible game" of Argentina's party competition. The return of Peronism to the government in the 1973 election (after almost 20 years of proscription) marked the economic and political culmination of the ISI period, but it ended in political turmoil after the death of President Juan Perón.

Determined to dismantle the ISI policy structure and dissolve the social base of Peronism, the military regime of 1976 opened a new phase. In this period, wage redistribution was avoided by political control. The politics of redistribution shifted increasingly toward the resources of the public sector, with the armed forces emerging as major competitors in the tug-of-war for fiscal resources. Despite wage freezes and improvements in tax collection, fiscal discipline was further eroded by the military itself, which became a major claimant on government funds through defense expenditures and transfers to public enterprises in the heavy industry sector, many linked to the military structure. Toward the end of the 1970s, capital inflows provided temporary relief, though leading to a much more constrained fiscal situation once world macroeconomic conditions deteriorated in the early 1980s and the accumulated external debt had to be repaid. The conduct of monetary policy was further complicated by the opening up of the capital account, the continuous dollarization of the economy, and the newly liberalized but poorly regulated financial sector. Moreover, because inflation generally remained high during this period, the Olivera-Tanzi effect worked against the possibility of placing fiscal accounts under control.

In the context of a weak fiscal and financial position, the full liberalization of the capital account in 1978 opened a new chapter. The currency became the target of speculative attacks along the lines of Krugman's model (1979) and extended in Calvo (1996), leading to further dollarization of the economy and to recurrent and sudden depletions of foreign exchange reserves.

With the return to democracy, the Radical Party, trying to woo the labor sector, a traditional Peronist bastion, increased salaries while trying to maintain a competitive exchange rate, which exacerbated inflation. When policies were changed with the 1985 Austral Plan, it was clear that an anti-inflationary posture yielded important electoral rewards, and the Alfonsín administration won the first mid-term election in that year. However, the economic and political conflict regarding use of the exchange rate as a nominal anchor to tame inflation, or as a real price to allocate real resources, continued unresolved during the Radical government. The collapse of world agricultural prices in the second half of the 1980s added to the administration's economic difficulties. The combination of all these factors led to more frequent and more explosive crises. The electoral defeats of the Radical Party were related to high and accelerating inflation that culminated in the hyperinflationary episode of 1989. The politics of redistribution was thus displaced by the politics of (hyper)inflation.

A new phase began in the early 1990s, with the emergence of a broad coalition in favor of stability. The adjustments needed mainly in the fiscal accounts and in terms of opening up the economy were made less difficult by a greatly improved international context in the 1990s. Capital flows returned to Argentina (marking the end of the 1980s debt crisis) and terms of trade improved. The Convertibility Law, which transformed the central bank into a currency board, provided a strong institutional foundation for stability, practically eliminating the possibility of passive monetary policies accommodating sectoral or factor demands.

In addition, distributional conflicts appeared to have diminished in intensity, and supportive international conditions and domestic growth facilitated, at least initially, the economic transition for some of the affected groups. Due to larger capital inflows, credit in dollars expanded significantly among middle and even lower-middle income groups, who had become very fearful of a devaluation. The post-1991 anti-devaluation coalition also included other groups heavily indebted in dollars, such as the government itself, the banking system, and private sector investors who participated in the privatization process and took on a significant amount of external debt to finance the acquisitions.

The decline of labor unions—a result of economic forces such as the restructuring and downsizing of the industrial sector, as well as political developments that weakened their clout within the Peronist Party— also changed the economic and political components of the traditional Peronist alliance and opened the way for a different social and political coalition more preoccupied with inflation.

In sum, a new and broadly based coalition emerged in the first half of the 1990s that prioritized monetary stability over unemployment. The members of the coalition had vivid memories of hyperinflation, along with a different perception of costs and benefits of exchange rate policies, due to changes in the structure of the economy and in their relative position in this new structure.

Looking to the future, the main question is whether the stability of the coalition can be maintained, given the strains posed by unemployment levels not experienced in Argentina since the Great Depression. Popular complaints about unemployment and unequal distribution of economic growth, in addition to other claims for improved governance and social issues, may be changing the country's economic and political picture. These pressures will most likely be exacerbated by the difficult international climate that began with the 1997 Asian devaluations, and which worsened because of the financial crises in Russia and Brazil. Given that context, it would not be surprising if more voices are raised in Argentina blaming the current exchange rate system for the deteriorating economic conditions and asking for its change, presumably by letting the peso float. Although the economic validity of this proposal is dubious (the experience of past crises in Argentina and elsewhere show the negative impact of devaluations in economies with widespread dollarization and vulnerable financial systems), a prolonged recession with high levels of unemployment could well lead to mounting political pressures "to do something." For some social groups and political forces, abandoning the Convertibility Plan may therefore look like an increasingly attractive option.

The polar opposite would be to fully dollarize the economy (i.e., buy out all physical pesos in the economy with the dollars held by the central bank), an option that had been suggested by the Menem administration.[37] Full dollarization would also require accounts now held in pesos to be redenominated in dollars, which could be done if confidence in the banking system is maintained.[38] Argentina's financial system has been strengthened by changes since 1996, mainly in the form of buyouts by international banks, increased capital and banking reserves, and the central bank's securing of contingent lines of liquidity from international private banks. Therefore, a hypothetical run on the currency, which can be stopped by dollarization, does not have to become a run on the banking system.

With the quasi-full dollarization of the Convertibility Law, or with a total conversion of pesos to dollars, the problem for the government and the private sector indebted in dollars would still be one of solvency and how to generate revenues through taxes (public sector) or cash flow through economic activities (private sector) to service the debt. These prospects could be seriously eroded by a deep recession. If the Convertibility Plan were abandoned, economic agents with debts in dollars and income in pesos would also face the additional problem of access to foreign currency.

---

[37] Full dollarization is not significantly different from the current system. The main difference would be the loss of about $500-$600 million in revenues by the central bank, corresponding to interest received on foreign currency reserves invested abroad. The proponents of dollarization present as a countervailing benefit the possible reduction in some of the components of the country risk premium paid by Argentina, mainly those linked to lingering doubts in the markets regarding the continuation of the current exchange rate parity.

[38] After the 1995 crisis, banks were allowed to hold the required reserves for peso deposits in U.S. dollars.

In the medium term, it may well be that more creative forms of monetary and exchange rate arrangements will be implemented. Two alternatives, which embody very different economic and geopolitical programs, would be a formal dollarization of the Argentine economy in the context of a monetary agreement with the United States, or the creation of a regional currency in MERCOSUR, most likely linked to a basket of currencies. These options will have their own distinctive political economy considerations.

In the short run, however, the key concern is how to balance the distribution of the fiscal costs and benefits involved in confronting difficult economic conditions. Of particular concern is how to manage the fiscal revenues to assuage expanding social demands, deal with high unemployment levels, improve the competitiveness of the private sector, and pay for the external debt. Distributional issues still revolve around the public budget, and the operation of the current exchange rate regime may well depend upon how these different pressures play out. The key to Argentina's most critical task—consolidating economic stability along with democratic institutions—is the transparent, efficient and equitable management of fiscal accounts.

References

Almansi, A., and C. Rodríguez. 1989. *Alternativas de Estabilización*. CEMA Working Paper No. 67. August.

Balassa, B. 1986. *Outward Orientation*. World Bank Development Research Department Discussion Paper148, Washington, DC.

_____. 1985. Policy Experiments in Chile, 1973-83. In G.M. Walton (ed.), *The National Economic Policies of Chile*. New York: JAI Press.

_____. 1977. *Policy Reform in Developing Countries*. Oxford: Pergamon Press.

Balassa, B. et al. 1971. *The Structure of Protection in Developing Countries*. Baltimore: Johns Hopkins University Press.

Basualdo, E., and D. Aspiazu. 1991. *Cara y Contracara de los Grupos Económicos: Estado y Promoción Industrial en la Argentina*. Buenos Aires: Cántaro.

Braun, O., and L. Joy. 1967. A Model of Economic Stagnation-A Case Study of the Argentine Economy. *Economic Journal*: 868-87.

Bruton, H. 1989. Import Substitution. In H. Chenery and T. Srinivasan (eds.), *Handbook of Development Economics*. Amsterdam: North Holland.

Buiter, W. 1986. *Fiscal Prerequisites for a Viable Managed Exchange Rate Regime*. NBER Working Paper 2041. National Bureau of Economic Research,Cambridge, MA.

Calvo, G. 1996. *Varieties of Capital-Market Crises*. University of Maryland Working Paper. May.

_____. 1991. The Perils of Sterilization. *International Monetary Fund Staff Papers* 38(4): 21-26.

Calvo G., and E. Mendoza. 1996. Mexico's Balance of Payments Crisis: A Chronicle of a Death Foretold. *Journal of International Economics* 41: 235-64.

Calvo, G., and C. Végh. 1999. Inflation Stabilization and BOP Crises in Developing Countries. In J.B. Taylor and M. Woodford (eds.), *Handbook of Macroeconomics*. North Holland.

_____. 1991. Exchange Rate-Based Stabilization under Imperfect Credibility. International Monetary Fund, Washington, DC. Mimeo.

Calvo, G., L. Leiderman, and C. Reinhart. 1996. Capital Flows to Developing Countries in the 1990s: Causes and Effects. *Journal of Economic Perspectives* 10(2): 123-39.

_____. 1993. Capital Inflows and Real Exchange Rate Appreciation in Latin America: The Role of External Factors. *IMF Staff Papers* 40: 108-51.

_____. 1992. *Capital Inflows to Latin America: The 1970s and the 1990s*. IMF Working Paper. International Monetary Fund, Washington, DC.

Canitrot, A. 1980. La Disciplina como Objetivo de la Política Económica: Un Ensayo sobre el Programa Económico del Gobierno Argentino desde 1976. *Estudios CEDES* 6.

Canova, F. 1995. Vector Autoregressive Models: Specification, Estimation, Inference and Forecasting. In M. Hashem Pesaran and M. Wickens (eds.), *Handbook of Applied Econometrics.* Blackwell Handbooks in Economics.

Cavallo, D., and R. Domenech.1988. Las políticas macroeconómicas y el tipo de cambio real: Argentina, 1913-1984. *Desarrollo Económico* 28(111): 375-400.

Cavallo, D., and Y. Mundlak. 1982. Agriculture and Economic Growth in an Open Economy: The Case of Argentina. *Research Report* 36. International Food Policy Research Institute, Washington, DC,

Claassen, E., and J. De la Cruz Martinez. 1994. *Dollarization and its Impact on the Economy: Argentina, Bolivia and Uruguay.* Inter-American Development Bank Economic and Social Department Working Paper, Washington, DC.

Corbo, V., and J. de Melo. 1987. *External Shocks and Policy Reforms in the Southern Cone: A Reassessment.* World Bank Development Research Department Discussion Paper 241, Washington, DC.

Corbo, V., and J. de Melo (eds.). 1985. Liberalization with Stabilization in the Southern Cone of Latin America. *World Development.* Special Issue.

Corden, W.M. 1990. *Exchange Rate Policy in Developing Countries.* PRE Working Paper 412. World Bank, Washington, DC.

Corrigan, E.G. 1996. *Building a Progressive and Profitable National Banking System in Argentina.* New York: Goldman Sachs.

Destler, I.M., and C.R. Henning. 1989. *Dollar Politics: Exchange Rate Policymaking in the United States.* Washington, DC: Institute for International Economics.

Devarajan, S., J. Lewis, and S. Robinson. 1993. External Shocks, Purchasing Power Parity, and the Equilibrium Real Exchange Rate. *World Bank Economic Review* 7(1): 45-63.

Díaz-Alejandro, C. 1970. *Essays on the Economic History of the Argentine Republic.* New Haven, CT: Yale University Press.

_____. 1963. A Note on the Impact of Devaluation and the Redistributive Effect. *Journal of Political Economy* 71.

Díaz-Bonilla, E. 1996. *The Washington Consensus and the Myth of the Tequila Effect.* Fundación Andina Working Papers, Buenos Aires.

_____. 1989. Consistencia, credibilidad y sustentabilidad. Notes for FAO Macroeconomics Course. Santiago.

Di Tella, G. 1987. Argentina's Most Recent Inflationary Cycle, 1975-85. In R. Thorp and L. Whitehead (eds.), *Latin American Debt and the Adjustment Crisis*. Pitt Latin American Series, University of Pittsburgh Press.

Drazen, A., and E. Helpman. 1986. Stabilization with Exchange Rate Management. Working Paper 41-86. Tel Aviv University, Foerder Institute for Economic Research.

Edwards, S. 1984. *The Order of Liberalization of the Balance of Payments*. World Bank Staff Working Papers 710, Washington, DC.

Edwards, S., and S. Teitel (eds.). 1986. Growth, Reform, and Adjustment: Latin America's Trade and Macroeconomic Policies in the 1970s and 1980s. *Economic Development and Cultural Change*.

Fair, R.C. 1996. Econometrics and Presidential Elections. *Journal of Economic Perspectives* 10(3): 89-102.

Frieden, J. 1994. Exchange Rate Politics: Contemporary Lessons from American History. *Review of International Political Economy* 1(1): 81-103.

_____. 1991. *Debt, Development, and Democracy*. Princeton: Princeton University Press.

Gowa, J. 1983. *Closing the Gold Window: Domestic Politics and the End of Bretton Woods*. Ithaca, NY: Cornell University Press.

Haggard, S., and R. Kaufman. 1990. *The Political Economy of Inflation and Stabilization in Middle-Income Countries*. PRE Working Paper 449, World Bank, Washington, DC.

Hoffmaister, A., and C. Végh. 1996. Disinflation and the Recession-Now-Versus-Recession-Later Hypothesis: Evidence from Uruguay. *IMF Staff Papers* 43: 355-94.

International Monetary Fund (IMF). 1998. *Argentina, Recent Economic Developments, 1998*. Washington, DC: International Monetary Fund.

_____. 1995. *Argentina, Recent Economic Developments, 1995*. Washington, DC: International Monetary Fund.

Kiguel, M. 1994. Exchange Rate Policy, the Real Exchange Rate, and Inflation: Lessons from Latin America. *Cuadernos de Economía* 31(93): 229-49.

Kiguel, M., and N. Liviatan. 1992. The Business Cycle Associated with Exchange Rate-Based Stabilization. *World Bank Economic Review* 6(2): 279-305.

Kirshner, J. 1995. *Currency and Coercion*. Princeton: Princeton University Press.

Krugman, P. 1979. A Model of Balance-of-Payments Crises. *Journal of Money, Credit, and Banking* 11(3): 311-25.

Krugman, P., and L. Taylor. 1978. Contractionary Effects of Devaluation. *Journal of International Economics* 8.

Laban, R., and F. Sturzenegger. 1994a. Distributional Conflict, Financial Adaptation and Delayed Stabilizations. *Economics and Politics* 6(3): 257-76.

_____. 1994b. Fiscal Conservatism as a Response to the Debt Crisis. *Journal of Development Economics* 45(2): 305-24.

Lewis-Beck, M., and T. Rice. 1992. *Forecasting Elections.* Washington, DC: Congressional Quarterly Press.

Little, I., T. Scitovsky, and M. Scott. 1970. *Industry and Trade in Some Developing Countries.* London: Organization for Economic Cooperation and Development/Oxford University Press.

Liviatan, N. 1993. *Proceedings of a Conference on Currency Substitution and Currency Boards.* World Bank Discussion Paper 207, Washington, DC.

Maier, C. 1987. *In Search of Stability: Explorations in Historical Political Economy.* Cambridge: Cambridge University Press.

Mundlak, Y., D. Cavallo, and R. Domenech. 1989. *Agriculture and Economic Growth in Argentina, 1913-1984.* International Food Policy Research Institute Research Report 76, Washington, DC.

Murillo, M.V. 1997. From Populism to Neoliberalism: Labor Unions and Market-Oriented Reforms in Argentina, Mexico, and Venezuela. Harvard University Department of Government, Cambridge MA. Doctoral dissertation.

Odell, J. 1982. *U.S. International Monetary Policy: Markets, Power, and Ideas as Sources of Change.* Princeton: Princeton University Press.

O'Donnell, G. 1973. *Modernization and Bureaucratic-Authoritarianism: Studies in South American Politics.* Berkeley, CA: Institute for International Studies.

Ostiguy, P. 1992. *Los Capitanes de la Industria: Grandes Empresarios, Política, y Economia en la Argentina de los Años Ochenta.* Buenos Aires: Legasa.

Rodriguez, C.A. 1993. Money and Credit under Currency Substitution. *IMF Staff Papers* 40(2): 414-26.

Schadler, S., M. Carkovic, A. Bennett, et al. 1993. *Recent Experiences with Surges in Capital Inflows.* International Monetary Fund Occasional Paper 108, Washington, DC.

Schamis, H.E. 1999. Distributional Coalitions and the Politics of Economic Reform in Latin America. *World Politics* 51(2).

_____. 1991. Reconceptualizing Latin American Authoritarianism in the 1970s: From Bureaucratic-Authoritarianism to Neoconservatism. *Comparative Politics* 23(2).

Sims C., J. Stock, and M. Watson. 1990. Inference in Linear Times Series with Some Unit Roots. *Econometrica* 58 (January):113-44.

Stein, E., and J.M. Streb. 1998. Political Stabilization Cycles in High-Inflation Economies. *Journal of Development Economics* 56(1): 159-80.

Tornell, A., and A. Velasco. 1995. *Money-Based Versus Exchange Rate-Based Stabilization with Endogenous Fiscal Policy.* NBER Working Paper 5300, National Bureau of Economic Research, Cambridge, MA.

Williamson, J. (ed.). 1994. *Estimating Equilibrium Exchange Rates.* Washington, DC: Institute for International Economics.

_____. 1991. Advice on the Choice of an Exchange Rate Policy. In E.M. Claassen (ed.), *Exchange Rate Policies in Developing and Post-Socialist Countries.* San Francisco: ICS Press.

World Bank. 1993. Argentina, Public Finance Review. From Insolvency to Growth. World Bank Country Department IV, Washington, DC.

_____. 1988. Argentina, Industrial Sector Study. World Bank Industrial Development Division, Washington, DC.

CHAPTER FOUR

The Dilemma of Inflation vs. Balance of Payments: Crawling Pegs in Brazil, 1964-98

Marco Bonomo and Maria Cristina T. Terra[1]

Under both authoritarian and democratic governments, the Brazilian economy has experienced periods of chronic high inflation and severe balance of payments crises in recent decades. Exchange rate policy has figured prominently in attempts to address these problems. There have been numerous heterodox stabilization attempts, but only two have proven successful: the first, undertaken at the beginning of the military regime, and the last, the Real Plan. During most of the 1964-98 period studied here, the exchange rate regime in Brazil was a crawling peg.[2] Since January 1999, however, the exchange rate has been allowed to float, ending the long period of the crawling peg regime.

Political economy determinants at least in part shaped exchange rate policy in Brazil over the past 30 years. Two complementary methodologies are used in this chapter to analyze these factors. The first investigates the historical context of exchange rate policy through an account of the political economy of that policy. The driving force affecting exchange rate policy was the tradeoff between the positive effect of a depreciated exchange rate on the balance of payments and its negative effect on inflation. The exchange rate policy resulting from this tradeoff, however, depended on the political environment. An analytical framework is sketched

---

[1] Marco Bonomo and Maria Cristina T. Terra are on the faculty of the Graduate School of Economics at the Getulio Vargas Foundation in Rio de Janeiro.

[2] The two exceptions are from 1964 to 1967, when exchange rate policy was characterized by infrequent and large devaluations, and from July 1994 to February 1995, when there was a floating exchange rate regime. From March 1995 to January 1999, there was an official target zone system. However, in practice, it worked like a crawling peg.

to interpret the history of real exchange rate policy, and it is then extended to encompass short-run election cycles.

The second methodology is statistical. A Markov Switching Model (MSM) is used to statistically characterize the exchange rate regimes, labeled as overvalued or undervalued real exchange rates, and the influence of political economy variables on regime changes. The results partially support the interpretation pursued in the analytical methodology. According to these statistical results, there is an election cycle. The probability of an overvalued exchange rate is higher in the months preceding elections, while the probability of an undervalued exchange rate is higher in the months following elections.

Analytical Framework

The present framework does not intend to encompass all the complexity of the different forces affecting the making of exchange rate policy over the period studied. It does, however, identify and highlight the main recursive dilemmas involving exchange rate policy choice.

There were clear changes in the administration of the crawling peg regime in Brazil. The frequency and size of exchange rate adjustments changed over time, resulting in alternating periods of appreciation and depreciation of the real exchange rate (RER). The choice of exchange rate adjustment procedure has nonetheless appeared purposeful, aiming to achieve a particular path for the real exchange rate.

If there are nominal rigidities in the economy, nominal exchange rate changes affect its real value, which allows exchange rate policy to be affected by political factors. There is a limit to discretion, though. If one sets an RER that produces large imbalances in the balance of payments, this level is unlikely to be sustainable in the long run. It is plausible to assume that in the long run the RER level is determined by economic variables such as external constraints and structural economic variables. Thus, the concept of equilibrium RER is appropriate for representing the RER long-run trend. It then makes sense to study the short-run misalignment produced by the exchange rate policy as determined by political economy variables.

The Inflation vs. Balance of Payments Tradeoff and Policymaker Preferences

It is beyond the scope of this chapter to formulate a rigorous model that encompasses all aspects of determining short-run exchange rates in Brazil.

However, it is useful to characterize policymaker preferences in terms of the main tradeoff identified in the country's recent history: a more devalued exchange rate is bad for inflation and good for the balance of payments. Government preferences can thus be modeled in terms of the variables included in this tradeoff. Policymakers dislike current account deviations from the level compatible with the country's intertemporal budget constraint, and they also dislike inflation rate deviations from the optimal level.

Policymakers' indirect preferences can then be represented as a weighted average of a function of the discrepancy between the current account and its intertemporal equilibrium level, and a function of inflation rate deviations from its optimal level:

$$U\left(e\right) = af_c\left(CA\left(e,X\right) - CA*\left(e*(X),X\right)\right) + f_\pi\left(\pi(e,X) - \pi*\right),$$

where a is a relative weight that measures the importance to the policymaker of the current account vis-à-vis inflation, CA (e, X) represents the current account as a function of the RER e and a vector X of exogenous (to the simple framework) variables, π (e, X) represents the inflation rate also as a function of e and X, $CA*$ is the current account level consistent with an equilibrium RER, and $\pi*$ represents the optimal inflation level.

It is assumed that both f_c and f_π functions increase in the negative range up to zero, and then start to decrease. It is also assumed that they decrease at an increasing rate when the absolute value of the discrepancy increases. Political economy literature typically uses quadratic functions for their simplicity, although here it is plausible to assume that the first function is asymmetric, with negative deviations from the sustainable level being more penalized than positive deviations.

The current account is posited as a positive function of the RER due to its effect on the trade balance. As discussed above, short-run RER behavior is different from the long-run trend. The equilibrium RER is the rate that would produce a smooth trajectory for the current account path, compatible with the country's intertemporal budget constraint.

As for the effect on the inflation rate, it should first be observed that to depreciate the RER it is necessary to devalue the nominal exchange rate at a faster rate than the difference between domestic and foreign inflation. The faster rate of devaluation fosters inflation of prices of tradables, which fuels the overall inflation rate. This short-run inflationary impact becomes permanent when there is widespread formal and informal indexation. To keep the RER at the new and more depreciated level, the devaluation rate must equal the new (higher) inflation differential. Hence, in indexed high-inflation economies, RER depreciation will engender, ceteris paribus, a higher inflation rate.

The weights attributed to the two functions, describing the policymaker's preferences as political objectives, should vary among policymakers. A more appreciated exchange rate results in lower inflation and cheaper imports, which benefit a large number of dispersed economic agents, to the detriment of a small number of concentrated economic interests such as exporters and domestic tradables producers. A policymaker may place a very high weight on a current account balance, to the detriment of inflation control, because he favors exporters and producers who compete with imports. At the other extreme, he could place a very low weight on adjustment of the current account because he needs political support, and inflation control is essential for that goal. Democracy as opposed to dictatorship thus tends to favor a lower current account weight, because the interests of a dispersed and large number of small economic agents have a better chance of being represented in the electoral process. However, even a dictatorship needs some political support. Sometimes the dictatorship is in a fragile political situation and needs to make decisions geared to gain, or at least not lose, political support. In this case it will place a higher weight on inflation control.

In summary, the government chooses the optimal RER so as to maximize its welfare function, balancing the tradeoff between the current account and inflation. The weight given to each policy objective depends at least in part on political economy factors, as the policy choice affects different groups in society in distinct ways.

Different Policymakers and Asymmetry of Information

The RER generally appreciates before elections and depreciates after elections. This pattern is captured for Brazilian data in the econometric exercise performed below, and for other Latin American countries in Frieden, Stein and Ghezzi (1999). In Brazil, the electoral cycles can be explained by imperfect information on policymakers' preferences. A situation may be considered where there are two different types of policymakers, with one placing a higher relative weight on the current account than the other. As a consequence, the type that places a higher relative weight on the current account would choose a more depreciated real exchange rate.

If the public knew policymakers' preferences, the policymaker more concerned with inflation would always win elections. An interesting and realistic situation arises when the public cannot observe policymakers' preferences. In such a situation, it may be worthwhile for the policymaker concerned with external sector performance to mimic the policymaker concerned with inflation, so as to have some chance of being reelected.

Bonomo and Terra (2000) construct a formal model inspired by this insight. The model assumes two possible types of policymakers, one committed to the tradables sector and the other to the nontradables sector.[3] However, since the nontradables sector has a higher number of votes, the policymaker who represents this sector would always win elections if the electorate knew the policymaker's preferences in advance. The policymaker may affect the relative gains of the two sectors by choosing expenditures on nontradable goods and in this way altering the equilibrium real exchange rate. The public, for its part, tries to extract information on the policymaker's preferences by observing the RER. However, economic policy is observed with noise, since there are exogenous shocks to the external sector after the policy is chosen. Thus, a given external sector performance is compatible with different combinations of policies and shocks. The policymaker who represents the tradables sector tries to disguise himself by choosing expenditures so as to appreciate the real exchange rate and improve the likelihood of his reelection. Due to noise, however, it is not necessary for him to imitate perfectly the other type to maintain a chance of being reelected. Moreover, since the tradables sector is hurt by a more appreciated exchange rate, the policymaker will choose exchange rate policy by weighting his immediate interests (the depreciated exchange rate raises the sector's gain) against his long-run interests, which depend on his reelection (the probability of which increases with a more appreciated RER). A political budget cycle is also generated in the model, as government intervenes in the exchange rate market by taxing tradable goods producers and spending on nontradable goods.

There is considerable literature on economic policy cycles generated by policymakers' political economy considerations in asymmetric information contexts. In Persson and Tabellini (1990), unemployment cycles are generated during election periods, whereas in Rogoff and Sibert (1988) and Rogoff (1990), cycles are in taxes and expenditures. Ghezzi, Stein and Streb (1999) relate more closely to the idea presented here. They explain exchange rate valuation/devaluation cycles during election periods, but the reason for the cycles is different from the one presented here. In this model there are two types of policymakers: competent and incompetent. The competent policymaker needs to tax less than the incompetent one does, hence, the incompetent policymaker may be willing to mimic the competent one by devaluing less before an election to increase his chances of being reelected.

---

[3] Policymakers in Alesina (1987) also have different preferences. However, in that study the probability of reelection is exogenous, whereas in Bonomo and Terra (2000) the probability of reelection depends on the actions of policymakers.

Exchange rate policy is seen here as being used to deal with external and internal imbalances. Different policymakers will have different tradeoffs between the two policy objectives. The main difference is that one preference is more popular than the other and therefore yields a greater chance of reelection. As pointed out by Ghezzi, Stein and Streb (1999), before elections, policymakers, independent of their preferences, would have a bias towards fighting inflation and pursuing a higher-than-average RER. If the policymaker committed to the tradable goods sector is elected, there will be a real devaluation after the election. As a consequence, one should observe an electoral cycle where, on average, the RER appreciates before elections and depreciates after them.

History of Exchange Rate Policy in Brazil from 1964-98[4]

The analytical framework presented above serves as a guide for historical study, although it does not consider all the complexities of several episodes. The framework does, however, try to identify those who most benefited or were most hurt by exchange rate policy throughout the period studied. The balance of payments vs. inflation tradeoff is identified, as well as the election cycle.

Infrequent and Large Devaluations: 1964-67

The year 1964 marked the beginning of the military government, and in that year the exchange rate was unified.[5] Until 1967, exchange rate policy was characterized by infrequent and large devaluations, causing substantial real exchange rate variability. High domestic inflation by international standards, combined with a fixed nominal exchange rate, led to a rapid real exchange rate appreciation and an appreciation-devaluation cycle that lasted from eight to 14 months on average (see Figure 4.1). According to Simonsen (1995), foreign currency displayed a corresponding cycle: the external credit supply rose after a large devaluation, then declined until an intense speculative movement made a new devaluation inevitable.

---

[4] Two useful sources for an economic perspective on the recent history of exchange rate policy are Dib (1985) and Baumgarten (1996). Dib provides an account of external sector policy, including exchange rate policy, from the 1950s to the end of the 1970s. Baumgarten analyzes the exchange rate policy up to and including the Real Plan.

[5] A system of multiple exchange rates had been introduced in 1953 by SUMOC (the agency responsible for coordinating monetary and exchange rate policy) in the context of the Bretton Woods agreement. The substantial difference between domestic and international inflation rates made it difficult for the economy to comply with the requirement of fixed exchange.

Figure 4.1. Real Exchange Rate
April 1964 - April 1968

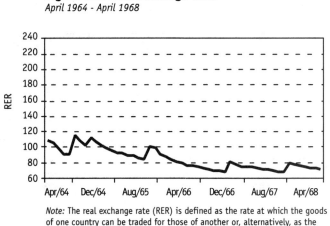

Note: The real exchange rate (RER) is defined as the rate at which the goods of one country can be traded for those of another or, alternatively, as the ratio of the price of tradables to nontradables. A lower RER indicates greater international competitiveness.

The real exchange rate appreciated over this period, but real wages fell at a higher rate,[7] thus maintaining export competitiveness. The result was reduced inflation and an improved trade balance. Domestic industry was the principal beneficiary of policy during this period, as high tariffs ensured demand for domestic tradable goods. Imported inputs and labor, moreover, became cheaper in real terms. Because of the 1964-65 recession, however, gains from these policies were concentrated among surviving firms, particularly multinational subsidiaries.[8]

Workers were the main losers during this period.[9] While the recession increased unemployment, those who remained employed experienced a decline in real wages.[10] Nor did workers benefit from real exchange rate appreciation by way of cheaper imported consumer goods. Imports concentrated in oil, intermediate and capital goods fell to 4 percent of GDP in 1965.

---

[7] According to the Departamento Intersindical de Estatística e Estudos Sócio-Econômicos (DIESSE), an independent institution specialized in labor-related statistics.

[8] The 1964-65 recession distributed the benefits of this policy unequally. Restrictions on profit remittance imposed in 1962 were lifted, prompting Brazilian subsidiaries of multinational firms to look for capital from their foreign parent companies. Small national firms did not have the same alternative, since they were subject to the unfavorable credit conditions of the period.

[9] Exporters were not necessarily losers because the fall in real wages was likely to have more than compensated for the real exchange rate appreciation.

[10] That reduction was the result of government policy. In a repressive environment where the main union leaders were banned, a national wage policy was instituted, under which wages were adjusted according to a formula that implied real wage reductions whenever the government underestimated the inflation rate for the period, which happened systematically.

Figure 4.2. Real Exchange Rate
July 1968 - July 1973

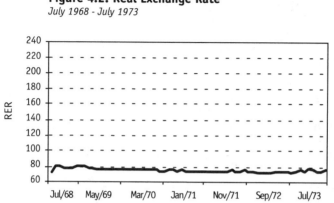

Introduction of a Mini-Devaluation System: 1968-73

A period of nominal exchange rate mini-devaluations, conducted initially almost on a monthly basis, began in 1968. This system would last for the whole period studied, with the exception of a few intervals during price stabilization attempts.

As shown in Figure 4.2, the real exchange rate remained stable during this period, which coincided with high growth rates and export diversification.[11] Imports continued to be concentrated in oil and, to a lesser extent, intermediate and capital goods, and there was a trade balance surplus for most of the period. The stability of the real exchange rate seems to have contributed to the attractiveness of foreign loans, which in turn led to an accumulation of reserves.

The introduction of a mini-devaluation regime, however, represented an acknowledgment that domestic inflation rates would be much higher than international rates. In fact, the economic team led by Delfim Neto, who served as Finance Minister from 1967 to 1974, explicitly favored growth over inflation control. The mini-devaluation system, under which exchange rates were indexed to inflation, was designed to stimulate exports and foreign indebtedness, at the price of increasing inflationary inertia. This contrasted with wage adjustments, which were designed to prevent past inflation from fueling future inflation.

---

[11] Coffee accounted for around 40 percent of total exports in 1964 but declined to 20 percent in 1973 (see Table 4.1).

The mini-devaluation system and the use of wage indexation helped people live with inflation. But they also increased the cost of fighting inflation. On the one hand, they decreased the cost of a given level of inflation to society and, therefore, to the policymaker. On the other, as the cost of fighting inflation increased, the real exchange rate appreciation necessary to achieve a given reduction in inflation became higher. Inflation control thus became a lower priority, while the tradeoff between improving the balance of payments and fighting inflation worsened.

Failure to React to the First Oil Shock: 1974-79

Oil prices quadrupled at the end of 1973, transforming the trade balance from a modest surplus to a deficit of $4.7 billion in 1974. The current account likewise deteriorated from a $1.7 billion deficit in 1973 to a $7.1 billion deficit in 1974 (Table 4.1). While most oil importing countries reacted to the oil shock by devaluing and controlling aggregate demand through fiscal and monetary restrictions, the Brazilian government kept the real exchange rate constant (see Figure 4.3) and refrained from severely restricting aggregate demand. The government reduced imports through measures that smacked of import substitution, [12] but oil imports were excluded from the restrictions. The government apparently intended to minimize the effect of the oil price shock on inflation and growth.

While import restriction had an immediate effect, [13] the global recession dampened exports. Meanwhile, the country made use of high liquidity in international capital markets to finance the current account deficit. Consequently, foreign debt increased by $20 billion. [14]

At first glance, this strategy looks strange coming from a military government, which would appear to be in a better position to impose macroeconomic adjustments than a democratic one. The armed forces, however, were divided. A moderate group was associated with President

---

[12] The measures designed to restrict imports included tariff increases, the interdiction imposed on Brazilian state enterprises from buying foreign goods for which there was a similar Brazilian product, and the compulsory deposit of 100 percent of the import's value for six months, without any interest paid. In order to stimulate import substitution of capital and intermediary goods, subsidized credit and tax exemptions were granted to activities linked to the production of such goods. Also, substantial public investments were devoted to this goal, including investment in oil exploration (see Carneiro, 1990).

[13] The coefficient of imports fell from 12 percent in 1974, a historical high, to 7.25 percent in 1978.

[14] Industrial policy for export stimulation and import substitution had a high cost in terms of fiscal performance, causing a substantial budget deterioration. This policy left the next government an unpleasant heritage: high inflation, extremely heavy external debt service, and a deteriorating fiscal position (see Carneiro, 1990).

Table 4.1. Brazil: Economic Statistics, 1964-97

	Inflation FIPE (%)	Inflation (%)	GDP growth (%)	Public sector borrowing requirements (% of GDP)
1964	84.38			
1965	45.55		0.03	
1966	38.10		0.23	
1967	24.40		0.03	
1968	25.02		0.05	
1969	21.77		0.11	
1970	18.39		0.10	
1971	20.66	17.59	0.03	
1972	16.09	15.74	0.11	
1973	13.88	15.55	0.12	
1974	34.94	34.54	0.14	
1975	30.11	29.33	0.08	
1976	38.90	46.26	0.05	
1977	38.34	38.80	0.10	
1978	43.12	40.82	0.05	
1979	67.82	77.19	0.05	
1980	85.55	110.27	0.07	
1981	89.11	95.18	0.09	6.38
1982	100.70	99.73	-0.04	7.61
1983	168.29	211.01	0.01	4.60
1984	184.18	223.81	-0.03	2.84
1985	236.69	235.57	0.05	4.68
1986	67.64	62.37	0.08	3.81
1987	371.03	365.96	0.07	5.93
1988	1,033.55	933.62	0.04	5.12
1989	2,210.71	1,764.87	-0.00	7.37
1990	1,105.88	1,794.84	0.03	-1.43
1991	481.09	478.09	-0.05	0.19
1992	1,144.39	1,149.05	0.00	1.74
1993	2,752.90	2,489.11	-0.01	0.72
1994	648.10	929.32	0.04	-1.14
1995	24.41	21.98	0.06	4.99
1996	9.40	9.27		3.75
1997		4.34		

Table 4.1. (cont.)

Oil*/Total imports	Coffee/total exports	Current Account (Millions of US$)	Terms of trade	World interest rates
	0.53	81.00	189.02	3.55
	0.44	283.00	219.96	3.95
	0.44	(33.00)	208.05	4.88
	0.43	(264.00)	191.73	4.33
	0.41	(508.00)	188.62	5.34
	0.35	(281.00)	183.91	6.69
	0.34	(562.00)	187.62	6.44
	0.27	(1,307.00)	175.44	4.34
	0.25	(1,489.00)	172.37	4.07
	0.20	(1,688.00)	183.24	7.03
0.20	0.11	(7,146.50)	139.72	7.87
0.22	0.10	(6,968.00)	127.62	5.82
0.27	0.21	(6,520.00)	141.61	4.99
0.30	0.19	(5,049.00)	157.18	5.27
0.30	0.15	(6,996.00)	142.17	7.22
0.35	0.13	(10,516.00)	124.40	10.04
0.41	0.12	(12,831.00)	104.98	11.61
0.48	0.07	(11,764.00)	95.56	14.08
0.49	0.09	(16,317.00)	93.29	10.72
0.51	0.10	(6,834.00)	93.90	8.62
0.48	0.09	33.00	95.78	9.57
0.41	0.09	(280.00)	94.50	7.49
0.20	0.09	(5,311.00)	108.42	5.97
0.26	0.07	(1,452.00)	102.81	5.83
0.22	0.06	4,156.00	107.75	6.67
0.19	0.05	1,002.00	107.93	8.11
0.21	0.04	(3,823.00)	114.82	7.51
0.16	0.04	(1,450.00)	117.57	5.41
0.15	0.03	6,089.00	109.29	3.46
0.08	0.03	20.00	109.07	3.02
0.07	0.05	(1,153.00)	114.01	4.27
0.05	0.04	(18,136.00)	115.31	5.51
0.01			114.99	5.04

Sources: Boletim do Banco Central do Brasil, FUNCEX, *International Financial Statistics* (IMF).
*Oil and natural gas.

Figure 4.3. Real Exchange Rate
January 1974 - January 1979

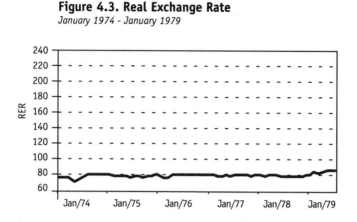

Castelo Branco, the first military president (1964-67), while a hard-line group aligned itself with Emílio Garrastazu Médici, president during the "miracle years" of 1969-74. [15] President Ernesto Geisel (1974-79), Médici's moderate successor, needed to produce high growth rates in order to maintain legitimacy among the military, and the military as a whole relied heavily on the entrepreneurs' support for civilian legitimacy, particularly as the government lost the parliamentary elections of 1974 in spite of the country's economic performance. Favoring high growth rates, entrepreneurs were unwilling to support a macroeconomic adjustment policy. The Brazilian response to the first oil shock thus shows that a dictatorship, precisely because of its fragile legitimacy, may be less able to take necessary but bitter measures than a democratic regime.

Although the oil shock depreciated the equilibrium real exchange rate, the government chose to keep the real exchange rate constant, inducing overvaluation. Real exchange rate stability over the period, as shown in Figure 4.3, thus marked a change in exchange rate policy.

The need for political legitimacy thus made the government prioritize inflation over the balance of payments. Beyond controlling inflation, though, official concerns included preventing a recession that could result from an adjustment of the current account. That is, a sharp real exchange rate depreciation could have equilibrated the current account but would have taken its toll in lower output and higher inflation.

---

[15] Skidmore (1988) analyzes the dispute between the two groups during the period of military government.

Figure 4.4. Real Exchange Rate
July 1979 - July 1980

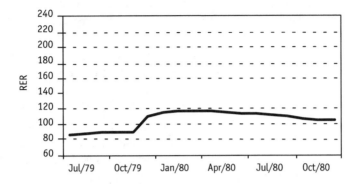

Pre-setting Exchange Rate Adjustment to Affect Inflationary Expectations: 1979-80

In March 1979, João Figueiredo succeeded Geisel, and former Finance Minister Mário Henrique Simonsen was named Minister of Planning in a new institutional design that concentrated all important economic decisions in his ministry. Simonsen, pursuing a more traditional macroeconomic adjustment policy, sought to control aggregate demand by fiscal and monetary measures, thus curbing inflation and improving external accounts.

Political pressures, though, forced Simonsen to resign. Entrepreneurs objected to the prospect of an orthodox adjustment and, according to a July 1979 survey conducted by the biweekly magazine *Exame*, only 19 percent of businessmen rated the minister as "excellent" or "good" (see Goldenstein, 1985). Exporters objected to the withdrawal of fiscal incentives, which were not offset by accelerated devaluation. Farmers, who enjoyed strong support in Congress, opposed Simonsen's resistance to increased agriculture subsidies, especially as they were defended by Delfim Neto, the Minister of Agriculture and former Minister of Finance during the "miracle years." President Figueiredo himself may not have wanted to incur the political costs of unpopular measures, especially as his predecessors had enjoyed the benefits of imprudent expansionary policies.

Simonsen was replaced by Delfim Neto, who at first followed a heterodox strategy based on price controls. By the end of 1979, the exchange rate was devalued by 30 percent, causing a RER depreciation (see Figure 4.4). Simultaneously, primary product exports were taxed at 30 percent, fiscal incentives to manufacture exports were removed, and the imports value deposit requirement of 360 days was lifted. The devaluation was thus complemented by measures with opposite effects on exports and imports: importers' and exporters' incentives were not substantially altered, while government revenue increased due to these fiscal changes. The government also tried to influence inflationary expectations by pre-setting the 1980 devaluation at 40 percent, well below 1979 inflation of 77 percent, a measure also aimed at reconciling the lower interest rates needed for growth with the incentives to foreign debt needed to improve the balance of payments.

This endeavor took one year, and it failed completely. Inflation accelerated, RER appreciation approached 1979 levels, and the balance of payments continued to deteriorate, with a substantial loss of reserves. [16, 17]

The government chose this maxi-devaluation instead of accelerating the mini-devaluations for two reasons. First, exporters would benefit immediately. Second, a maxi-devaluation would impose an instantaneous loss on debt holders, but it would not decrease incentives for new loans, since there would be less devaluation in the near future. In the end, because the mini-devaluation rule was broken, the effect could be the opposite, since uncertainty about future policy increased.

As Brazil's situation illustrates, the main cause of exchange rate policy tension is the tradeoff between inflation and the balance of payments. Delfim Neto attempted to skirt this dilemma by combining the maxi-devaluation's short-run balance of payments incentives with the preset devaluation's influence on inflationary expectations. The failure of this policy, however, undermined the balance of payments incentives. The same real exchange rate pattern would repeat itself during most heterodox stabilization attempts after democracy was reestablished.

---

[16] One important cause of the inflation acceleration was the new wage policy, implemented in October 1979, when wage adjustment periodicity was increased to twice a year. Had inflation remained constant, this would have amounted to a substantial increase in real wages, in a context where the second oil shock and the balance of payment adjustment would have required a fall in real wages. As mentioned by Simonsen (1995), inflation increased from 45 percent a year between July 1978 and July 1979 to 45 percent a semester, or 110 percent a year, between December 1979 and December 1980 (see Table 4.1). Moreover, wages between one and three minimum wages (a large proportion in Brazil) would be adjusted every semester by 1.10 times the inflation rate. As a consequence, the higher the inflation, the higher the real wage increase.

[17] Deterioration of the balance of payments had several causes. On the one hand, the trade balance was negatively affected by the second oil shock, and by speculative imports and postponement of exports due to the exchange rate policy's lack of credibility. On the other hand, besides the international interest rate increase (see Table 4.1), there was a rise in the spread charged to Brazil because of the declining international credibility of the country's policies. These factors contributed to further increasing the current account deficit. The control of domestic interest rates, and increased uncertainty over future exchange rate policy and the country's capacity to honor its external debt, contributed to the retraction of foreign loans, resulting in a substantial loss of reserves.

Figure 4.5. Real Exchange Rate
January 1981 - January 1985

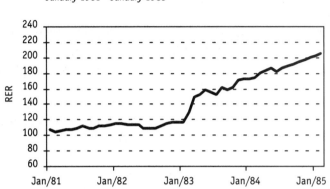

External Adjustment as a Priority: 1981-85

In 1980, the government returned to an orthodox approach that used mini-devaluations based on inflation differentials, which stabilized the real exchange rate (see Figure 4.5). The radical policy reversal resulted in a 5 percent reduction in GDP and a decrease of 10 percent in industrial production, without substantial progress on inflation. On the other hand, the trade balance improved from a $2.8 billion deficit to a $1.2 billion surplus. [18]

The policy reversal affected the supply and demand of foreign loans. On the demand side, the combination of domestic credit restrictions, [19] the return to a sensible exchange rate policy, and the lifting of interest ceilings seemed to have induced increased demand for foreign loans. On the supply side, the orthodox approach improved the international credibility of government policy. As a result, external debt increased 14 percent. Inflows into the capital account, however, led to only a small increase in reserves, already at a dangerously low level.

In August 1982, the world recession and the Mexican moratorium aggravated the Brazilian situation. Brazilian exports decreased by $3 billion while interest payments grew, foreign loans practically disappeared, and reserves dwindled. The government had no choice but to seek an

---

[18] The result was less spectacular due to substantial deterioration in the terms of trade (see Table 4.1). However, the continued increase in interest rates partially compensated for improvement in the trade balance, resulting in a modest reduction of the current account deficit from $12.8 billion to $11.7 billion (see Table 4.1).

[19] Quantitative limits to credit expansion by financial institutions were imposed in March 1980 and renewed for 1981 and 1982 (see Bonomo, 1986).

IMF agreement, though the decision was announced only after the November elections for legislative seats and the first direct gubernatorial elections since 1966.

In February 1983 the government announced another 30 percent maxi-devaluation, this time followed by a continuous mini-devaluation policy. The effect of these policies on the RER[20] was another year of sharp recession, and more than a doubling of inflation (see Table 4.1). These conditions produced formal and informal indexation, as well as inflation rate insensitivity to aggregate demand. The recession, though, enhanced the performance of the external sector and led to a 1983 trade surplus of $6.5 billion.[21]

By opting for a maxi-devaluation, the government chose to improve the balance of payments rather than reduce inflation. This complemented other stimuli such as contraction of aggregate demand, fiscal incentives, and favorable credit conditions for the production of export and import substitutes. In distributive terms, however, decreasing real wages and an increasing real exchange rate shifted income from workers to tradable sector entrepreneurs.[22]

The New Republic and Fighting Inflation: 1985-92

The return to democracy in Brazil was accompanied by a long period of real exchange rate appreciation (see Figure 4.6) and several price stabilization attempts. Fixed exchange rates during the initial phase of the stabilization plan typically resulted in a real exchange rate appreciation, followed by a partial recovery in preparation for the next plan. Overall, however, substantial real exchange rate appreciation reflected the government's emphasis on price stabilization rather than the balance of payments,[23] a change in priorities made possible by current account gains in the early 1980s.

---

[20] At the same time, the strict fiscal and monetary policies negotiated with the IMF, combined with the wage indexation reduction, should have attenuated the inflationary impact of the devaluation.

[21] However, this time the recovery of the U.S. economy boosted demand for exports, and there was only a small deterioration in the terms of trade. The stimulus given by the more permanent real exchange rate depreciation was possibly an important element of such an amazing tradable sector performance. The decrease in real wages, due both to the recession and the new wage policy, further contributed to the sector's profitability.

[22] This was not necessarily true for unionized workers in the tradables sector.

[23] Terra (1998, 1997) presents empirical evidence on the effect of the balance of payments crisis on the inflation rate in developing economies.

Figure 4.6. Real Exchange Rate
March 1985 - March 1993

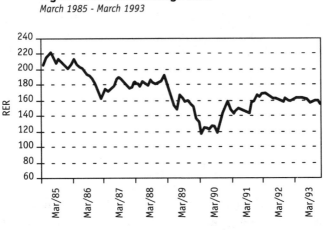

The Gradualist Failure and the Mini-Devaluation Formula: 1985

In March 1985, a civilian government came to power. However, the elected president, Tancredo Neves, a member of the opposition during the entire military period, died before being sworn in. The elected vice-president, José Sarney, the former chief of the military-headed government party, thus became the first civilian president since 1964. With Sarney as president rather than Neves, the government was less able to withstand political pressures, and the president's search for legitimacy would subsequently influence his economic decisions.

The cabinet inherited from Neves included an orthodox economist, his nephew Francisco Dornelles, as Minister of Finance. While continuing daily mini-devaluations, Dornelles immediately changed the formulas for exchange rate adjustment and monetary correction. The adjustment formulas were now based on geometric mean inflation for the three previous months, rather than current inflation. This new adjustment formula had two main impacts. On the one hand, it reduced uncertainty over future nominal devaluations, because past inflation was known in advance, whereas current inflation would be known only by the end of the month. On the other hand, the real exchange rate became more sensitive to inflation movements, appreciating with the acceleration of inflation, and depreciating with its reduction. Sarney had little political capital to spare, so when Dornelles failed to bring inflation down in six months, he was replaced by Dilson Funaro, who more closely supported Sarney's short-term political concerns.

Funaro emphasized lower inflation and restored the rule of basing devaluations and monetary indexation on current inflation. The rule based on geometric means appears to have bad dynamic properties, since high inflation in the past would feed back on future inflation through the mini-devaluations, increasing inflation inertia. By making the policy change after the inflation peak of 14 percent in August, Funaro realized an opportunistic gain by preventing this high rate from fueling into future inflation.

The Cruzado Plan: 1986

During the second half of 1985, inflation reached approximately 15 percent a month. As November 1986 gubernatorial and legislative elections approached, the alternative of a heterodox stabilization plan became politically appealing. The Argentine Austral Plan and the Israeli stabilization program were examples of heterodox stabilization plans where prices were frozen in order to coordinate price setting at a new equilibrium (see Heymann, 1991, for Argentina, and Bruno, 1989, for Israel).

On February 28, 1986, the government announced the Cruzado Plan, which fixed the nominal exchange rate at the previous day's level. A fixed exchange rate was intended to fight inflation by preventing an increase in the price of imports in domestic currency and by signaling a commitment to low inflation rates. The plan was sweetened by expansionary fiscal and monetary policies, a wage conversion rule that assured substantial immediate real gains, and wage adjustment formulas designed to protect real earnings.

The Cruzado Plan immediately produced huge excess demand, and charging a premium over legal prices became widespread (see Modiano, 1990). Favorable external conditions initially prevented serious deterioration in the trade balance, but by September a worsening trade balance caused anticipation of a maxi-devaluation. This in turn prompted postponement of exports and anticipation of imports. When the black market premium reached 90 percent, the government broke with the fixed exchange rate rule and devalued by 1.8 percent in October, at the same time announcing a return to mini-devaluations at unspecified intervals (see Modiano, 1990). Breaking the rules without a clear alternative, in an environment where the exchange rate was considered overvalued, only increased expectations of a maxi-devaluation. This produced further deterioration in the balance of trade.

Exchange rate rigidity contributed to higher real wages, but high levels of protection in the tradable goods sector encouraged producers to concentrate on the overheated domestic market. The situation was not sustainable in many aspects. Producers had an incentive to increase prices and profits, fueling inflation, and eroding real wage gains. The current account deterioration made the maintenance of a fixed exchange rate unsustainable. However, there is evidence that the government was able to provide some credibility for the unsustainable regime, since it won the November elections by a landslide. The fact that there were no losers in the short run contributed to its electoral success.

One week after the elections, the government resumed daily devaluations and announced measures to control aggregate demand. The trade balance nonetheless worsened, and reserves plunged to $5 billion in February 1987, down from $10.4 billion in June 1986. At this point, the government stopped paying interest on external debt owed to private banks. This decision, in part intended to exploit nationalist sentiment, failed completely. The government neither recovered its popularity nor obtained better conditions for external debt payment.

The Cruzado Plan displayed a well-defined exchange rate cycle. The government used an appreciating exchange rate policy to stabilize inflation before elections, but after elections undertook bitter corrective measures, including exchange rate devaluation.

Other Stabilization Attempts: 1987-90

A succession of short-lived stabilization attempts followed the Cruzado Plan. Funaro's replacement, Luis Carlos Bresser Pereira, undertook the first in June of 1987. The plan superimposed monetary and fiscal control on heterodox rent control and deindexation measures. During the three months preceding the plan, Bresser Pereira induced a 10.5 percent real exchange rate depreciation, allowing for a lower exchange rate devaluation during implementation of the plan. However, the stabilization attempt failed. Inflation gradually increased, reaching 14 percent in December, when Bresser Pereira resigned. Inflation led to an overall exchange rate appreciation of 6.4 percent during the Bresser Pereira term.

The next finance minister, Mailson da Nóbrega, took office with a simple monetary and fiscal control plan labeled the "Rice and Beans Policy" and designed to prevent hyperinflation. Inflation was initially held below 20 percent a month, but by December it had reached 28.8 percent, and in January 1989, Nóbrega gave up his initial pledge.

He subsequently formulated a new heterodox policy, called the Summer Plan. Like the Bresser Plan, this program combined heterodox deindexation and rent controls with orthodox monetary and fiscal controls. The exchange rate was devalued by 18 percent to reach the parity of one new cruzado with one dollar, a measure intended to produce a sense of currency strength.

The Summer Plan nonetheless failed due to its lack of credibility, the result of the defeat of its predecessors. Persistent inflation and a rising black market premium forced the government to resume mini-devaluations based on inflation. Real exchange rate appreciation subsequently continued through the 1989 election season and until the March 1990 presidential inauguration.

The Collor Plans: 1990-92

In November 1989, Fernando Collor narrowly defeated leftist candidate Luís Inácio da Silva in a run-off election, the first direct presidential election in almost 30 years. While Collor initially lacked the support of any major political force, in the second round he acquired conservative support by providing the only alternative to da Silva.

During the months preceding Collor's inauguration, inflation was increasing rapidly and the nominal exchange rate was not adjusted at the same speed, leading to a real appreciation of approximately 35 percent from October to March. The reason for the real appreciation was probably the government's attempt to prevent open hyperinflation before the new government took office. Collor came to power with plenty of political capital. He surprised economic analysts with an extremely radical plan that included freezing financial assets,[24] suspending government debt payments, and imposing new price controls. The government also announced an important change in the exchange rate. Legal transactions in foreign currency would no longer be centralized in the central bank. An official foreign exchange market called the "commercial market" was created running parallel to the floating market for restricted financial transactions, which had been created in 1989. Although the change was operationally important, in practice the government continued to determine the exchange rate level through massive intervention in the newly created market.

The real exchange rate was devalued from March to July to make up for previous currency overvaluation. Then, apparently to control inflation aggravated by increasing oil prices, the government maintained a stable nominal exchange rate for two months. As the inflation rate exceeded 12 percent a month, the real exchange rate returned in September to the appreciated level of March. As the trade surplus was narrowed and inflation persisted, the central bank intervened, causing a continuous real currency devaluation from September to January.

---

[24] Liquidity was reduced from 30 percent to about 8 percent of GDP.

The second Collor Plan was launched in January 1991, when monthly inflation exceeded 20 percent. Relying heavily on the deteriorating instrument of price freezes, the plan had only short-run success, as monthly inflation returned to double digits in June. A more orthodox economic team empowered in May favored an exchange rate depreciation policy, including a 14 percent exchange rate devaluation on the last day of September, on top of mini-devaluations throughout the period.

During the Collor government, devaluations alternately lagged behind inflation, in an attempt to prevent hyperinflation, or were accelerated to make up for inflation-induced overvaluations. On average, the real exchange rate remained more appreciated than in preceding periods.

These measures were accompanied by structural reforms. The privatization of state-owned companies, for instance, contributed to capital inflow, which in turn allowed for a more appreciated real exchange rate. On the other hand, steep tariff reductions were intended to make the exchange rate policy effective for regulating competition between imports and domestically produced goods.

The failure of these measures sealed Collor's political fate. His popularity among workers declined because he had frozen assets without defeating inflation. He also lost elite support because trade reform and appreciation of the real exchange rate affected the tradables sector. Without allies, Collor was impeached on corruption charges in September 1992 and replaced by Vice President Itamar Franco.

The Real Plan and Its Antecedents: 1993-98

In May 1993, incoming Finance Minister Fernando Henrique Cardoso implemented a new, less interventionist stabilization plan. Inflation had reached 40 percent a month and continued to increase, so it was clear that any government successful in controlling inflation would enjoy years of popularity. Cardoso was part of a government supported by a congressional majority and was himself a candidate to succeed Itamar Franco in the presidential elections of October 1994. At the beginning of that year, however, opposition candidate da Silva was leading the polls by a comfortable margin.

Cardoso's plan included a hyper-indexation phase in preparation for deindexation.[25] In March 1994, the government created an inflation-

---

[25] A fiscal adjustment called the Fundo Social de Emergência was also negotiated in the Congress. This measure freed a portion of government revenues that were matched with specific expenditures by the Constitution of 1988. This allowed the government to reduce expenditures and improve the fiscal budget.

indexed unit of account, the *unidade real de valor* (URV), with stable purchasing power.[26] Its use became widespread within a few months. The value of the URV in domestic currency was initially fixed at the same value as one dollar in domestic currency, and during this phase, the government intervened in the dollar market whenever the dollar value would become greater than the URV value. Although the exchange rate policy was important in fighting inflation, this was not a typical exchange rate-based stabilization, since some flexibility in the exchange rate policy was preserved. The plan was to extinguish the old unit of account on July 1 and to transform the URV into the new currency. From then on, the value of the dollar could depart from the value of the new currency (see Franco, 1996).

This kind of stabilization was preferred over an exchange rate-based stabilization pegged to the dollar for several reasons. First, stabilization with a free convertibility regime and fixed exchange rate could buy credibility, but it would reduce the range of future policy options. Second, this kind of stabilization would not be as effective in Brazil, a large closed economy, as it would be in a small and open dollarized economy. Last, since a possible victory of the left would lead to capital outflow, it was not prudent to have a policy of free convertibility.

Floating Exchange Rate and Real Appreciation: July 1994-February 1995

Inflation plummeted from over 40 percent before July to around 3.5 percent during the third quarter of 1994, and in October, Cardoso was elected president in a landslide. Shortly thereafter, the government introduced a new currency, the *real,* at a one-to-one parity with the dollar. The government let the currency appreciate as a result of capital inflows, however, and by February 1995 real exchange rate appreciation totaled 18 percent.

The exchange rate level provoked considerable debate. While entrepreneurs and exporters complained that the exchange rate policy favored external competition, consumers benefited from lower prices of imports and tradables. The dispersed interests of the electorate prevailed over the organized and concentrated power of the tradables industry.

Both the real exchange rate appreciation and the boom during the second semester of 1994 led to deterioration in the trade balance: the monthly $1 billion surplus turned into a $700 million deficit. The Mexican crisis at the end of December brought uncertainties about the possibility of financing large future current account deficits. Exchange

---

[26] Since the degree of dollarization was low in the Brazilian economy, it was necessary to create a new unit of account with stable purchasing power and stimulate its use.

Figure 4.7. Real Exchange Rate
January 1994 - July 1996

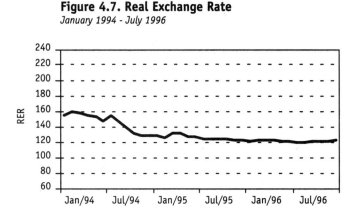

rate policy was altered in March 1995 to a target zone regime after a 7 percent devaluation.

Return of the Mini-Devaluation: 1995-98

In March 1995, the government implemented an exchange rate band regime. The exchange rate was devalued by 6 percent, and the *real* was allowed to float in a band of roughly 5 percent (see Figure 4.7). Following the establishment of periodic spread exchange rate auctions in July 1995, the central bank successfully signaled a much narrower band. In practice, the regime was similar to a crawling peg.

While the real exchange rate remained stable, with a slight devaluation trend, the nominal exchange rate was devalued at a rate of roughly 0.6 percent from the end of 1996 onward. Continuous falling inflation resulted in higher rates of real devaluation, which amounted to approximately 2.5 percent in 1997.

However, the sustainability of this policy came into question because of growth in the current account deficit from the end of 1994 onward. The exchange rate appreciation in the second semester of 1994 and the reduction in tariff protection during the Collor government stimulated imports, which showed impressive growth. In some sense that was natural and desirable, since the import coefficient in Brazil was one of the smallest of the world, and imports would help stabilization by relieving excess demand and increasing domestic competition. The fall in inflation contributed to relative price transparency, enhancing the effect of imports.

The ability to maintain a stable real exchange rate with a considerable current account deficit depended on foreign capital inflows. The

Mexican crisis of December 1994 and the Asian crisis of October 1997 prompted a sharp reduction in capital inflows. Privatization of large state companies, which attracted a continuous flow of foreign direct investment, helped provide the capital necessary to sustain the current account deficit.

Brazilian currency also remained stable during the Russian crisis in 1998. Current account deterioration and capital outflow led to a loss of international reserves, in spite of loans resulting from an IMF agreement. In January 1999, the government announced a moderate exchange rate devaluation, and a new exchange rate target zone. The exchange rate was allowed to float as a response to a speculative attack two days after the announcement, and it has been floating ever since.

Exchange Rate Levels as Regimes: A Quantitative Assessment

This section statistically characterizes exchange rate behavior by estimating a Markov Switching Model (MSM) with time-varying probabilities. The dependent variable is the RER misalignment, and the political explanatory variables affect the transition probabilities.

It is first necessary to rationalize the choices of both the dependent variable and the statistical specification. The choice of RER level results from pure economic and political economy factors. It is assumed that economic factors have a more permanent effect on the RER, whereas political economy factors influence its cyclical component. Were the economic factors constant, it would suffice to look at the behavior of the observed RER in order to extract the impact of political economy components on exchange rate policy choice. That is not the case, however. Over the period studied, there were substantial changes in the terms of trade, the international financial environment, and domestic imbalances, just to name a few variables that affected the equilibrium RER.

The evolution of the equilibrium RER captures the long-run RER trend, and, hence, the effect of economic variables on it. The difference between the actual RER and its equilibrium value, denoted as *RER misalignment*, is the part of RER movement that is not explained by the economic variables used. This empirical study will test whether political economy variables can explain this RER misalignment.

The influence of political economy variables is characterized in the following way. The government has a discrete policy choice of maintaining the misalignment fluctuating around an overvalued or undervalued level; that is, it chooses from two different regimes for the misalignment rate mean. Since changing policy is costly, one should expect this choice to have some persistence. Explanatory variables of misalignment regime choice can be divided into two types: observable and unobservable. Due to the presence of unobservable variables, the regime choice seems stochastic. In this context, observable political economy variables should be modeled as affecting the probability of changing regimes, rather than determining the regime.

An MSM captures the exchange rate regime choice characterization described above. In such a model, the time series behavior of the dependent variable follows an auto-regressive process ruled by alternative states (or regimes), which have different means and/or variances. In the model specification used, there are two possible states that differ in their means: an overvalued and an undervalued regime. Hence, the RER misalignment is modeled as following an auto-regressive process, and the process mean may change over time, depending on which regime is prevalent. Political economy variables enter the model by affecting the probability that the regime changes.

An important advantage of using the MSM over other empirical specifications that characterize discrete choices is that it does not require previous identification of the regimes by researchers. The characterization of regimes is a result of the estimation procedure. The choice of the MSM can be justified both by its characterization of the empirical features of the exchange rate series (see Kaminsky, 1993; Bollen, Gray and Whaley, 1998; and Diebold, Lee and Weinbach, 1993), and by its appealing interpretation.

Markov Switching Model

In the specification of the MSM chosen, there are two possible states (or regimes) that will be labeled 0 and 1. If the economy in t is in state 0, the dependent variable behavior in t will be that of an AR1 with auto-regressive parameter a and mean $m(0)$. Otherwise, the behavior in t will be that of an AR1 process with the same auto-regressive parameter a but with mean $m(1)$, which is different from $m(0)$. This means that the dependent variable fluctuates randomly around a certain mean. That stochastic oscillation is modeled through the AR1 specification. A change of policy regime would be reflected in the change of mean. The policy regime is modeled as an unobservable state variable, which is governed by a first order Markov process.

Let e be the degree of RER misalignment, and s an unobservable variable that takes values 0 or 1, depending on the regime. Then:

$$(1) \qquad e_{t+1} - \mu(s_{t+1}) = \alpha(e_t - \mu(s_{t+1})) + \sigma\varepsilon_{t+1},$$

where the mean ($\mu(s_{t+1})$) is a function of the regime, and $\{\varepsilon\}$ are i.i.d. with the standard normal distribution.

The regime variable is a discrete variable with two possible values. The transition matrix M gives the probabilities of switching states:

$$M = \begin{vmatrix} p_t^{00} & p_t^{01} = \left(1 - p_t^{00}\right) \\ p_t^{10} = \left(1 - p_t^{11}\right) & p_t^{11} \end{vmatrix},$$

where pij gives the probability of moving from state i to state j.

If $\mu(0)$ is higher than $\mu(1)$, state 0 can be identified with an overvalued exchange rate regime and state 1 with an undervalued exchange rate regime. A higher p^{ii} means a higher probability of continuing in state i, therefore a lower probability of changing states. Thus, the expected time of permanence in state i, when it is visited, is increased, yielding a higher unconditional probability of being in state i.

The transition probabilities may be assumed constant, as in Hamilton (1989), or time varying, as in Diebold, Lee and Weinbach (1993). When the transition probabilities are constant, the MSM amounts to a pure univariate time series model. In this case, the influence of no other variable is introduced into the behavior of the exchange rate variable: only its past behavior explains its future behavior.

Alternatively, it is assumed that the probability of switching states depends on political economy variables. The specification of the explanatory variables' effect on the probability of transitions is:

$$(2) \qquad p_t^{ii} = \frac{exp(q_t^{ii})}{1 + exp(q_t^{ii})}$$

$$q_t^{ii} = \beta_i + \sum_{k=1}^{K} \lambda_i^k X_i^k + \xi_t, \text{ for } i = 0,1,$$

where X_i^k is an explanatory variable of the transition probability.

Note that p^{ii}, being defined as a logistic function of q^{ii}, has a value between 0 and 1. Then, q^{ii} is modeled as depending linearly on the explanatory variables.

The model is estimated by maximum likelihood (Hamilton, 1994, and Diebold, Lee and Weinbach, 1993).

Empirical Implementation

The empirical investigation performed has two objectives. One is to identify whether an MSM can characterize the exchange rate variable. For that purpose an MSM is estimated with constant probabilities and compared to an autoregressive process of first order AR(1) specification. Then, the equation that specifies the transition probabilities, equation (2), becomes:

$$(2.a) \qquad p_t^{ii} = \frac{exp(\beta_i + \xi_i)}{1 + exp(\beta_i + \xi_i)}.$$

The other objective is to test whether political economy variables affect the probability of being in an appreciated exchange rate regime. That is achieved by using the MSM with time varying transition probabilities, where the transition probabilities are functions of political economy variables, and comparing it to the constant probability specification. The exercise was performed using no more than two political economy variables at a time, because otherwise the number of parameters to be estimated would be too large in comparison with the number of observations available. In this specification, equation (2) becomes:

$$(2.b) \qquad p_t^{ii} = \frac{exp(\beta_i + \lambda_i^1 X_t^1 + \lambda_i^2 X_t^2 + \xi_i)}{1 + exp(\beta_i + \lambda_i^1 X_t^1 + \lambda_i^2 X_t^2 + \xi_i)},$$

where X_i^1 and X_i^2 are two political economy variables.

The political economy variables used are the following:

• *Dummy variable for the dictatorship period.* This variable takes the value of 1 during the period of dictatorship and the value of 0 otherwise. This is based on the assumption that governments during dictatorships did not have to worry about election results. The expected result is that the probability of either remaining in or changing to the undervalued regime should be lower during dictatorship than during democracy.

• *Dummy variable for pre-election periods.* In Brazil, elections are always during the months of September, October or November. This value is 1 from March of the election year to the month when elections take place. This periodicity was chosen for the election dummy because election campaigns in Brazil start peaking only after *Carnaval* in February. Although there were elections during the dictatorship, they had less influence on power than in the democratic period; therefore the policymaker should be subject to fewer electoral considerations when choosing economic policy. Hence, the estimations were also performed for a pre-election dummy taking the value of 1 only for elections during the democratic period and the two first elections of dictatorship, when there was still the expectation that the military government would not stay in power for long.

• *Dummy variable for post-election periods.* This dummy variable takes the value of 1 during the 12 months following an election, for elections during democratic periods, and for the first two elections of dictatorship.

The dependent variable, RER misalignment,[27] is calculated as the difference between the logarithm of the RER and its equilibrium value. Both the RER and the equilibrium value used are the series calculated and estimated in Goldfajn and Valdés (1999). They calculate the RER as a trade-weighted average of bilateral RERs, including trade partners responsible for at least 4 percent of Brazilian trade. The equilibrium RER is the predicted value from the regression of the RER on the fundamentals, which are the terms of trade, the level of government spending, and the degree of openness (see Goldfajn and Valdés, 1999). The data range is from 1964 to 1996.

A real exchange rate overvaluation indicates that the RER is more valued than it should be according to its equilibrium level, and the opposite is true for the undervalued regime.

Results

Figure 4.8 presents RER misalignment and election dummy evolution through time. The left axis shows the value of exchange rate misalignment, and the right axis presents the value of the election dummy. This figure shows a concentration of negative misalignments or exchange rate overvaluation during the periods prior to elections. The effect is especially strong during the democratic period.

Table 4.2 summarizes the estimation results. Each row presents the result of a different specification, depending on which variables are being used to explain the transition probabilities between exchange rate regimes. Table 4.3 presents the estimated transition probabilities for each specification of Table 4.2.

The test begins by estimating a univariate model, which is a Markov Switching Model with constant probabilities. The results in row (1) of Table 4.2 suggest the existence of two regimes. The overvalued regime has mean

---

[27] The results of a different set of estimations using RER as a dependent variable are presented in Bonomo and Terra (1999). The results using an RER misalignment dependent variable were more robust and in conformity with the predictions of the analytical framework presented above. As argued above, RER misalignment is in fact the more appropriate variable to look at when explaining the effect of political economy variables on the choice of an exchange regime.

Figure 4.8. RER Misalignment and Election Dummy Devolution over Time

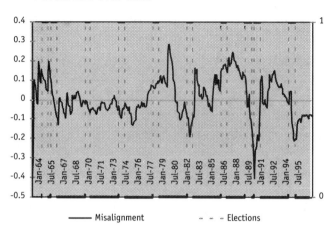

—————— Misalignment   — — — Elections

—0.081, and the undervalued regime has mean 0.012. As for the constant transition probabilities, if the economy is in the overvalued regime, the probability it will remain there is 84.5 percent, whereas if the economy is in the undervalued regime, the probability the economy will remain there is 96.4 percent, as shown in Table 4.3.

The MSM specification is then tested to determine whether it is justified. An AR(1) model for the RER misalignment is then estimated, and the results are presented in row (0) of Table 4.2. The hypothesis of two regimes against the null of an AR(1) can be tested based on a likelihood ratio test. However, the asymptotic distribution of the statistics is not chi-squared as usual. García (1998) derives the asymptotic distribution for this statistic. For the case of an auto-regressive factor of 0.95, the 1 percent and 5 percent critical values of this distribution are 12.08 and 8.48. The likelihood ratio in this case is 35.55. The linear model is rejected at less than 1 percent.

After the estimation of the univariate two regime specification, different political economy variables are included as possible variables that affect the transition probabilities. Row (2) presents the results when a political regime dummy is used as an explanatory variable of the transition probabilities. It is interesting to note that in this specification the misalignment mean in the overvalued regime is not significantly different from 0. During the dictatorship, the probability of remaining in the overvalued regime is higher (this probability is 73.3 percent during democracy and close to 97.4 percent during dictatorship), and the probability of remaining in the undervalued regime is lower than during the democratic period (95.3 percent during democracy and 70.6 percent during dictatorship). If a likelihood

Table 4.2. Estimation Results Summary of Political Variables (Dependent Variable: Exchange Rate Misalignment)

$$e_{t+1} - \mu(s_{t+1}) = \alpha(e_t - \mu(s_{t+1})) + \sigma\varepsilon_{t+1}$$

$$p_t^{ii} = \frac{exp(\beta_i + \lambda_i^1 X_t^1 + \lambda_i^2 X_t^2 + \xi_i)}{1 + exp(\beta_i + \lambda_i^1 X_t^1 + \lambda_i^2 X_t^2 + \xi_i)}, \quad where \quad p_t^{ii} = Pr\left[S_{t+1} = i \,|\, S_t = i\right]$$

Explanatory variables of the transition probabilities	Mean		Constant part of probability		X1 coefficient		X2 coefficient		Auto-regressive factor	Standard deviation	Likelihood function value	Likelihood ratio test χ2 p-value	
	Overvalued $\mu(0)$	Undervalued $\mu(1)$	Overvalued $\beta 0$	Undervalued $\beta 1$	Overvalued $\lambda 01$	Undervalued $\lambda 11$	Overvalued $\lambda 02$	Undervalued $\lambda 12$	α	σ		Inclusion of X1	Inclusion of X2
(0) AR(1) - One regime case	0.000 (0.14)								0.940 (54.32)	0.035	756.11		
(1) Constant probabilities	-0.081 (-2.07)	0.012 (13.48)*	1.702 (3.85)	3.293 (9.85)	(70.39)	(23.78)			0.964	0.027	791.66		
(2) X1-Political regime	-0.036 (-0.92)	0.056 (15.30)*	1.008 (1.89)	3.007 (6.24)	2.596 (3.81)	-2.131 (-2.76)			0.964 (67.76)	0.027 **	798.45	0.000	
(3) X1-Pre-elections	-0.083 (-2.2)	0.011 (12.64)*	1.272 (2.17)	3.902 (7.53)	0.784 (0.92)	-1.692 (-2.41)			0.962 (70.1)	0.027 **	794.70	0.014	
(4) X1-Pre-election during democracy	-0.082 (-2.11)	0.011 (13.17)*	1.425 (2.59)	3.788 (8.23)	0.432 (0.50)	-2.201 (-3.08)			0.963 (69.03)	0.027 **	795.65	0.005	
(5) X1-Pre-election during democracy X2-Pre-election during dictatorship	-0.082 (-2.50)	0.011 (13.19)*	1.226 (2.18)	3.897 (8.04)	0.635 (0.74)	-2.321 (-3.27)	14.881 (0.01)	-0.575 (0.51)	0.962 (70.78)	0.027 (24.98)	796.60		0.168
(6) X1-After-election during democracy	-0.078 (-1.92)	0.015 (14.34)*	2.184 (-3.12)	3.421 (8.84)	-0.745 (-0.83)	-0.996 (-1.34)			0.965 (71.94)	0.027 **	792.73	0.144	
(7) X1-Political regime X2-Pre-election during democracy	-0.037 (-1.01)	0.057 (15.68)*	0.455 (0.59)	18.372 (0.02)	3.119 (3.70)	-17.498 (-0.02)	0.407 (0.43)	-16.659 (-0.02)	0.963 (69.93)	0.027 **	802.87	0.000	0.003
(8) X1-Political regime X2-After-election during democracy(-1.01)	-0.040	0.055 (14.19)*	-0.090 (-0.11)	3.481 (5.74)	4.328 (4.27)	-2.953 (-3.32)	-2.791 (-2.96)	0.884 -0.90	0.964 (69.33)	0.028 **	800.49	0.000	0.043

Note: Asymptotic t-ratios are in parentheses.

*This is the t-ratio of the difference between the mean of the two regimes.

**Value larger than 99.99.

Table 4.3. Estimated Transition Probabilities for Each Specification in Table 4.2 (Dependent Variable: Exchange Rate Misalignment)

Explanatory variables of the transition probabilities	Probabilities when dummies equal 0		Probabilities when dummy X1=1		Probabilities when dummy X2=1	
	Overvalued	Undervalued	Overvalued	Undervalued	Overvalued	Undervalued
(1) Constant probabilities	0.846	0.964				
(2) X1-Political regime	0.733	0.953	0.974	0.706		
(3) X1-Pre-elections	0.781	0.980	0.887	0.901		
(4) X1-Pre-elections during democracy	0.806	0.978	0.865	0.830		
(5) X1-Pre-elections during democracy X2-Pre-elections during dictatorship	0.773	0.980	0.865	0.829	1.000	0.965
(6) X1-After-elections during democracy	0.899	0.968	0.808	0.919		
(7) X1-Political regime X2-Pre-elections during democracy	0.612	1.000	0.973	0.706	0.703	0.847
(8) X1-Political regime X2-After-elections during democracy	0.478	0.970	0.986	0.629	0.053	0.987
(9) X1-Minister of Finance change	0.841	0.975	0.817	0.925		

ratio test is performed for the inclusion of the political regime dummy, the null of constant probability is rejected at 1 percent.

The second set of political economy variables used to explain the transition probabilities are the pre-election dummies, and the results are in rows (3), (4), and (5) of Table 4.2. Rows (3) and (4) present the results when a dummy variable for the pre-election period is used as a possible explanatory variable of the transition probabilities. Both the pre-election for the whole period and the pre-election during democracy dummies have the same qualitative impact over the transition probabilities: proximity of elections increases the probability of the economy remaining in the over-valued regime and decreases the probability of remaining in the underval-ued regime. The impacts of these variables on the transition probability are significant for the undervalued regime, but not for the overvalued one. Both results indicate that there is a higher unconditional probability of an overvalued regime before elections.

When rows (3) and (4) of Table 4.3 are compared, the negative impact of the pre-election dummy is larger when only democratic periods are taken into account. For the pre-election dummy, the probability of the economy remaining in the undervalued regime changes from 98 percent in normal times to 90.1 percent during pre-election periods, whereas for the pre-election during democracy dummy the probability changes from 97.8 percent during normal times to 83 percent during pre-election periods.

The likelihood ratio test indicates that the inclusion of the pre-election during democracy dummy is significant at 1 percent, while the inclusion of the pre-election dummy is significant at 2 percent.

The difference between the impact of pre-election during democ-racy and during dictatorship is made clear in estimation (5), which uses both a pre-election during democracy dummy and a pre-election during dictatorship dummy. All coefficients have the expected sign, but only the coefficient of the pre-election during democracy dummy for the underval-ued regime is significant (see Table 4.2). The probability of the economy remaining in the undervalued regime when it is there in normal times is 98 percent. In pre-election during dictatorship, the probability changes to 96.5 percent, whereas in pre-election periods during democracy this probability changes to 82.9 percent (see Table 4.3). In summary, during pre-election periods, the probability of the economy remaining in the undervalued re-gime decreases, and the effect is larger during democratic periods than during dictatorship. The inclusion of the pre-election during dictatorship dummy (row 5) in the model with only the pre-election during democracy dummy (row 4) is rejected at any conventional significance level.

The post-election during democracy dummy has a negative impact on both transition probabilities, producing an ambiguous effect on the regime unconditional probabilities. However, neither one is significant, as shown in row (6) of Table 4.2. Moreover, the inclusion of that variable in the constant probability model is rejected.

Row (7) combines the political regime and the pre-election during democracy dummies. The probability of remaining in the overvalued regime is higher during dictatorship and during pre-election periods, although only the impact of dictatorship is significant. The impact of these dummies on the probability of remaining in the undervalued regime is not significant. The inclusion of the political regime dummy is tested by comparing the specification in row (7) with the specification in row (4). As for the inclusion of the pre-election during democracy dummy, the specification in row (7) is compared with the specification in row (2). Both tests reject the null hypothesis of the restricted specification at any conventional significance level.

The next specification uses the political regime and the post-election dummies as explanatory variables for the transition probabilities. As shown in row (8) of Table 4.2, the political regime dummy has a positive impact on the probability of remaining in the overvalued regime (during democracy the probability is 47.8 percent and during dictatorship it is 98.6 percent), and a negative impact on the probability of remaining in the undervalued regime (the probabilities are 97 percent and 62.9 percent for the democratic and dictatorial periods, respectively). The post-election dummy has a negative impact on the probability of remaining in the overvalued regime, and a positive impact on the other probability. The post-election dummy coefficient for the undervalued regime is the only one that is not significant. The inclusion of both the political regime and the post-election dummies individually pass the likelihood test at a 5 percent significance level.

In summary, dictatorship favored an overvalued currency. A misalignment cycle around elections is identified: an overvalued currency is more likely before elections, while there is a higher probability of changing from an overvalued to an undervalued currency immediately after elections. The election cycle proved stronger during the democratic period than during the dictatorial period.

Interpretation

The results are divided into two groups: those related to political regime, and those related to election. Each group will be interpreted in turn.

The results related to the political regime are not in accordance with initial predictions. The prior was that the military government would be more concerned than a democracy with the balance of payments vis-à-vis inflation. The reason was that a strong balance of payments performance would benefit a group of well-organized citizens from the tradables sector. The underlying assumption in the prior was that an overvalued exchange rate would hurt the tradables sector. However, this is not true if protection is high and the bulk of imports are intermediate goods for the tradables sector. As discussed in the historical analysis above, this was the case in Brazil until the late 1980s.[28] In such an economic environment, an overvalued exchange rate would have little impact on the balance of payments and would benefit tradables sector agents. Thus, it is not surprising that there was a higher unconditional probability of the overvalued regime during dictatorship.[29]

During democracy, voters' assessment of government policies became important. Since voters do not know the policymakers' preferences, incumbents have an incentive to behave as if they had popular preferences. This means that before elections, incumbents tend to set a more appreciated exchange rate in order to influence voters. The subsection above describes evidence of an exchange rate election cycle during democracy, and this empirical pattern fits the asymmetric information framework.

Conclusions

Exchange rate policy in Brazil has been a crawling peg throughout the period studied, with the exception of two short periods. The main policy choice has basically been the administration of the crawling peg, which could lead to either real exchange rate appreciation or depreciation. The main forces guiding this exchange rate policy choice were the result of a tradeoff between inflation and the balance of payments. Exchange rate policy that results in a real exchange rate appreciation reduces inflation but deteriorates the balance of payments; the reverse is true for a real exchange rate depreciation. These two effects of exchange rate policy, however, do not have a symmetric effect on the different members of society: inflation reduction benefits a large number of dispersed agents, whereas balance of payments improvement benefits a more concentrated group of exporters

---

[28] The predictions of the analytical framework would be expected to be valid if the present protection structure had previously existed.

[29] The Geisel government (1974-79) had a major influence on the results when it did not adjust the exchange rate during the first oil shock.

and import-competing domestic industries.

The analytical framework posited that choices of policymakers depend on the relative weight they placed on the balance of payments as opposed to inflation reduction. In particular, policymakers in need of popular support would place a relatively higher weight on reducing inflation. Hence, democratic governments are likely to place more weight on inflation reduction than are dictatorial governments. An election cycle can also result if policymakers differ on the relative weights they place on their policy objectives, and if the public can only observe policymakers' choices, not their preferences.

The analytical framework predictions were tested empirically. A Markov Switching Model with time-varying transition probabilities was used to characterize the exchange rate regimes and the influence of the political economy variable on them. The dependent variable chosen was the real exchange rate misalignment with respect to its equilibrium level. Real exchange rate misalignment is a more appropriate measure for the exercise performed. In trying to identify political economy factors that affect exchange rate policy, it is advisable to capture the effects of other exogenous purely economic variables. The misalignment measure controls for the effects of the economic variables, and the political economy variables should explain the remaining variations.

During the dictatorship period, the probability of the economy remaining in the undervalued regime was smaller than during the democratic period, and the reverse is true for the probability of remaining in the overvalued regime. This is in contrast with the analytical predictions. This finding can be reconciled with the analytical framework if one takes into account the economic environment during the dictatorship period, which was characterized by high protection for finished goods and reliance by domestic industry on imports of intermediate goods. The election cycle was also identified: the probability of an appreciated exchange rate is higher in the months preceding elections, while the probability of a depreciated exchange rate is higher in the months following elections. Moreover, the election cycle proved stronger during the democratic period than during the period of dictatorship.

References

Alesina, A. 1987. Macroeconomic Policy in a Two-Party System as a Repeated Game. *The Quarterly Journal of Economics* 102: 651-78.

Baumgarten, M. 1996. Modelos de Taxa de Câmbio Real de Equilíbrio: uma Aplicação para o Brasil. Pontifícia Universidade Católica do Rio de Janeiro. Masters thesis.

Bollen, N., S. Gray, and R. Whaley. 1998. Regime Switching in Foreign Exchange Rates: Evidence from Currency Option Prices. *Journal of Econometrics.*

Bonomo, M. 1986. Controle de Crédito e Política Monetária em 1981. Pontifícia Universidade Católica do Rio de Janeiro. Masters thesis.

Bonomo, M., and M.C. Terra. 2000. Election and Exchange Rate Policy Cycles. Fundação Getulio Vargas, Escola de Pós-Graduação em Economia, Rio de Janeiro. Mimeo.

_____. 1999. The Political Economy of Exchange Rate Policy in Brazil: 1964-1997. Research Network Working Paper R-367 and *Ensaios Econômicos EPGE*, No. 341. Fundação Getulio Vargas, Escola de Pós-Graduação em Economia, Rio de Janeiro, and the Inter-American Development Bank, Washington, DC.

Bruno, M. 1989. *Israel's Crisis and Economic Reform: A Historical Perspective.* NBER Working Paper No. 3075, National Bureau of Economic Research, Cambridge, MA.

Carneiro, D. 1990. Crise e Esperança: 1974-80. In M. Abreu (ed.), *A Ordem do Progresso.* Rio de Janeiro: Editora Campus.

Dib, M. 1985. *Importações Brasileiras: Políticas de Controle e Determinantes da Demanda.* Rio de Janeiro: Banco Nacional de Desenvolvimento Econômica e Social.

Diebold, F.X., J.H. Lee, and G.C. Weinbach. 1993. Regime-Switching with Time-Varying Transition Probabilities. In C. Hargreaves (ed.), *Nonstationary Time Series and Cointegration.* New York: Oxford University Press.

Franco, G. 1996. *The Real Plan.* Texto para Discussão No. 354, Pontifícia Universidade Católica do Rio de Janeiro, Departamento de Economia.

Frieden, J., E. Stein, and P. Ghezzi. 1999. The Political Economy of Exchange Rate Policy in Latin America. Inter-American Development Bank, Washington, DC, and Harvard University, Cambridge MA. Mimeo.

Garcia, R. 1998. Asymptotic Null of the Likelihood Ratio Test in Markov Switching Models. *Journal of International Economics* 39: 763-88.

Ghezzi, P., E. Stein, and J. Streb. 1999. Elections and the Timing of Devaluations. Inter-American Development Bank Research Department Working Paper 396, Washington, DC.

Goldenstein, L. 1985. Da Heterodoxia ao FMI - a política econômica de 1979 a 1982. Universidade Estadual de Campinas, Brazil. Masters thesis.

Goldfajn, I., and R. Valdés. 1999. The Aftermath of Appreciations. *Quarterly Journal of Economics* 114: 229-62.

Hamilton, J. 1994. *Time Series Analysis*. Princeton, NJ: Princeton University Press.

_____. 1989. A New Approach to the Economic Analysis of Nonstationary Time Series and the Business Cycle. *Econometrica* 57: 357-84.

Heymann, D. 1991. From Sharp Disinflation to Hyperinflation, Twice: The Argentine Experience, 1985-1989. In M. Bruno, S. Fischer, E. Helpman, et al. (eds.). *Lessons of Economic Stabilization and its Aftermath*. Cambridge, MA: MIT Press.

Kaminsky, G. 1993. Is There a Peso Problem? Evidence from the Dollar/ Pound Exchange Rate: 1976-1987. *American Economic Review* 83: 450-72.

Modiano, E. 1990. A Ópera dos Três Cruzados. In M. Abreu (ed.), *A Ordem do Progresso*. Rio de Janeiro: Editora Campus.

Persson, T. and Tabellini, G. 1990. *Macroeconomic Policy: Credibility and Politics*. Harwood Academic Publishers.

Rogoff, K. 1990. Equilibrium Political Budget Cycles. *American Economic Review* 80: 21-36.

Rogoff, K., and A. Sibert. 1988. Elections and Macroeconomic Policy Cycles. *Review of Economic Studies* 55: 1-16.

Skidmore, T. 1988. *De Castelo a Tancredo*. Rio de Janeiro: Editora Paz e Terra.

Simonsen, M.H. 1995. Inflação e Política Cambial. In *30 Anos de Indexação*. Rio de Janeiro: Editora da Fundação Getulio Vargas.

Terra, M.C.T. 1998. Openness and Inflation: A New Assessment. *Quarterly Journal of Economics* 113: 641-48.

_____. 1997. Debt Crisis and Inflation. *Revista de Econometria* 17: 21-48.

CHAPTER FIVE

Something for Everyone: Chilean Exchange Rate Policy since 1960

José De Gregorio[1]

Chile has experimented since 1960 not only with several exchange rate regimes, but also with various approaches to economic policy. The country followed strategies ranging from import substitution in the 1960s to full-fledged populism in the early 1970s. Since then, Chile has adopted an open free market economy with conservative macroeconomic management. But implementation of macroeconomic policies has changed according to the external environment as well as internal developments. Such objectives as inflation management, macroeconomic stability, outward orientation, competitiveness and structural reform have played different roles in the choice of exchange rate regime and stabilization policies. At the same time, economic policy has not been implemented in isolation from pressures from interest groups and political economy considerations. Indeed, many decisions have taken into account interest group pressures as well as the need to build support for policies, and as a result some compensation mechanisms have come into play.

Economic performance has varied widely during this period. The economy showed moderate growth in the 1960s, extreme inflation and then stabilization and recovery from recession in the 1970s, and finally a major recession-recovery cycle followed by high growth since the 1980s.

This range of economic performance makes Chile an interesting case study in exchange rate policy over the last 30 to 40 years. During the past 15 years, in particular, exchange rate policy has been the focus of

---

[1] José De Gregorio is an economist with the Department of Industrial Engineering of the Center for Applied Economics at the University of Chile.

public attention and discussion regarding economic policy. As a consequence of the 1982 crisis and the economy's strong performance since the mid-1980s, the private sector as well as the government have given high priority to maintaining competitiveness. Understanding the country's current situation, though, requires an analysis of the Chilean experience from 1960 to the present. This, in turn, calls for an examination of what has determined the choice of exchange rate regime, with special emphasis on political economy factors.

Evolution of Exchange Rates and Policies

The real exchange rate in Chile has fluctuated widely since the 1960s (Figure 5.1), primarily due to changes in such economic fundamentals as terms of trade, productivity, and the degree of openness. In addition, changes in nominal exchange rate policies have had persistent effects on the behavior of the real exchange rate, and the use of these rates to achieve competitiveness or reduce inflation has further produced significant effects.[2] Another notable characteristic of Chile's exchange rate policies was the country's strong restrictions on foreign exchange transactions for most of the period from 1960 to 1990, with the exception of the late 1970s and early 1980s. The 1990s saw almost complete liberalization of foreign exchange markets.

Classification of Exchange Rate Regimes

In order to classify exchange rates regimes, four different regimes are each defined by a discrete variable (1 to 4):

1) *The fixed exchange rate* regime is usually implemented to achieve low inflation. It is also characterized by a liberalization of most foreign exchange transactions and unification of exchange rate markets. Since 1960, there has twice been partial liberalization of capital flows in Chile, but the two experiences differed slightly. During the first, the country was a relatively closed economy that followed an import substitution strategy, while, during the second, the economy was fairly open. Both experiences, however, occurred at a time when economic policy tended toward increasing openness.

2) The *crisis management* regime usually occurs in periods when the authorities adopt some form of float and introduce segmentation in

---

[2] For descriptions of exchange rates policies, see Ffrench-Davis (1973, 1979), De Gregorio (1986), Edwards and Cox-Edwards (1987), Dornbusch and Edwards (1994), Meller (1996), Williamson (1996) and Cowan and De Gregorio (1998).

Table 5.1. Exchange Rate Regime

	Regime		Regime		Regime
1960	1	1973	2	1986	3
1961	1	1974	3	1987	3
1962	1	1975	3	1988	3
1963	2	1976	3	1989	3
1964	2	1977	3	1990	3
1965	3	1978	3	1991	3
1966	3	1979	1	1992	4
1967	3	1980	1	1993	4
1968	3	1981	1	1994	4
1969	3	1982	2	1995	4
1970	3	1983	3	1996	4
1971	2	1984	3		
1972	2	1985	3		

foreign exchange markets. These periods follow exchange rate crises. At this stage there is no clear exchange rate regime, only attempts to control the loss of reserves, rising inflation and financial distress.

3) *The crawling peg* with exchange rate controls regime basically consists of a policy of small devaluations of the exchange rate according to a rule that is oriented to maintain some level for the real exchange rate. The exchange rate can be fixed at the level of the crawling peg or it can be allowed to float within a narrow band. Most of the crawling peg episodes have been characterized by segmentation in the foreign exchange market.

4) The *wide band* regime is a system consisting of a wide exchange rate band around some central parity, with few controls on the foreign exchange rate market. The central parity can be chosen in a manner similar to that of the crawling peg, but the exchange rate is allowed to float in a wide range. This is the closest that the Chilean economy has been to a floating regime.

Table 5.1 presents the classification of the exchange rate regime according to these categories. The reasons for this classification are discussed below along with a description of exchange rate policies.

Exchange Rate Policies from 1960-96

The 1960s began with a fixed exchange rate regime. Following devaluations of 18 percent in late 1958 and 25 percent in January 1959, the exchange rate was fixed at 1.05 Escudos per U.S. dollar in January 1959 in order to achieve price stability. The foreign exchange market was unified, and free access to it was established. Between 1960 and 1962, there was a 12 percent real appreciation, a decline in inflation, and a sharp increase in the current account deficit. With the external situation deteriorating following the liberalization of foreign exchange, liberalization was reversed and foreign trade restrictions reintroduced at the start of 1962. The exchange rate system was abandoned in October 1962, and in the next couple of years exchange rate policy and capital account management were oriented to close the external gap. Restrictions in the foreign exchange market were reintroduced and intensified during 1963-64.

The crawling peg system was first implemented in April 1965, with a couple of small devaluations per month. The policy remained essentially the same until 1970, with varying degrees of restrictions on foreign exchange and foreign trade, depending to a large extent on short-term balance of payments conditions. For example, restrictions were tightened in 1967 in response to a deteriorating external situation. By the late 1960s, there were three official exchange rates: one for most trade transactions (the *corredores* rate), a second rate that applied to the banking system (used mainly for financial obligations), and a third rate for copper exports. The latter was in practice a tax, though small. Over 1963-65, this dual system was used more intensely as the economy entered a balance of payments crisis. The gap between the general exchange rate for exports and the rate for copper was on average 11 percent during this period, reaching a maximum of 18 percent in 1964.

At the start of the Allende government in late 1970, there was a new attempt to fix the exchange rate. But a rapid rise in inflation caused substantial real appreciation. The policy response was to devalue and to increase segmentation in the foreign exchange market. By 1973, there were at least six official exchange rates, with a ratio of 1:52 between the maximum and the minimum. There was also massive intervention in foreign trade, with the average tariff running around 100 percent.

Figure 5.1 shows that the real exchange rate during the 1960s was substantially lower than the real post-1974 exchange rate. As mentioned above, multiple exchange rates with a number of restrictions and trade protection may have allowed the economy to endure such an appreciated real exchange rate without a wide current account deficit.

After the military took power in 1973, its first exchange rate measure was a 300 percent devaluation of the most important rates in order to restore competitiveness. The multiple exchange rate regime was collapsed to just three rates. A crawling peg with four devaluations a month was implemented. However, each rate was adjusted differently, with the

Figure 5.1. Real Exchange Rate
(Index 1986=100)

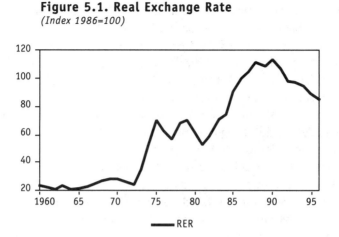

RER

goal of achieving exchange rate unification. In August 1974, the exchange rate for copper exports was unified, at which time two exchange rates remained. The final unification occurred one year later. Macroeconomic discipline was achieved, but inflation was still high, despite the large decline in activity. By 1974, the real exchange rate reached its maximum depreciation since the 1960s.

Inflation remained in the three digits in 1976, declining to 64 percent in 1977. During these years, the crawling peg system was based on pre-announced daily devaluations indexed to domestic inflation. In June 1976 and March 1977, however, two 10 percent revaluations were implemented, officially justified by the fact that the real exchange rate was too depreciated and the external conditions would allow for an appreciation. In February 1978, the system of daily indexed devaluations was abandoned in favor of a *tablita* that set the rate of the crawl according to inflationary targets. The *tablita* was inaugurated with a 2.5 percent monthly devaluation and ended with a 0.75 percent devaluation in the last quarter of 1978. Inflation remained high and stabilized at around 30 percent, despite the reduction in the rate of nominal devaluation. In late 1978, a *tablita* was announced for all of 1979, with a 15 percent devaluation. Despite the attempt to curb inflation through reduction of the devaluation rate, high inflation persisted. The year 1978 closed with 30 percent inflation, the same rate prevailing in June 1979.

With disappointing progress on inflation, the exchange rate was fixed in June 1979. The value of the currency was set at 39 Escudos/US$, which was 6 percent higher than the prevailing *tablita*. The rest of the story is well known. Faced with deteriorating internal and external conditions, the fixed exchange rate regime collapsed in June 1982.

The devaluation of 1982 was followed by a period of instability, with discrete devaluations, a short period of floating, segmentation of the foreign exchange rate market and so on. In August 1982, the exchange rate was again set according to a crawling peg based on a purchasing power parity (PPP) rule. Although the rules have changed, the basic mechanism of daily mini-devaluations, begun in the 1960s, has remained in place up to the present. In order to help firms under financial distress because of high leverage in dollars, several programs to help debtors were implemented in the early 1980s. They are discussed below.

In late September 1982, the exchange rate was allowed to move within a narrow band of ± 2 percent, which subsequently widened. The central parity was determined according to daily devaluations based on the differentials between domestic and foreign inflation. There were changes in the rate of crawl as well as the basket of currencies used to set the central parity.

After stability returned to exchange rate policy, several substantial devaluations, in addition to the daily "mini-devaluations," were implemented during the 1980s. The first and largest of these was a 23.7 percent devaluation in September 1984. It was followed by devaluations of 9 percent in February 1985 and 5 percent in June 1985.

The crawling rate was set following a PPP rule. Devaluations were carried out on a daily basis as the difference between domestic and foreign inflation, which in terms of U.S. dollars was estimated at an annual rate of 1 percent when the system was reintroduced. Then in March 1983 the discount was set to zero to induce a depreciation. This figure was changed to 0.6 percent in 1985 as foreign inflation was discounted, and subsequent rates of 3.6 percent, 0 percent, and 1.2 percent were used to finally reach a discount of 2.4 percent in July 1992.

In late 1995 a downward drift (appreciation) of 2 percent was added to the PPP rule. In effect, the discount allowed for an "equilibrium" 2 percent real appreciation in the central parity; that is, a PPP -2 percent rule. The central parity was set according to a basket of currencies, but the weights were changed on different occasions.

When the band was first implemented in September 1982, a ± 2 percent width was set around the central parity. In mid-1989, the band was widened to ± 5 percent, with further increases to ± 10 percent in January 1992 and ± 12.5 percent in January 1997. As in the 1980s, the central parity was changed on several occasions during the 1990s, but these changes involved revaluations instead of devaluations. There were four revaluations:

the central parity was revalued by 2 percent in June 1991, followed by 5 percent in January 1992, 10 percent in December 1994, and 5 percent in January 1997.

In the period from the debt crisis to 1990, continuous devaluations of the nominal exchange rate resulted in a continuous real depreciation. Devaluation without inflation was achieved because these devaluations contributed mainly to correcting a large misalignment that had occurred in the early 1980s.[3] Between 1981 and 1988, the period of persistent depreciation, the average devaluation was 30 percent per year, while average inflation was only 20 percent per year. It is interesting to note that real depreciation continued even in the second half of the 1980s, when there was no need to devalue discretely. The depreciation of the dollar in the second half of the 1980s, after the sharp appreciation of the first half of the decade, allowed for a depreciating rate with respect to the dollar, an even lower inflation rate, and a depreciation of the real exchange rate.

In 1990, the situation reversed, and exchange rates started appreciating. The economy had reached full employment by 1988, external accounts appeared to be sound, and productivity growth was significant. Chile had also returned to voluntary capital markets. In this context, tensions in the exchange rate market appeared and the period of "high" (depreciated) real exchange rates ended. From 1990-96, the real exchange rate appreciated at an average annual rate of 4.6 percent.

An important policy implemented during the 1990s, with a debatable degree of success, was an unremunerated reserve requirement on most capital inflows, which currently amounts to an entry fee of about 3 percent. This has been used as a complement to macroeconomic policy, with the objective of allowing both tight monetary policy and a "weak" currency.

The Political Economy of Exchange Rate Regimes

Decisions on exchange rate policy are not made a vacuum. This is particularly true in terms of policy objectives such as achieving a desired level for the real exchange rate, as well as that rate's interaction with other goals such as promoting specific sectors or controlling inflation. The choices made are not necessarily the technically optimal ones, since they often are subordinated to other objectives and represent the result of interaction between different interest groups. In this respect, it is important to

---

[3] For details on real exchange rates determinants, see De Gregorio (1996) and Céspedes and De Gregorio (1999).

show how Chile's economic system evolved from an import substitution strategy to trade liberalization, and how the exchange rate played an important role as a compensation mechanism. Also important in Chile was the evolution of the exchange rate system from one oriented to competitiveness to one focused on controlling inflation. Throughout this process, political economy factors, ideas and institutions played a role in determining specific choices.

From Import Substitution to Liberalization

From the 1960s until 1974, Chile was a classic example of inward-looking development based on import substitution. The exchange rate thus had to accommodate this strategy. Although the crawling peg was introduced in the 1960s to preserve competitiveness and stability, Figure 5.1 shows that the real exchange rate was highly appreciated when compared to post-1974 levels. To avoid excessive imports and an unsustainable external imbalance, this rate was sustained by high tariffs and other trade restrictions.

A clear description of the interaction between the exchange rate and trade regimes appears in a 1976 speech by Sergio de Castro, one of the leading figures in Chile's trade liberalization. He was explaining the problems Chile had with the Andean Pact in liberalizing its trade regime. On import substitution and appreciation he said:

> Obviously that policy [appreciated exchange rate] allowed for the import of capital goods and raw materials at relatively low prices to support the industrialization that was being promoted. As a result...it also motivated the importation of all sorts of goods. If the policy had remained in effect, it would obviously have created a large deficit in the balance of payments. The tariff policy designed to avoid a balance of payments crisis prohibited, or applied extremely high duties to, products that could be produced domestically.

Regarding the exchange rate and trade regimes, de Castro went on to argue:

> It should be emphasized that the exchange rate and tariff policies are inversely linked...In this way, a particular sector that is left unprotected when the tariffs are lowered receives compensatory protection from an automatic rise in the real exchange rate.

The exchange rate regime prevailing until 1978 was clearly oriented to compensate the industrial sector as well as other protected sectors for the loss of protection.[4] It was also designed to promote exports. Of course, as basic open macro theory would suggest, a depreciation of the real exchange rate is the natural outcome of trade liberalization, and hence the objectives of the authorities were consistent with expected outcomes. The objective of achieving competitiveness was already evident in "El Ladrillo," the name given to the document prepared by the "Chicago boys" during Pinochet's government, which is considered to be the economic program of the military regime.[5] According to this document:

> The maintenance of the exchange rate in real terms is a requisite to moving a significant amount of resources to the export industry. Consequently, *while stability of prices is still not achieved,* it is indispensable that the central bank continue devaluing periodically and frequently enough to avoid large or predictable devaluations that could induce speculation...It is fundamental that the exchange rate policy not change. If, for example, it is expected that the exchange rate will increase less than domestic prices [real appreciation], there will be a devastating effect on the allocation of resources, since the risk of investing in the export sector will be increased...

The clear intention of the policy was to open up the economy and compensate for reduced protection by means of the exchange rate, as well as to promote exports. However, the exchange rate was not the only compensation given to entrepreneurs in order to obtain their support for reforms, particularly opening up the economy. Reforms were deep and widespread, and several other mechanisms had to be used. Edwards and Lederman (1998) provide an insightful discussion on the political economy of Chile's trade reform. In a relatively short period of time, from 1974 to 1979, tariffs were drastically reduced—from an average of 100 percent, with many selective controls, to a flat 10 percent and no other controls—and this reduction was possible because there existed the necessary support to un-

---

[4] It is debatable when authorities changed from the compensation objective to the anti-inflation objective, since in February 1978 the *tablita* had already been implemented, anchoring the rate of crawl to future expected inflation. However, the regime in 1978 is classified as a crawling peg, although it later moved to a fixed exchange rate regime.

[5] The document was called "Economic Program for Development" and was given to important figures in the military government in September 1973.

dertake the reform. Some of the components of the reform program provided compensation to the private sector. This was the case for large-scale privatizations, some of which were at bargain rates (Hachette and Luders, 1992), and financial liberalization, which allowed existing and emerging conglomerates to participate in financial activities that had been highly regulated prior to 1974. On the other hand, more direct compensation mechanisms included the repression of labor unions and the appointment of leaders of entrepreneurial associations to the cabinet. The first important instance was the appointment of the leader of the organization of farmers as Minister of Agriculture, and this mechanism was regularly used to build private sector support for the reforms (Campero, 1991).

Finally, it is important to bear in mind that reforms were also favored by the fact that, in 1973, the country was in one of its deepest economic and political crises of the century, and therefore there was ample popular support for introducing drastic reforms.

Summarizing, one can argue that from 1974 to 1979 the exchange rate regime was consistent with the compensation needed to implement a deep trade reform and the drastic switch from import substitution to outward-oriented development.

Inflation and a Fixed Exchange Rate

As described above, after 1978 the exchange rate policy began shifting toward an anti-inflation objective, which culminated with the fixed exchange rate from June 1979 to June 1982. From a political economy point of view, there are two main questions that arise in this period. The first is why, after a strong position favoring competitiveness, there was the change of emphasis toward using the exchange rate as the anchor to fight inflation. The second is what were the compensation mechanisms used to maintain support for the economic program after several years of pro-competitiveness discourse.

Regarding the change of emphasis in exchange rate policy, it is difficult to find a single strong answer, but there are at least three important factors that may help to explain this change:

• *The role of ideas.* The economic team was mostly educated at the University of Chicago. As was made clear in "El Ladrillo" (see the italicized section in the quotation above), the use of the crawling peg, or mini-devaluations, was considered a useful tool before price stability was achieved. In a more stable situation, it was believed, inflation would quickly converge with international levels. According to one high-level official, Julio Dittborn, deputy director of the planning office (ODEPLAN) at the time, "in light of existing information...fixing the exchange rate would lead us quickly to domestic inflation similar to international inflation" (cited by Arellano and Cortázar, 1982). Thus, the issue of real appreciation was not considered to be important. Moreover, the real exchange rate was at record levels (depreciated), hence there was room for a degree of appreciation.

• *Inflationary disappointment and temptation.* After shock treatment to reduce inflation in 1974 with a money-based stabilization, there was only modest progress in controlling inflation. By the end of 1976, inflation was 174 percent, declining in 1977 to 64 percent. Thus, moving to an exchange rate-based stabilization, under the view that the law of one price should hold, could help to bring progress faster. Indeed, in 1978 inflation decreased to 30 percent. It is important to note, however, that the decision to fix the exchange rate was taken before achieving price stability, since by June 1979 yearly inflation was still 30 percent.

• *A suitable external environment.* At this time, large amounts of funds in the international economy were available for developing countries, and Chile's financial markets were open to the rest of the world. Financing a widening current account deficit was therefore not seen as a problem.

The 1979-82 experience bears some similarities with the fixed exchange rate of the late 1950s in terms of "inflationary disappointment." From 1955 to 1958, Chile undertook the "Misión Klein-Sacks," an economic program designed by an American consulting firm, which had previously worked in Peru. The firm proposed a broad reform program that showed partial success (Ffrench-Davies, 1973). But after inflation declined from levels of 70-80 percent in 1954-55 to 17 percent in 1957, it jumped again to around 30 percent in 1958. A notable inflationary success was achieved in 1960-61, when the exchange rate was fixed, with inflation declining to 5.5 percent and then 9.5 percent, figures not previously seen in Chile in the post-war era, and not seen again until the 1990s.[6]

In the context of an appreciating exchange rate and a pro-openness objective, one may wonder how it was possible to sustain the fixed exchange rate regime of the late 1970s and early 1980s. First of all, the main "compensation" was an economic boom. This boom, associated with the stabilization program, is a typical consequence of exchange rate-based disinflations (see Calvo and Végh, 1998). The average rate of growth from 1977 to 1981 was 7.9 percent. Growth was particularly important in the early 1980s, since this marked the beginning of a recovery from the 1974

---

[6] A difference in the two cases is that the crisis of 1962 was clearly caused by a fiscal imbalance, with a fiscal deficit of about 5 percent of GDP, while the crisis in 1982 was with a fiscal surplus, but with a financial crisis closely resembling the Asian crisis of the late 1990s.

recession. This compares strikingly with a -3.2 percent average decline in output in the previous five years.[7] Low tariffs and an appreciating exchange rate also allowed for cheap imports of consumer goods as well as industrial sector inputs. This overall economic scenario, with strong growth in output and even stronger growth in consumption, generated ample support for the stabilization strategy.[8]

There were additional reasons that explained ongoing support for the fixed exchange rate. Edwards and Lederman (1998) stress the fact that the opening of the capital account and the liberalization of financial markets allowed the major *grupos* (conglomerates) to obtain financing abroad under very favorable conditions, at a time when interest rates for domestic lending were very high. Therefore, while experiencing difficulties in their tradable activities, corporate conglomerates enjoyed large spreads in interest rates domestically and were able to obtain financing and make profits in their nontradable businesses. The appointment of entrepreneurs to the cabinet also continued, involving them in policymaking and making them partners in major decisions.

By late 1981, as the crisis approached, support started declining. For example, Jorge Alessandri—president of Chile from 1958 to 1964 and one of the main figures among entrepreneurs—criticized the economic situation on the eve of the devaluation of 1982 (*El Mercurio*, April 17, 1982). Although he did not ask directly for a devaluation, he suggested that tariffs could be increased. The official line of course was to argue that a devaluation would bring only chaos and inflation, and therefore did not represent a valid option.

Crisis and Compensation Revisited: Subsidies to Debtors during the 1982 Crisis

After the devaluation of 1982, the government needed to rebuild support in order to undertake an adjustment and prevent social unrest from threatening the military regime. Indeed, 1983 was perhaps the year when the military government faced its greatest threat. One solution was to return to a degree of populism and appoint more pragmatic ministers, in contrast to

---

[7] Similarly, in the early 1960s, an expansion of output gave support to the fixed exchange rate regime, since output grew 4.4 percent in the period 1959-62, compared to 1.8 percent in the previous four years. However, the currency crisis of 1962 did not result in a major recession, since strong output growth continued in subsequent years.

[8] In 1980, there was a plebiscite to approve a new constitution, and the results, despite questions about the legitimacy of the election, showed that the government enjoyed broad popular support. Certainly the economic situation was a key factor in that support.

the "Chicago boys." These ministers raised tariffs and introduced several measures to alleviate the difficulties faced by particular groups. But they either did not have the strength to change the underlying basis of the economic model, or perhaps did not have the intention to do so.

In the aftermath of the crisis, several measures were announced to compensate for losses and the costs arising from the regime's broken commitment to the exchange rate.[9] Although the crisis was widespread and deep, without benefiting any sector in particular, some early announcements may also have helped to defend the model among entrepreneurs. Only a few days after the devaluation, the finance minister announced the privatization of such public enterprises as an electric company (Chilectra), the telephone company, and a maritime shipping firm.

Although many instruments were used to obtain support for the adjustment and accompanying privatizations, particular schemes were implemented to relieve debtors and manage the crisis in order to avoid a major collapse. After allowing the exchange rate to float in August 1982, the authorities decided to implement a preferential exchange rate system for all debts in foreign exchange (or denominated in foreign exchange) contracted before August 1982 with financial institutions operating in Chile or directly with foreign banks. This preferential exchange rate could be used to pay interest and principal, and no prepayment was allowed. The rate was set as the exchange rate that would have prevailed on August 6, 1982 if the policy of mini-devaluations had been maintained, expressed in *Unidades de Fomento* (UF),[10] with a 5 percent surcharge.

Since the mini-devaluation rule was applied with a discount for foreign inflation, the preferential and the official exchange rate should have converged. However, the existence of the preferential exchange rate, pegged in UFs, imposed constraints on the central bank's ability to conduct exchange rate policy, since each time the bank would decide to devalue, it would widen the gap between the two exchange rates. This was what in fact happened. The gap between the official exchange rate and the preferential exchange rate, which began at about 26 percent and declined systematically to 17 percent in mid-1984, increased sharply after the devaluations of September 1984 and February and June 1985, reaching a maxi-

---

[9] To many, one of the main difficulties faced in the early 1980s was the inability of wages to adjust, since labor legislation imposed 100 percent indexation as a floor for new negotiations. Therefore, one of the first measures implemented after the devaluation was the elimination of the automatic wage adjustments.

[10] *Unidad de Fomento* is a unit of account indexed daily to the variation of the Consumer Price Index in the previous month.

mum of 63 percent in July 1985.

During its period of application, the preferential exchange rate underwent a variety of changes. These included a shift in the form of payment from cash to bonds, and a revision of eligibility requirements. The most important change was the exclusion of exporters in early 1984, since they were benefiting from exchange rate depreciations. In June 1985 the gradual elimination of the preferential exchange rate was announced, to be achieved by linearly reducing the gap between rates, which was scheduled to disappear in December 1986.

Although the preferential exchange rate was the main subsidy to debtors, in September 1984 a "de-dollarization" of debts was allowed. Debtors could refinance their debts at an exchange rate of 93 Escudos/US$, instead of the post-devaluation rate of 115 Escudos/US$. There was a maximum allowed for these operations and special treatment for debts under the preferential exchange rate system.

The amount of these subsidies was sizable. Between 1982 and 1985, the subsidy for the preferential exchange rate was $2.9 billion, and the de-dollarization of 1984 cost $232 million. The average costs of these two mechanisms was 3.5 percent of GDP per year between 1982 and 1986.

The June 1979-June 1982 appreciation initially enjoyed popular support, as cheap imports, and financing for them, became available. While the subsequent devaluation came at a time when it was broadly seen as inevitable, it represented a major change in the rules of the game. These arrangements, for those who were highly indebted in foreign exchange, are an example of how the losers, in particular the larger ones, are compensated in order to obtain support for government policies.

Back to Competitiveness

After the 1982 crisis and a period of instability, exchange rate policy returned to a crawling peg system. During the second half of the 1980s, the economy made a strong recovery from the 1982-83 recession. This period was characterized by strong export growth and a greatly depreciated real exchange rate (Figure 5.1), which, according to the official measure that includes all main trading partners, reached a historic high by 1990. This set the stage for the economic program of the Aylwin administration, the first elected presidency after the military regime. Regarding exchange rate policy, the program was very clear: the exchange rate must be kept stable to stimulate efficient exports and import substitution.

The commitment to a depreciated exchange rate was strong, although unsuccessful, as the real exchange rate appreciated. As shown below, this was the result of an undervalued currency in 1990. The lack of capital flows in the 1980s allowed an artificially depreciated real exchange rate, but as capital inflows resumed with force in the early 1990s and the economy kept growing, the real exchange rate appreciated. There was a trend of appreciation between 4 percent and 5 percent during the 1990s, and the authorities were unable to stop it.

Even the Frei administration, which began in 1994, was strong in its desire to avoid appreciation. In his first important speech, at a meeting called "Entrepreneurs of the World," the finance minister announced that the government would seek a stable real exchange rate. Real appreciation nonetheless continued. Flexibilization of the exchange rate band, based on a center crawling with PPP, was subsequently introduced in order to permit the exchange rate to appreciate.

Two main instruments were used to avoid, or at least slow, real appreciation. First, there was a massive accumulation of reserves. Second, capital controls were introduced in 1991 and revised definitively in 1992 to slow down inflows. Also introduced was an unremunerated reserve requirement of 30 percent for one year for capital inflows, with some exceptions and loopholes. As time went on and more loopholes were discovered, the mechanism was perfected, mainly through the increase of its scope. By 1998, the reserve requirement covered most inflows, with the exception of foreign direct investment and the issue of new stocks sold as American Depository Receipts (ADRs) abroad. In June 1998, the reserve requirement was reduced to 10 percent.

Regarding compensation, two aspects need to be mentioned. First, the average annual growth rate of the economy over the past 10 years was about 8 percent. Therefore the claims for compensation are rather weak. Even the agricultural sector, which has perhaps faced the greatest difficulties, has had problems in asking for compensation, since its productivity and production have grown strongly. Therefore, as in the late 1970s and early 1980s, with appreciation during the fixed exchange rate period, vigorous growth has reduced the strength of complaints. Moreover, the official position has usually been that appreciation is not a serious problem, since the economy, including the tradable goods sector, has been growing at a healthy rate.

From the point of view of large conglomerates and the leadership of entrepreneurial organizations, there are also some similarities with the appreciation of the early 1980s. In spite of capital controls, large firms with access to international financial markets have been able to obtain long-term financing at international rates from the unremunerated reserve requirement, with a small fee that declined as the length of borrowing increased. This, in addition to an appreciating exchange rate, has made the cost of financing very low.

The Choice of Exchange Rate Regimes

In general, exchange rate policies are designed in conjunction with other policies. In particular, as is evident from the Chilean experience, the degree of openness, foreign exchange controls, and controls on capital flows are closely linked to exchange rate policies. The first set of variables accounts for policies related directly to the exchange rate regime. They are the following:

- Black market premium (BMP): indicates the tightness of foreign exchange and capital controls. It has also been used as an indicator of overall distortions of economic policy.
- Tariffs: the average level of tariffs.
- Quantitative restrictions indices: in addition to tariffs, several quantitative restrictions have been used to regulate trade flows in Chile. There is one index for imports and another for exports, though the latter was used only for the 1960-62 period. The indices are updated from Ffrench-Davis (1973) and de la Cuadra and Hachette (1990), and take values between 0 and 20, where 20 indicates the absence of quantitative controls.
- Trade liberalization index: updated from de la Cuadra and Hachette (1990), which summarizes all the previous indicators to measure the degree of trade openness and distortions on foreign exchange markets.

The second set of variables can be interpreted as variables related to economic fundamentals. Figures 5.2 to 5.7 show the evolution of the main variables, which are the following:

- Terms of trade, based on central bank and World Bank data.
- Fiscal variables: overall fiscal surplus and the ratio of government consumption to GDP.
- Current account deficit as a percentage of GDP.
- Inflation: CPI inflation.
- Unemployment rate: the unemployment rate of Greater Santiago is used, instead of national figures, because this is the only series for which data since 1960 are available.
- GDP growth and GDP per worker.
- Reserves as a percentage of M1 and M2, in order to have a measure of external vulnerability.

Figure 5.2. Black Market Premium
(Ratio of black market and official rate)

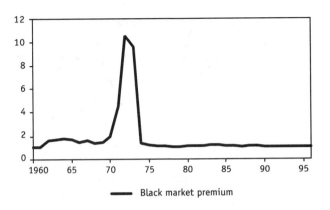

Black market premium

Figure 5.3. Trade Regimes: Liberalization Index and Tariffs

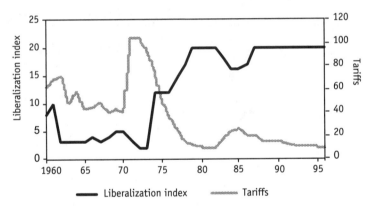

Liberalization index ⸻ Tariffs

- Net foreign assets: this is net foreign assets of 1960 plus accumulated current account deficit, taken from Broner, Loayza and López (1997).
- External environment: measures of international inflation (U.S. CPI), copper prices, and percentage of countries with a fixed exchange rate regime (from Goldfajn and Valdés, 1998) were used as external indicators. In particular, the latter variable was used to indicate world trends in macroeconomic management.

Some of the previous variables could also be given a political economy interpretation. For example, inflation may be related to eco-

Figure 5.4. Current Account and Terms of Trade

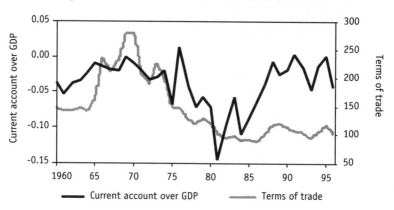

Figure 5.5. Annual Inflation Rate
(Log scale)

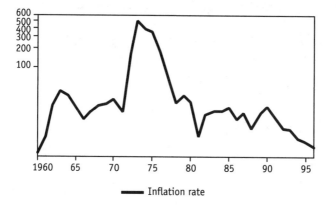

nomic fundamentals because it could reflect weakness in fiscal policy, or it could be interpreted as a political economy variable related to the weight the economy places on inflation vis-à-vis unemployment. Fiscal policy variables such as unemployment and net foreign assets (external indebtedness) could also be related to political economy factors. Finally, characteristics of the economic structure and some institutional factors could be related to political economy factors. Several variables were constructed, with the following used in the empirical investigation:

- Structure of the economy: data on composition of output and employment by main sectors of economic activity were

Figure 5.6. Unemployment Rate
(In percent)

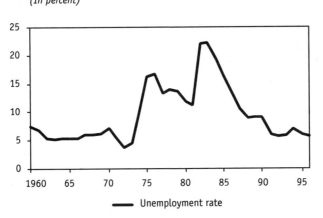

Unemployment rate

constructed. Both variables present a similar evolution over time, hence the share of manufacturing output and the share of exports in GDP were used to measure the relative importance of the import substitution and the export sector, respectively.[11] The reason for this classification is that in Chile, exports have been traditionally associated with mining and agriculture, while manufacturing has traditionally been an import substitution sector. All of these data were based on national accounts. In addition, line 22d of the IMF's *International Financial Statistics* (bank claims on private property as a share of GDP) was used to measure financial development, particularly the development of the banking system. This variable corresponds to the claims of the banking system (excluding the central bank) on the non-banking private sector as a percentage of GDP.

- While data on the importance of labor unions are scarce and unreliable, a series on unionization (percent of the labor force belonging to unions) was constructed based on Ministry of Labor data. However, because of inconsistencies in the series, the data

---

[11] It is possible that during major recessions the increase in the share of a particular sector may be the result of a decline in GDP rather than a trend increase in the production of that sector. For this reason, alternative use was made of shares of sectors constructed with respect to a Hodrick Prescott-filtered measure of the GDP. However, the results did not change significantly.

Figure 5.7. GDP Growth Rate
(In percent)

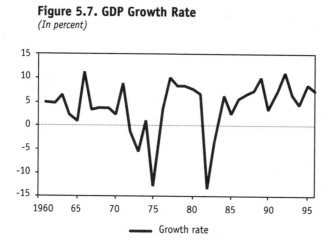

Figure 5.8. Real Exchange Rate Misalignment, 1960-96
(In percent)

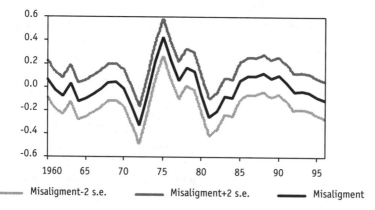

for 1974-79 were assumed to be constant and equal to the value of 1980, which was 13 percent, while in 1973 it was 24 percent. So it was assumed that from 1974 to 1980 unionization was constant at 13 percent, a substantial drop considering that unionization had been increasing since 1960. Some scattered data on the number of strikes and unions were obtained, but not with enough observations or reliability to use them in the empirical section.

Table 5.2. Exchange Rate Regimes: Tariffs

	Fixed	Crisis	Crawling peg	Band	All the sample
0 – 20%	3	1	7	5	16
20 – 70%	2	2	12	0	16
70 – 110%	1	3	1	0	5
Average tariffs	39.2	52.8	31.3	10.5	32.1
Standard deviation	31.3	34.6	16.5	0.9	23

Exchange and Trade Policies

Tables 5.2 through 5.4 are contingency tables for the four categories of exchange rate regimes and other indicators of economic policy. Each entry represents the number of years (37 in total) where a given regime coincides with a given range for the other variables. At the bottom of each table is the average for each variable across regimes and its standard deviation (s.d.).

Table 5.2 shows the relationship with the average level of tariffs, where the level of tariffs is divided into three ranges: from 0 to 20 percent, from 20 to 70 percent, and from 70 to 110 percent. As can be seen, crises occurred when there were high tariffs. Whether these high tariffs were a response to the crisis or part of overall foreign trade policy is not clear. Indeed, the three observations for very high tariffs coincide with the years 1971-73, when the economy was increasingly closed to foreign trade and macroeconomic management was out of control. However, it is natural to think that during currency crises, increasing

Table 5.3. Exchange Rate Regimes: Index of Trade Liberalization

	Fixed	Crisis	Crawling peg	Band	All the sample
1 - 8%	2	5	6	0	13
8 - 16%	1	0	6	0	7
16 - 20%	3	1	8	5	17
Average ITL	13.5	5.5	13	20	12.8
Standard deviation	7.5	7.1	6.6	0	7.3

Table 5.4. Exchange Rate Regimes: Black Market Premium (BMP)

	Fixed	Crisis	Crawling peg	Band	All the sample
0-5%	3	0	4	5	12
5-10%	2	1	4	0	7
10-50%	0	0	9	0	9
50% and up	1	5	3	0	9
Average BMP	13.3	386.7	27.1	0.6	79.6
Standard deviation	23.4	419.3	27.1	0.5	209.1

tariffs is a typical response to depreciation of the currency. This happened in Chile in the 1980s after the debt crisis. Crawling peg systems are oriented toward maintaining some competitiveness, and they have been used in periods of tariffs in the low and middle range. During the 1990s, tariffs were low and the exchange rate regime used a wide band.

Similar patterns are observed in the trade liberalization index (Table 5.3). Recall that the higher the value of the index, the more open is the economy. Regarding crises, it is observed that, in addition to the early 1970s, there is a reaction toward reducing the degree of openness; of the six cases, five coincided with an index between 1 and 8. The two periods of a fixed exchange rate regime occurred with both relatively open (early 1980s) and relatively closed (early 1960s) economies, and in both experiences there was a tendency toward liberalization.

Finally, Table 5.4 compares the exchange rate regime with the black market premium. Unification of the foreign exchange rate market characterized the two periods with a fixed exchange rate and, as the table shows, these were also periods with a low black market premium. The single exception occurred on the eve of the crisis of the early 1960s, when the premium started increasing before the abandonment of the regime and foreign exchange controls were used to defend the currency. As expected, crises have a high black market premium, in most cases above 50 percent. Crawling peg periods, however, have low, moderate and high exchange rate premiums. Finally, the experience of the 1990s is characterized by a small black market premium.

Overall, the results, though with few data, show several interesting relationships. There is a tendency toward a more closed economy and a high black market premium in times of crisis, while attempts to increase liberalization coincide with periods of fixed exchange rates. Crawling pegs have been used during periods of middle range and low tariffs, and the wide band has been used in a period of significant openness. Overall, one could initially conclude that more flexible exchange rate regimes have prevailed when the economy is more open, and the political economy interpretation would suggest that this is done in order to maintain competitiveness. A more complete analysis is presented below on the relationship between the exchange rate regime and other economic and political economy variables.

Measuring Real Exchange Rate Misalignment

A key variable needed to analyze the choice of the exchange rate regime is the degree of misalignment of the exchange rate. To construct a measure of misalignment, an equilibrium real exchange rate (q^*) must be defined and compared with the actual real exchange rate (q). More precisely, the misalignment, M, is defined as q-q^*, where the real exchange rate is measured as the unit of domestic goods per unit of foreign goods (ep^*/p). Therefore, a negative value for M implies an overvalued currency (the real exchange rate is "too low" or appreciated), while a positive value represents an undervalued exchange rate.

The first step in estimating the equilibrium real exchange rate was to estimate a structural equation for the real exchange rate (log). The predicted value was then smoothed using a Hodrick-Prescott Filter, and that value was considered to be the equilibrium real exchange rate. This assumes that a smooth real exchange rate allows persistent real exchange rate misalignments, which have characterized the Chilean economy from 1960 to 1996. The regressions were performed for those years, which represented the entire sample. In order to obtain reasonable estimates, a dummy variable was introduced for the constant and the fiscal variable for the post-1974 period. During the 1960s and early 1970s, there were multiple exchange rates, a low degree of openness and pervasive capital controls, which make it difficult to believe that there was a stable relationship for the real exchange rate.[12]

---

[12] In a previous version, regressions for the period 1974-96 were estimated. They are used in the analysis of the next section. For the period 1960-74, the variable misalignment was not used. In this version the entire sample is used, though the results do not change significantly when a restricted sample is used.

The explanatory variables in the real exchange rate equations are:

1) GDP per worker, as a measure of productivity and to capture the Balassa-Samuelson effect by which higher levels of productivity (in the tradable goods sector compared to the nontradable goods sector and across countries) imply a more appreciated real exchange rate. One should rigorously compare domestic productivity with productivity in the rest of the world. This was found to work better for the entire sample from 1960 to 1996.

2) Government consumption over GDP, as a measure of pressure on the relative price of nontradables as long as the government spends a larger portion of GDP on nontradables. This variable may also capture the intertemporal effects of increases in government expenditure. This variable is measured based on *International Financial Statistics* data for government final consumption, which is on average about 12 percent in the estimation period. The fiscal surplus was also used to proxy for the effects of fiscal policy.

3) Net foreign assets (log). An economy's need to generate current account surpluses depends on its net assets position in relation to the rest of the world. If net assets are positive and large, the economy will have an appreciated real exchange rate, as it will need smaller surpluses to pay back debts, hence a negative sign is expected. This series is constructed as the accumulated current account surplus, starting with an estimate in 1960.

4) Terms of trade (log). Depending on the strength of income and substitution effects, the sign may be either positive or negative, but in general one would expect the sign to be negative, indicating that an improvement in the terms of trade causes an appreciation (De Gregorio and Wolf, 1994).

5) Finally, an indicator of openness was used to capture the fact that more open economies should have a more depreciated real exchange rate. As economies open more, they need more resources devoted to the tradable goods sector in order to maintain full employment, hence the real exchange rate must appreciate. However, this variable is also amenable to political economy factors. In an open economy, more sensitivity toward the tradable goods sector will tend to favor a weak currency. In addition, import substitution sectors, which are most affected by the reduction of tariffs, can be implicitly compensated with a weak currency.

The results from the estimations of equilibrium real exchange rates are presented in Table 5.5, which uses the multilateral real exchange rate published by the central bank. In general, the results are in line with the theoretical predictions and other estimations for the Chil-

Table 5.5. Real Exchange Rate

	(1)	(2)	(3)
Chilean labor productivity	-1.004	-1.496	
	(-3.68)	(-7.49)	
U.S. labor productivity	1.415	2.052	
	(3.97)	(7.81)	
Relative labor productivity			-1.009
			(-3.58)
Net foreign assets (log)	-0.154	-0.168	-0.187
	(-4.84)	(-5.00)	(-7.09)
Fiscal surplus	0.009	0.013	0.011
	(1.44)	(1.98)	(1.79)
Openness			1.197
			(2.91)
Sample	1960-1996	1960-1996	1960-1996
R^2	0.99	0.98	0.98
Adjusted R^2	0.98	0.98	0.98
Durbin Watson	1.84	1.89	1.54
Observations	37	37	37

Note: t-statistics in parenthesis. Equations (1), (2), (3) include a dummy for the 1974-96 period for fiscal surplus and the constant.

ean economy, although neither the terms of trade nor government expenditures were statistically significant. As noted above, the fiscal surplus was significant only in the post-1974 period. The rest of the coefficients have the expected sign. An increase in labor productivity in Chile (measured in logarithmic form) produces a real appreciation, while an increase in foreign productivity produces a real depreciation; both results are consistent with the Balassa-Samuelson effect. Moreover, when the difference in labor productivity is entered in regression (3), the coefficient is about -1. An increase in relative productivity of 1 percent produces an appreciation on the order of 1 percent. An increase in net foreign liabilities, on the other hand, induces a depreciation. A 10 percent increase in foreign liabilities leads to a depreciation of 1.5 percent. The only significant fiscal variable was the post-1974 budget surplus, which indicates that an increase in the surplus by 1 percent of GDP leads to a 1 percent real depreciation. Finally, openness, measured by the index of liberalization, also plays a significant role in the real exchange rate, as a greater degree of openness is associated with a more depreciated real exchange rate. As explained above, the trade liberalization of the 1970s was accompanied by a deliberate effort to maintain a depreciated real exchange rate. Of course, there are theoretical reasons that explain why this attempt was successful, since a reduction in tariffs is associated with a depreciated real exchange rate. As argued above, it was also consistent with the need to compensate import substitution industries for the loss of competitiveness stemming from reduced protection.

Misalignment is measured by using regression (3), although the results are not very different when computed with other regressions. The stabilization of the mid-1970s resulted in a very depreciated real exchange rate, which started appreciating significantly with the *tablita*. Substantial depreciation followed the debt crisis, though appreciation began again in the early 1990s, but with a more flexible exchange rate regime. The Chilean experience is one where misalignments tend to be very persistent (see also Broner, Loayza and López, 1997).

A First Look at the Data

With the basic data for the analysis, it is first necessary to examine the behavior of the variables across the different exchange rate regimes. This is done in Tables 5.6.A and B. Inflation has been lower in the band period, which corresponds to the 1990s. It is interesting to note that the periods with a crawling peg are characterized by higher inflation and lower growth than the periods with a fixed exchange rate. Both periods with a fixed exchange rate, though, ended in a crisis, which is an indication of the boom-bust cycle of exchange rate-based stabilization (Calvo and Végh, 1998), as noted previously of their role as a compensation mechanism. The periods are also characterized by wide current account deficits. The terms of trade were not exceptionally low during crises, so deficits are not purely a result of an unfavorable external environment.

The data show that the relationship between the exchange rate regime and the misalignment is consistent with the discussion in the previous section. The real exchange rate is relatively undervalued during periods of a crawling peg. Therefore, crawling pegs have a bias toward competitiveness, while fixed exchange rate regimes have a bias toward controlling inflation. Crises are associated with misalignments, since they present the highest overvaluation.

Fiscal figures show that, during the fixed and band exchange rate regimes, fiscal accounts were in surplus or a slight deficit, hence the collapse of the fixed regimes cannot be attributed to a fiscal problem, except for the crisis of 1962. Moreover, during the period with a wide band, the 1990s, the fiscal position has been the strongest and the level of government expenditure the lowest.

Table 5.6.A. Variables Statistics by Exchange Rate Regime

Regime		Inflation (%)	GDP growth (% of GDP)	Current account (% of GDP)	Terms of trade index	Copper price (cUS$/pound)	One month US$ libor	BMP[1]
Fixed	Mean	20.4	6.6	-6.7	129.8	59.4	8.9	113.3
	S.d.	13.9	1.5	4.1	17.2	33.3	6.0	23.4
Crisis	Mean	133.0	-0.4	-3.8	167.3	53.2	7.0	486.7
	S.d.	191.4	8.2	2.8	49.6	18.1	3.5	419.3
Crawling peg	Mean	66.7	4.0	-3.3	152.8	75.8	7.5	127.1
	S.d.	105.7	5.3	3.3	63.3	24.0	1.8	27.1
Band	Mean	9.7	7.4	-2.3	104.6	106.4	4.5	100.6
	S.d.	2.6	2.5	2.0	8.9	16.7	1.2	0.5
All the sample	Mean	62.2	4.1	-3.8	145.0	73.6	7.2	179.6
	S.d.	112.0	5.6	3.4	53.7	28.1	3.2	209.1

Regime		Reserves (% of GDP)	Long and medium foreign debt	Real exchange rate	Misalignment sample 1960-96[2]	Fiscal surplus (% of GDP)	Government expenditure (% of GDP)	Government consumption (% of GDP)
Fixed	Mean	6.6	26.9	30.9	-3.7%	-0.1	24.2	12.0
	S.d.	6.6	10.4	16.2	13.5%	5.3	5.1	1.6
Crisis	Mean	2.3	30.8	23.4	-14.3%	-7.8	28.8	13.2
	S.d.	4.2	13.0	10.5	12.2%	4.4	9.7	2.9
Crawling peg	Mean	6.5	51.6	49.6	7.0%	-1.0	26.1	12.6
	S.d.	6.0	26.2	24.5	12.5%	2.6	5.8	1.9
Band	Mean	22.4	31.6	68.3	-6.3%	2.1	20.2	9.3
	S.d.	2.0	3.6	4.0	3.4%	0.3	0.7	0.3
All the sample	Mean	8.0	41.5	44.8	0.0%	-1.5	25.6	12.1
	S.d.	8.0	22.9	23.9	14.1%	4.4	6.4	2.2

[1] BMP: observed dollar exchange rate over official rate.
[2] Estimation based on equation (3), Table 5.5.

Sectoral composition of output, exports and employment do not show clear patterns across exchange rate regimes, and they are relatively stable. Only in the latest period is there some increase in the share of exports of manufactures, although production of manufactures declines slightly compared to other periods. These figures show the major change that has taken place within industry, which has become export-intensive, whereas in the 1960s and 1970s industry was essentially producing import substitutes. Similar changes have taken place in agriculture, forestry and fishing. In all of these sectors, the share of exports increased during the 1990s, although the share of labor (and output) has declined significantly during the same period, reflecting the shift toward export-oriented, capital-intensive activities and away from traditional production for domestic markets. The level of the real exchange rate and the exchange rate regime are important in explaining these changes.

Clearly, in the 1990s (the period of the exchange rate band), financial development was the highest of any time in the period studied, measured by the relative size of M2 or credit from the banking system.

Table 5.6.B. Variables Statistics by Exchange Rate Regime

Regime		M1/GDP (% of GDP)	M2/GDP (% of GDP)	Claims on private sector (% of GDP)	Mining (% of GDP)	Manufactures, industry (% of GDP)	Construction transport, telecomm. (% of GDP)	Trade and services (% of GDP)
Fixed	Mean	9.1	12.3	31.5	10.0	20.7	11.6	48.4
	S.d.	0.5	6.3	16.7	0.5	1.2	1.0	3.2
Crisis	Mean	14.4	10.6	22.1	9.6	22.7	12.0	47.3
	S.d.	6.4	9.6	29.7	1.1	3.1	1.6	3.1
Crawling peg	Mean	8.7	18.3	34.6	10.0	20.7	11.6	47.4
	S.d.	0.8	13.2	26.7	0.6	2.3	1.1	2.1
Band	Mean	8.8	29.6	49.9	8.9	18.5	14.4	46.6
	S.d.	0.2	1.4	3.5	0.2	0.4	0.6	0.1
All the sample	Mean	9.7	17.7	34.2	9.8	20.7	12.0	47.4
	S.d.	3.3	12.1	24.6	0.7	2.4	1.4	2.3

Regime		Mining exports (% of total exports)	Agriculture exports (% of total exports)	Industry exports (% of total exports)	Total exports (% of GDP)	Share of labor in agric., forestry, fishing (%)	Unemployment (%)	Unionization (%)
Fixed	Mean	71.1	6.7	21.7	13.2	23.3	9.3	11.7
	S.d.	16.4	1.6	14.6	3.6	6.9	3.3	1.3
Crisis	Mean	80.4	4.7	14.3	10.8	21.5	7.7	17.8
	S.d.	11.8	2.9	8.4	2.8	5.5	7.1	7.3
Crawling peg	Mean	66.8	8.1	24.7	19.8	20.3	11.1	13.5
	S.d.	14.9	5.1	10.2	5.9	3.3	5.1	3.0
Band	Mean	46.3	11.3	42.4	22.2	16.5	6.0	13.5
	S.d.	2.2	1.3	1.7	1.5	1.2	0.5	1.1
All the sample	Mean	66.9	7.8	24.9	17.6	20.5	9.6	13.9
	S.d.	16.4	4.3	12.5	6.2	4.5	5.1	4.0

During crises, financial development declines substantially and M1/GDP increases.

Finally, unemployment appears to be somewhat greater during crawling peg regimes, but this is a consequence of the recovery from the (currency) crisis of 1982-83 that resulted in high unemployment for the next several years. Unionization has also tended to increase during crises, due to a large extent to the fact that the first to become unemployed are workers not affiliated with unions.

The Choice of Exchange Rate Regimes: Multinomial Analysis

Methodology

Given that the possible choices are $j = 1, 2, 3$ and 4, for the exchange rate regime, the following multinomial logit model can be estimated:[13]

$$Pr(Y_i = j) = \frac{e^{\beta_j \times X_i}}{\sum_{k=1}^{4} e^{\beta_{k'} \times X_i}} \quad (1)$$

However, if β_j is replaced by $\beta_j + z$ in the previous expression, the term $\exp(z \cdot X_i)$ cancels out and hence the probability is exactly the same. To solve this indeterminacy one needs to normalize one of the β's to zero. The crawling peg (j=3) is therefore chosen as the normalization, as it is the regime in most of the observations. Although the coefficients depend on the normalization, the marginal effects are independent of it. Therefore, equation (1) becomes:

$$Pr(Y_i = j) = \frac{e^{\beta_j \times X_i}}{1 + \sum_{k=1, k \neq 3}^{4} e^{\beta_{k'} \times X_i}}$$

for $j = 1, 2, 4$, and:

$$Pr(Y_i = 3) = \frac{1}{1 + \sum_{k=1, k=!3}^{4} e^{\beta_{k'} \times X_i}}$$

The parameters of these equations are not easy to interpret, especially since the effects of a given variable on the probability of a given regime are rather complicated. Therefore, in order to assess the impact of a given variable, it is possible to calculate the marginal effects of a change in a given variable on the probability of a given regime. The expression for the "marginal" effect of the vector X on the probability of a given regime (the gradient) is:

$$\frac{\partial Pr(Y_i = j)}{\partial X} = P_j [\beta_j - \sum_k P_k \beta_k]$$

---

[13] See Greene (1993, chapter 21).

where P_i is the probability of a given regime. Those probabilities are evaluated at the mean of the independent variables. In the presentation of the results, changes around the mean are normalized by 10 percent to have an indicator closer to elasticities.

It is important to make two clarifications before going into the results. First, the sample is relatively small, with only 37 data points and not enough variability, since 20 observations correspond to a crawling peg, five to a wide band, five to a fixed exchange rate, and six to crises. Obtaining strong results for experiences that have just five or six observations will be difficult. For this reason, the choice of the crawling peg is compared with the rest. And second, the definition of a crisis is also disputable since it is not properly a choice: it is the only alternative. Hence, the regression results may not only be measuring the choice of regime, but also the likelihood of currency crisis.

Results from Univariate Multinomial Logit

As a first pass on the data, Tables 5.7 and 5.8 present univariate regressions for the main variables. Each entry corresponds to the effect on the probability of choosing a given regime when the independent variable increases 10 percent around its mean. The mean of each variable in the sample is in the last row of each table. Table 5.7 examines the contemporaneous correlation, and Table 5.8 uses lagged independent variables to avoid potential problems of simultaneity.

The results for inflation are weak and small in magnitude, but they show that a fixed exchange rate regime is more likely to be chosen when past inflation is low. There is also a negative contemporaneous correlation between a fixed exchange rate regime and inflation. In contrast, when inflation is high the choice of a crawling peg is more likely. The results indicate, for example, that a previous increase in inflation by 6.4 percentage points increases the probability of choosing a crawling peg by 1.3 percent and reduces the probability of a fixed exchange rate by 1.2 percent. This result confirms statistically the discussion of previous sections, since low inflation may create the temptation to accelerate progress using the exchange rate as an anchor. In contrast, crawling pegs, by targeting the real exchange rate, may have the cost of allowing higher inflation in order to restore competitiveness.

The results for the terms of trade are puzzling because they are contrary to what should be expected at first. According to the results, fixed exchange rates are less likely when terms of trade improve. Since fixed exchange rates cause a real appreciation and external sustainability is their Achilles heel, one would expect that the choice of fixing may be most likely when terms of trade are relatively good. One possible reason for these

Table 5.7. Effect on Regimes: Probabilities of a 10 Percent Change (around mean) in Independent Variable Univariate Regression and Contemporaneous Independent Variable

	Inflation	Terms of trade	BMP	Unemployment	Exports on GDP	Manufactures on GDP	GDP growth	Credit to private sector	Misal[1]	Unionization
Fixed	-0.86%	-1.84%	-2.34%	-0.03%	-6.15%	-0.71%	8.84%	-0.31%	-9.3%	-5.26%
Crisis	0.54%	1.90%	11.39%	-1.55%	-2.22%	10.14%	-0.90%	-1.31%	-11.9%	4.26%
Crawling peg	0.32%	2.78%	-9.05%	3.80%	5.27%	-2.48%	-0.92%	0.18%	32.3%	0.85%
Band	0.00%	-2.84%	0.00%	-2.22%	3.10%	-6.95%	0.93%	1.43%	-10.9%	0.14%
Mean of variable (whole sample)	62.22	144.95	1.80	9.56	0.18	0.21	4.15	0.30	0	0.13912

Note: The measure of misalignment employed in Table 5.7 and 5.8 was estimated with equation (3) in Table 5.5, and the estimated effect corresponds to a ten-point change in the mean of misalignment.

Table 5.8. Effect on Regimes: Probabilities of a 10 Percent Change (around mean) in Independent Variable

Univariate regression and lagged independent variable

	Inflation	Terms of trade	BMP	Unemployment	Exports on GDP	Manufactures on GDP	GDP growth	Credit to private sector	Misal	Unionization
Fixed	-1.22%	-1.52%	0.00%	0.89%	-4.38%	-1.62%	0.98%	-0.47%	-11.2%	0.04%
Crisis	-0.08%	2.54%	0.79%	-3.20%	-0.61%	11.11%	0.04%	-1.63%	-12.7%	-4.19%
Crawling peg	1.30%	1.98%	-0.79%	48.76%	1.86%	-0.38%	-2.02%	0.68%	35.0%	4.20%
Band	0.00%	-3.00%	0.00%	-2.56%	3.13%	-9.10%	1.00%	1.43%	-11.8%	-0.06%
Mean of variable (relevant sample)	63.76	146.15	1.82	9.67	0.17	0.21	4.06	0.29	0	0.13912

Note: The measure of misalignment employed in Table 5.7 and 5.8 was estimated with equation (3) in Table 5.5, and the estimated effect corresponds to a 10-point change in the mean of misalignment.

results may be that what matters is not the level of the terms of trade, but rather their movements. However, the residuals from an AR(1) process for the terms of trade were also used, and the results did not change. There is nonetheless another explanation, also based on the results of the previous section on the determinants of the real exchange rate. A deterioration in the terms of trade leads to an exchange rate depreciation, and to offset its inflationary effects an inflation-adverse policymaker may choose to fix the exchange rate rather than accommodate with further inflation. This could be the dominant effect in the sample. The results also indicate that crisis occurs along with significant terms of trade shocks, an expected result.

The black market premium shows a strong contemporary correlation with exchange rate regimes, but not when lagged variables are used in the regressions. This confirms the idea discussed above that fixed exchange rate regimes coincide with liberalization of the capital account and of foreign exchange transactions. When unemployment is high and growth in the previous year is low, a crawling peg regime is likely to result. In contrast, high growth accompanies fixed exchange rate regimes, consistent with the initial boom of exchange rate-based stabilizations.

The results for misalignment are basically the same for contemporaneous and lagged variables, and similar to the results of Table 5.6. Undervaluation is likely to happen with crawling peg regimes, while the others have a tendency toward overvaluation. This reinforces the idea that the main objective of the crawling peg is linked to competitiveness.

With regard to the composition of economic activity, the share of manufactures increases in crises. This result, however, may be more of reverse causality, as in episodes of currency crisis the most affected sectors are nontradables. A large export sector makes a crawling peg or a more flexible regime such as the band more likely, while making fixed regimes less likely. This is consistent with the preliminary finding that openness is linked to an exchange rate regime that allows a weak currency to build support for the economic strategy. However, there could be a reverse causality problem, since a large exportable sector is the result of a real depreciation.

The effects of financial intermediation on the choice of regime are weak and the signs are the same as those of the share of exports. This result, although weak, is also puzzling, since one would expect the opposite rather than the same signs for the size of intermediation and the share of exports, since they would indicate the relative strength of very different interest groups. However, as corporate conglomerates grow in importance, and have ties with nontradable sectors (perhaps including the financial sector), the dividing line between interest groups in terms of productive sectors is blurred.

Unionization has a relevant coefficient only in the case of a fixed exchange rate and in crises. The results show that in periods of a fixed exchange rate, there is less unionization, as happened in the early 1960s and early 1980s. In turn, during crises, unionization increases, but this is mainly influenced by the experience in the early 1970s. Regarding lagged variables, high levels of unionization are less likely to be followed by a crisis and more likely to be followed by a crawling peg.

Multinomial Logit Results

Multiple regressions with different coefficients across regimes are bounded by the number of regressors, since some regimes have at most five observations. For this reason, only combinations of two variables were used in the case of multiple regressors. The more variables were introduced, the more the results changed for the sign and significance of the different variables.

Tables 5.9, 5.10 and 5.11 show several regressions using pairs of variables. Coefficients of a crawling peg are normalized to zero. The first panel in each table shows the results, the second the forecasting ability of the regression, and the third the impact of a change in a variable on the probability of a given regime.

In Table 5.9, lagged values of a black market premium and inflation, the results are in line with those of the univariate correlations, with the exception of the negative sign for the variable inflation in periods of crisis. The forecasting ability of this regression is relatively good, since it predicts correctly in 28 out of the 36 years in the sample, tending to overpredict periods of a crawling peg and underpredict periods of crisis. Table 5.10 replaces the lagged black market premium with the current ratio of exports to GDP, and the results are similar, confirming that the share of exports increases with a crawling peg and a band and declines in years of crisis and fixed exchange rates.

Finally, Table 5.11 shows regressions with misalignment and share of exports. It is important to consider these two variables together, since the competitiveness bias of some regimes is not necessarily to look for an undervaluation, but to boost exports. This can explain why the relative importance of the coefficients changes. Indeed, the results show that undervaluations are associated with a crawling peg, something observed also in univariate regressions, and overvaluations with periods of a fixed exchange rate. For crises and bands, the coefficient is negative, but smaller. On the other hand, a crawling peg is associated with a large export share, while the contrary occurs for a fixed exchange rate. Therefore, the results show that crawling peg regimes are essentially oriented toward competitiveness and export promotion, while fixed exchange rate regimes are related to misalignments and low inflation.

Table 5.9.A. Multinomial Logit Model: Lagged Inflation and Lagged Black Market Premium

	Fixed	Crisis	Band
Constant	39.7	-5.42	63.8
	(2.178)	(-1.800)	(1.598)
BMP (lagged)	-38.0	4.20	-59.9
	(-2.157)	(1.507)	(-1.520)
Inflation (lagged)	-0.01	-0.08	-0.12
	(-0.273)	(-1.545)	(-1.396)
Log-Likelihood	-20.3		
Restricted (Slopes=0) Log-L.	-42.2		
Chi-Squared (3)	43.8		

Note: t-statistics in parentheses. No results reported for crawling peg since it is used as normalization vector.

Table 5.9.B. Frequencies of Actual and Predicted Outcomes: Predicted Outcome Has Maximum Probability

	PREDICTED				
ACTUAL	Fixed	Crisis	Crawling Peg	Band	TOTAL
Fixed	2	0	1	2	5
Crisis	0	3	3	0	6
Crawling peg	1	0	19	0	20
Band	1	0	0	4	5
Total	4	3	23	6	36

Table 5.9.C. Effect on Regimes: Probabilities of a 10 Percent Change (around mean) in Independent Variable

	BMP Lagged (%)	Inflation (%)
Fixed	0.00	0.00
Crisis	4.84	-3.06
Crawling peg	-4.84	3.06
Band	0.00	0.00
Mean of variable (relevant sample)	1.82	63.76

Binomial Logit

A final set of results is presented in Table 5.12. Since there are few observations for a fixed exchange rate, band and crisis, while there are 20 observations for a crawling peg, the choice between a crawling peg and band or fixed exchange rate is analyzed. Management of the exchange rate in a currency crisis is not considered, since it is not really a choice. In addition, and as discussed before, crawling pegs have in general been associated with some form of capital or exchange controls, while fixed exchange rate periods in the 1990s, with a wide band, have been much more liberal. Therefore, one could also interpret the results as related to the choice of capital controls.

There are 31 observations, 20 of which are years of a crawling peg, and the remaining 11 band or fixed exchange rate. The results confirm most of the findings presented above. A crawling peg is most likely to accompany high inflation and a high share of exports. It is also the most probable regime when terms of trade are high. A significant portion of the crawling peg experiences occurred in the 1960s, during the Bretton Woods era, and therefore they are most likely to occur when the trend around the world is a fixed exchange rate. The black market premium is also higher with a crawling peg than with other regimes, indicating the presence of capital controls. Finally, crawling pegs have, more often than other regimes, coincided with low growth and high unemployment.

Conclusions

Despite relatively few observations over a 37-year period, which makes it difficult to obtain strong results, there is some evidence for the factors underlying the choice of exchange rate regime in Chile from 1960 to 1997. Of course, the results must be interpreted with caution. First, causality is not clear. For example, crawling pegs are likely when growth is low, but this is in part because crawling pegs have been used after currency crises to restore competitiveness. Second, the empirical results are basic descriptions of the relationships among the data. It is not possible to derive straightforward policy implications from those results, since they are not based on a model that connects all of the variables.

For example, the fact that fixed exchange rates are associated with a boom in economic activity does not imply that this is a policy to get out of a recession. The results indicate that low inflation and unification of ex-

Table 5.10.A. Multinomial Logit Model: Share of Exports on GDP and Lagged Inflation

	Fixed	Crisis	Band
Constant	4.3	8.39	1.32
	(1.775)	(2.289)	(0.481)
Exports on GDP	-26.7	-72.5	11.9
	(-1.992)	(-2.252)	(0.839)
Inflation (lagged)	-0.04	0.006	-0.30
	(-0.920)	(0.699)	(-2.096)
Log-Likelihood	-24.8		
Restricted (Slopes=0) Log-L.	-42.2		
Chi-Squared (3)	34.7		

Note: t-statistics in parentheses. No results are reported for the crawling peg, since it is used as normalization vector.

Table 5.10.B. Frequencies of Actual and Predicted Outcomes: Predicted Outcome has Maximum Probability

ACTUAL	PREDICTED				TOTAL
	Fixed	Crisis	Crawling Peg	Band	
Fixed	2	1	2	0	5
Crisis	0	5	0	1	6
Crawling peg	1	1	17	1	20
Band	0	0	2	3	5
Total	3	7	21	5	36

Table 5.10.C. Effect on Regimes: Probabilities of a 10 Percent Change (around mean) in Independent Variable

	Exports on GDP	Lagged Inflation
Fixed	-1.74%	1.05%
Crisis	-2.00%	0.079%
Crawling peg	3.73%	0.97%
Band	0.00%	0.00%
Mean of variable (relevant sample)	0.18	63.76

CHILEAN EXCHANGE RATE POLICY   193

Table 5.11.A. Multinomial Logit Model: Real Exchange Rate Misalignment and Share of Exports on GDP

	Fixed	Crisis	Band
Constant	2.81	4.35	-15.2
	(1.289)	(1.258)	(-1.600)
RER misalignment	-6.03	-14.8	-35.6
	(-0.95)	(-1.85)	(-1.92)
Exports on GDP	-24.8	-43.9	60.1
	(-1.70)	(-1.65)	(1.53)
Log-Likelihood	-25.8		
Restricted (Slopes=0) Log-L.	-44.1		
Chi-Squared (3)	36.5		

Note: t-statistics in parentheses. No results are reported for the crawling peg, since it is used as normalization vector.

Table 5.11.B. Frequencies of Actual and Predicted Outcomes: Predicted Outcome has Maximum Probability

ACTUAL	PREDICTED				Total
	Fixed	Crisis	Crawling Peg	Band	
Fixed	1	2	3	0	6
Crisis	2	3	0	1	6
Crawling peg	1	1	18	0	20
Band	0	0	2	3	5
Total	4	6	23	4	37

Table 5.11.C. Effect on Regimes: Probabilities of a 10 Percent Change (around mean[1]) in Independent Variable

	Misalignment[2]	Exports on GDP
Fixed	-7.34%	-5.92%
Crisis	-3.61%	-1.89%
Crawling peg	13.60%	6.91%
Band	-2.65%	0.89%
Mean of variable (relevant sample)	0	0.18

[1] Equation (3) in Table 5.5.
[2] The estimated effect corresponds to a 10-point change in the mean of misalignment.

change rate markets (measured through a reduction of the black market premium) are associated with fixed exchange rate periods. Moreover, low inflation precedes the choice of the fixed exchange rate regime, which suggests that such a policy is undertaken mainly by inflation-adverse policymakers seeking to use the exchange rate as an anchor. Indeed, there is a temptation to use the exchange rate in order to consolidate low inflation, as was observed in the late 1950s and late 1980s.

Overvaluation is another characteristic of periods of fixed exchange rate regimes. There is, of course, the issue of compensation and political sustainability for large changes in relative prices. Periods of fixed exchange rates are also associated with a strong expansion of economic activity, hence this reduces the pressures stemming from interest groups that in relative terms lose, since most sectors benefit from the boom. The two experiences with a fixed exchange rate regime in Chile, however, have ended in a currency crisis, followed by a period of instability and the introduction of capital controls and foreign exchange restrictions.

Political economy factors, as measured by the relative size of different groups, do not appear to play a direct important role in the determination of the regime. However, this does not imply that political economy plays no role in the choice of exchange rate regime. It is likely that important entrepreneurial groups are linked to several sectors, especially in both tradables and nontradables.

There are, however, indications that political economy factors have been behind some decisions regarding the exchange rate regime, as well as other related policies, such as the trade regime and subsidies given after currency crises. Inflation and unemployment, for instance, play a role in the choice of regime. During most of the period from 1960-97, exchange rate policy followed a crawling peg, with some form of capital controls. This situation changed beginning in 1990, when a widening exchange rate band was implemented. A crawling peg has been used, at the cost of inflation, to attain a depreciated real exchange rate. Periods of a crawling peg usually follow periods of high growth and low inflation.

Exchange rate policy is certainly determined jointly with other sets of policies that respond to the objectives of the authorities and interaction between interest groups. This is the case for the sharp undervaluation of the second half of the 1970s, which was clearly intended to compensate for the deep trade liberalization that exposed most of the economy to external competition, something previously unknown, given Chile's tradition of import substitution. More direct compensation mechanisms have been used regarding exchange rate policy, as in the case of subsidies to debtors in foreign exchange after the devaluation of 1982.

Table 5.12. Binomial Logit Estimations: The Choice of a Crawling Peg

	(1)	(2)	(3)	(4)	(5)
Growth			-0.281		-0.281
Test t			(-1.792)		(-1.773)
10% Effect			-2.5%		-2.5%
Terms of trade (log)	20.407				
Test t	(1.969)				
10% Effect	2.2%				
Inflation	0.116	0.143			
Test t	(1.554)	(1.864)			
10% Effect	0.1%	0.1%			
Reserves/ M2	-15.417				
Test t	(-2.130)				
10% Effect	-0.1%				
Industry share on GDP[1]	-69.540				
Test t	(-2.018)				
10% Effect	-0.1%				
Export share on GDP[2]		55.06		65.945	
Test t		(2.064)		(1.837)	
10% Effect		1.1%		11.2%	
Bmp		12.67		20.187	
Test t		(2.289)		(2.169)	
10% Effect		1.6%		22%	
Unionization					20.768
Test t					(0.868)
10% Effect					4.8%
Govt. expectation before elections			2.435		
Test t			0.4		
10% Effect			0.4%		
Unemployment				0.729	
Test t				(1.978)	
10% Effect				6.6%	
RER misalignment[3]			17.374		13.681
Test t			(2.233)		(2.272)
10 points Effect			31%		24%
Log-Likelihood	-8.9	-9.1	-13.4	-7.5	-13.7
Restricted (Coef=0)	-20.2	-20.2	-20.2	-19.1	-20.2
Chi-Squared	22.6	22.1	13.6	23.1	12.9
Predicted/Observations	29/31	28/31	25/31	26/31	26/31

[1] Sampled for the 1974-96 period.
[2] In equation (1), this variable was sampled for the 1974-96 period.
[3] In equation (3), this variable was sampled for the 1974-96 period.

References

Arellano, J., and R. Cortázar. 1982. Del Milagro a la Crisis: Algunas Reflexiones sobre el Momento Económico. *Colección Estudios CIEPLAN* 8: 43-60.

Baxter, M. 1994. Real Exchange Rates and Interest Rates Differentials: Have We Missed the Business-Cycle Relationship? *Journal of Monetary Economics* 33(1): 5-37.

Broner, F., N. Loayza, and H. López. 1997. Misalignment and Fundamentals: Equilibrium Exchange Rates for Seven Latin American Countries. World Bank, Washington, DC. Mimeo.

Calvo, G., and C. Végh. 1998. Inflation and BOP Crises in Developing Countries. In J. Taylor and M. Woodford (eds.), *Handbook of Macroeconomics*. Amsterdam: North-Holland.

Campero, G. 1991. Entrepreneurs under the Military Regime. In P. Drake and I. Jerks (eds.), *The Struggle for Democracy in Chile. 1982-1990.* Lincoln: University of Nebraska Press.

Céspedes, L., and J. De Gregorio. 1999. Tipo de Cambio Real de Equilibrio, Desalineamiento y Devaluciones:Teoría y Evidencia para Chile. Universidad de Chile, Santiago. Mimeo.

Cowan, K., and J. De Gregorio. 1998. Exchange Rate Policies and Capital Account Management: Chile in the 1990s. In R. Glick (ed.), *Managing Capital Flows and Exchange Rates: Lessons from the Pacific Basin.* Cambridge, UK: Cambridge University Press.

De Gregorio, J. 1996. Determinantes del Tipo de Cambio Real. In F. Morandé and R. Vergara (eds.), *Análisis Empírico del Tipo de Cambio en Chile.* Washington, DC: Centro de Estudios Públicos, Instituto Latinoamericano de Doctrina y Estudios Sociales/Georgetown University.

_____. 1986. Principales Aspectos de la Política Cambiaria en Chile: 1974-85. Notas Técnicas No. 81. Corporación de Investigaciones Económicas para Latinoamérica, Santiago.

De Gregorio, J., and H. Wolf. 1994. *Terms of Trade, Productivity and the Real Exchange Rate.* NBER Working Paper No. 4807, National Bureau of Economic Research, Cambridge, MA.

De la Cuadra, S., and D. Hachette. 1990. *Apertura Comercial: Experiencia Chilena.* Santiago: Universidad de Chile.

Dornbusch, R., and S. Edwards. 1994. Exchange Rate Policy and Trade Strategy. In B. Bosworth, R. Dornbusch and R. Labán (eds.), *The Chilean Economy: Policy Lessons and Challenges.* Washington, DC: Brookings Institution.

Edwards, S., and A. Cox-Edwards. 1987. *Monetarism and Liberalization: The Chilean Experiment.* Chicago: University of Chicago Press.

Edwards, S., and D. Lederman. 1998. *The Political Economy of Unilateral Trade Liberalization: The Case of Chile.* NBER Working Paper No. 6510, National Bureau of Economic Research, Cambridge, MA.

Ffrench-Davis, R. 1979. Las Experiencias Cambiarias en Chile: 1965-1979. *Colección Estudios CIEPLAN* 4: 39-78.

_____. 1973. *Políticas Económicas en Chile: 1952-1970.* Santiago: Editorial Nueva Universidad.

Goldfajn, I., and R.O. Valdés. Are Currency Crises Predictable? *European Economic Review* 42(2-35): 873-85.

Greene, W. 1993. *Econometric Analysis.* Second edition. New York: Macmillan Publishing Co.

Hachette, D., and R. Luders. 1992. *La Privatización en Chile.* San Francisco, Chile: Centro Internacional para el Desarrollo Económico.

International Monetary Fund. Various years. *International Financial Statistics.* Washington, DC: IMF.

Meller, P. 1996. *Un Siglo de Economía Política Chilena (1890-1990).* Santiago: Editorial Andrés Bello.

Williamson, J. 1996. *The Crawling Band as an Exchange Rate Regime: Israel, Chile and Colombia.* Washington, DC: Institute for International Economics.

CHAPTER SIX

A Long-lasting Crawling Peg: Political Determinants of Exchange Rate Policy in Colombia

Juan C. Jaramillo, Roberto Steiner and Natalia Salazar[1]

As witnessed by the remarkable longevity of its managed crawl, Colombia has had few major regime changes in its exchange rate policies since 1967. Policy shifts have come through variations in the rate of crawl, varying degrees of administrative restrictions on capital flows and, on occasion, ad hoc measures to generate multiple exchange rates.

Given this incremental approach, economic policy in general, and exchange rate policy in particular, should not be seen exclusively as a function of their intended effects, but also as the result of interaction between interest groups, politicians and bureaucrats in a context of institutional constraints. The fact that different economies facing similar problems and with comparable resources have performed differently cannot be explained solely with analytical frameworks. Macroeconomic optimality is only one of the factors affecting the choice of exchange rate policy, so other policy determinants must be investigated (Haggard and Webb, 1994).

Political and Institutional Background

Three Decades of Power-Sharing

The party system has changed less in Colombia than in any other country in the Western Hemisphere, with the possible exception of Mexico. Ac-

[1] Juan C. Jaramillo is with the Western Hemisphere Department of the IMF. Natalia Salazar and Roberto Steiner are on the faculty of the School of Economics of the University of the Andes.

cording to Dix (1990, p. 100), "what does distinguish the Colombian case is the failure of the country's political institutions, and notably its party system, to manifest changes comparable in magnitude to the new levels of social mobilization." On average over 1945-86, the two traditional parties commanded over 97 percent of the vote for the House of Representatives. Only once (in 1970) did their combined total fall below 90 percent. Between 1931 and 1982, only 12 percent of municipalities switched party allegiance. Almost without exception, moreover, every time dissident factions appeared, they invariably went back to their original partisan allegiance.

The failure of a third party to emerge is surprising considering that, from the late 1950s until the early 1990s, the two traditional parties converged in terms of policy and ideology.[2] Furthermore, Colombia's poor distribution of income and wealth has made it an ideal place for the emergence of a class-based party. However, the workforce has not been heavily employed in sectors that are prone to produce militant, class-oriented activism. Instead, coffee, the country's main product, is grown on thousands of small, family-operated parcels. This has fostered conservative, individualist values rather than radical or collectivist ones (Dix, 1990). In addition, coffee has been entirely owned by Colombian nationals, as have many of the country's other key industries. This might explain the lack of nationalistic attitudes, which are a frequent breeding ground for populist movements.[3]

Dix (1980) maintains that since 1958, Colombia can be characterized as a "consociational democracy," unique in that its subcultures do not originate in religious, ethnic or class differences.[4] The exclusive nature and

---

[2] This changed with enactment of a new constitution in 1991. In fact, the latter part of the next section explores the possible link between the 1994 electoral results and the distinct positions regarding economic policy between the two traditional parties.

[3] Nelson et al. (1971) mention as an additional element the organizational weakness of labor federations and "the hierarchical difference between them and the entrepreneurial class." As will be seen later in this chapter, labor's inability to promote a political movement did not constrain it from achieving important sporadic leverage, including the wage hike that deemed the 1962 devaluation a failure.

[4] Lijphart (1977, p. 1) describes a consociational democracy as one where "centrifugal tendencies inherent in a plural society are counteracted by the cooperative attitudes and behavior of the leaders of the different segments of the population." By means of proportionality rules, grand coalitions and mutual vetoes, leaders of different subcultures are able to provide reasonable stability to an otherwise polarized society. Other analysts have referred to Colombia as a "modified democracy," using qualifications such as "controlled," "oligarchic" or "bipartisan elitist." Some have even called it a "formally authoritarian democracy" or a "constitutional dictatorship" (Hartlyn, 1993).

familial and communal roots of the country's two traditional parties mark them as the functional equivalent of subcultures.[5]

Historically, the two traditional parties have been composed of prominent individuals, bound together through clientelistic relationships, with weak organizations and almost no programmatic content.[6] They are nonetheless effectively multi-class, as elites have sought popular support in their partisan competition for the perquisites of power. Furthermore, the relative openness of the regime, in terms of elections, division of powers and freedom of the press, granted it reasonable legitimacy among all social groups.

The two traditional parties' hold on power was enhanced in the late 1950s through a political coalition (the National Front or *Frente Nacional*). After several years of party violence, the leaders of the two traditional parties reached an arrangement by which both would share power for 16 years. Several factors led to this agreement. First, the usual conflict between the parties was increasingly superseded by popular resentment toward them. Second, the military's repressive actions and political ambitions became more uncomfortable than a coalition with a partisan foe. Third, the Liberals came to accept Colombia's status as an officially Catholic country. Finally, both parties agreed that the military would not be persecuted and that the Minister of Defense would come from its ranks.

The National Front consensus was based on three main provisions. Perhaps the most prominent was that the presidency would alternate between parties for the duration of the coalition. Throughout the political system, seats in Congress, departmental assemblies and municipal councils, all cabinet and government offices, and Supreme Court positions would be divided evenly between the two major parties to the exclusion of all others. To avoid partisan stalemates, nonprocedural decisions in all elective bodies required a two-thirds majority.

Though it can be criticized for having impeded social change, the National Front must be credited with greatly reducing inter-party violence

---

[5] Nelson et al. (1971, p. 218) suggest that "the traditional style of Colombian politics invokes an emotional, moralistic, and tenacious attachment to hereditary loyalties."

[6] According to Supelano (1992), in Colombia there has always been resistance towards the dominant theories of the day. Policy has generally been eclectic, depending more on the need to maintain the balance of power than on theoretical principles. Dix (1978) argues that the lack of ideology is not exclusive to the two traditional parties. The same can be said of General Rojas' ANAPO, at least circa 1970, when it made an important run for the presidency. A survey of its leaders suggests that their motivations were not ideological in the sense of having an all-encompassing approach to government. The movement instead reflected conservative Christian values, as Rojas was the candidate more opposed to divorce and birth control.

and returning the military to the barracks.[7] The two parties stopped quarrel-ing for control of the state, while reaping the gains of impressive economic growth. Resulting policies fostered stable growth and moderate inflation without openly discriminating against any activity.[8] Government policies favored coffee sector interests, however, and, to a lesser extent, other inter-ests (Hartlyn, 1993).[9]

The National Front formally ended in 1974, but several of its provi-sions were extended for four years.[10] Informally, the coalition lasted much longer. Every president until 1990 came from within its ranks, and Congress continued to be dominated by the two traditional parties. A referendum in 1990 man-dated the convening of a popularly elected Constituent Assembly that drafted a new constitution. Its provisions were designed to facilitate the creation and consolidation of new political movements, empower citizens, and advance po-litical and fiscal decentralization. Though many analysts have been skeptical of the practical implications of these provisions, the power-sharing schemes of the National Front did, for all practical purposes, end in 1991.

Economic and Institutional Connotations of the Polity

The characterization of Colombia as a consociational democracy where two parties explicitly or implicitly share power largely explains the country's eco-nomic policies. According to Haggard (1994, p. 238), Latin American countries with histories of high inflation have been those where the "urban popular sector" and labor groups have been incorporated into populist parties, within the context of relatively polarized party systems. In turn, the political difficulties of implementing macroeconomic adjustment programs have been less severe where decision-making has been centralized and less subject to rent-seeking pressures.

Two features distinguish Colombia from the typical Latin Ameri-can country. The most influential business group produces an export (cof-

---

[7] Recent violence has occurred outside of any power dispute between the traditional parties, although many of its causes can be traced back to the exclusive nature of the National Front (see Leal, 1995).

[8] According to Reveiz and Pérez (1986), heads of business associations during the National Front began to occupy, in a rather large proportion, positions in the executive branch.

[9] In sharp contrast with this interpretation, Bates (1997) argues that coffee producers, because they are so electorally important, have been highly influential in those periods when party competition has been significant, but have been subjected to the government's redistributive purposes when there was no partisan competition in national elections (i.e., the National Front years).

[10] A 1968 constitutional amendment prolonged parity in cabinet and administrative positions for four years and established that after this extension the party other than that of the Presi-dent would receive "equitable" cabinet and administrative positions.

fee) not linked to import substitution, and export promotion has been the cornerstone of policy since 1967. Colombia seems to fit Haggard's assessment of Asia in the sense that in that region it has been important "to maintain realistic exchange rates and to shift toward the promotion of manufactured exports"(1994, p. 241).

According to Urrutia (1991), there has generally been no "economic populism" in Colombia, at least not in the sense of Dornbusch and Edwards (1991). Macroeconomic policy has generally been conducted with the purpose of providing the stability deemed necessary to promote growth, rather than for redistribution purposes. This has been made possible not by populism, but by clientelism, which has given politicians an important say in the distribution of the national budget, while at the same time allowing them to reap the benefits of stability produced by a seldom politicized macroeconomic decisionmaking process.

As Archer and Soberg Shugart (1997) and Soberg Shugart and Nielson (1997) show, Colombia's electoral rules—members of Congress are elected by proportional representation rules applied to each district on the basis of factional rather than party lists—provide incentives for politicians to pursue personal, service-related votes instead of party-oriented votes.[11] Voters are tied to individual legislators, and obtaining votes depends heavily on how well the elected official delivers government services. In addition, parties have almost no control over the composition of their delegations in Congress. Nelson et al. (1971) argued that National Front political practices were supplementing the inter-party political and ideological debate with the politics of pressure groups.

To be sure, in spite of the strong bipartisan coalition, politics does not take place in a vacuum. Different regions hold different interests, and those interests are better served by different powers within the state. As a first approximation, it is interesting to differentiate between the (mainly Andean) coffee-growing region and the rest of the country. The former is heavily dependent on a primary export, while the latter has a much more diversified economic base.

Table 6.1 shows the regional origin of the heads of three key institutions: the Ministry of Finance, the Central Bank and the National Planning Department. The first is involved with all economic matters, the second primarily with exchange rate and monetary policy, and the third with long-term planning and fiscal policy. The coffee-growing region, with less

---

[11] The 1991 Constitution maintained this rule for the lower house of Congress. To facilitate matters for political minorities, Senate seats are now assigned by proportional representation rules applied in a national electoral district.

Table 6.1. Regional Origin of Policymakers

Región	Finance Minister[1] No.	%	Central Bank Governor[2] No.	%	Head of Planning Department[3] No.	%	Population 1993 (%)	GDP 1992 (%)
Antioquia	11	20			3	13	13.1	14.5
Atlántico					2	9	4.9	4.1
Boyacá	4	7					3.5	2.8
Caldas	9	16	1	25			2.8	2.1
Cundinamarca	16	29	2	50	13	57	19.7	27.4
Magdalena	1	2					3.0	1.6
Nariño					1	4	3.9	1.5
N. Santander	1	2					3.1	1.8
Quindío	1	2	1	25			1.3	1.5
Risaralda	1	2			2	9	2.3	2.4
Santander	4	7					4.8	5.5
Tolima	1	2					3.4	3.0
Valle	2	4			2	9	10.0	11.6
Others/na	4	7					24.2	20.2
Coffee growing region	23	42	2	40	5	22	22.9	23.6

[1] 1930-98.
[2] 1969-98.
[3] 1958-98.
Source: Authors' calculations based on Meisel (1996) and Yanovich(1997).

than a quarter of the population and GDP, has provided 40 percent of the Ministers of Finance and Governors of the Central Bank but only 22 percent of the Directors of the National Planning Department.

As noted above, until 1990 both houses of Congress were apportioned by proportional representation. Table 6.2 shows that, as a result, the regional origin of senators and representatives was very similar to the regional distribution of the population. However, the 1994 senate elections were based on proportional representation at the national level. The last two columns of the table indicate that the Caribbean region became overrepresented in the Senate, at the expense of the coffee- growing and Pacific regions, among others.

Table 6.3 contains information regarding abstention during the 1990 elections. For the presidential election, abstention in the coffee-growing region was in line with the national average, and much lower than in the Caribbean region. In congressional elections, however, abstention was much lower in the Caribbean region than in the country as a whole. It can be argued that the Caribbean region is a very active political actor in congressional elections, whose outcome is crucial in the formulation and distribution of the budget, but much less important in presidential elections, whose

Table 6.2. Regional Composition of Congress

	1974	1986	1990	1994	Population Distribution (1993)
Number of senators	112	114	114	100	
Regional composition (%)					
Caribbean	22.3	21.9	21.9	25.0	21.2
Antioquia	21.4	21.1	21.1	17.0	19.5
Pacific	18.8	18.4	18.4	15.0	18.0
Central	28.6	28.1	28.1	34.0	30.6
Santander	8.9	8.8	8.8	9.0	8.0
Coffee growing	25.9	25.4	25.4	20.0	22.9
Others	0.0	1.8	1.8	0.0	2.8
Number of representatives	199	199	199	163	
Regional composition (%)					
Caribbean	20.1	20.1	20.1	21.5	21.2
Antioquia	21.6	21.6	21.6	18.4	19.5
Pacific	18.1	18.1	18.1	16.0	18.0
Central	29.1	29.1	29.1	26.4	30.6
Santander	8.5	8.5	8.5	7.4	8.0
Coffee growing	26.1	26.1	26.1	21.5	22.9
Other	2.5	2.5	2.5	10.4	2.8

Source: Authors' calculations, based on Yanovich (1997) and Departamento Administrativo Nacional de Estadística (DANE).

Table 6.3. Abstention in the 1990 Elections
(Percentage of potential voters)

Region	Presidential election	Congressional election	
		Senate	House
Total[1]	56.4	43.9	44.8
Coffee growing[2]	56.7	45.2	45.0
Caribbean[3]	66.5	36.1	37.2

[1] Excludes Amazonas, Arauca, Casanare, Consulados, Guanía, Guaviare, Putumayo, San Andrés, Vaupés and Vichada.
[2] Includes "Viejo Caldas" (Caldas, Quindío, Risaralda), Tolima y Antioquia.
[3] Includes Atlántico, Bolívar, Cesar, Córdoba, Guajira, Magdalena y Sucre.
Source: Authors' calculations based on Registraduría Nacional del Estado Civil.

outcome is critical in the design of overall macroeconomic policy (including, until 1991, all matters related to exchange rate and monetary policy).

There is no doubt that all regions and economic interests are concerned with all types of economic policies, from the more technical issues of monetary and exchange rate management to the more political aspects of fiscal policy. However, Tables 6.1 through 6.3 give some support to the idea that certain regions and economic interests are more concerned with certain types of policies and are therefore more interested in politically capturing the institutions that develop these policies.

In other words, even though Colombia has displayed remarkable stability in economic policy, institutions are nonetheless run by people who reflect the interests of certain regions and economic activities. In particular, the all-important coffee-growing region seems to be much more active in presidential politics, which is key to determining exchange rate policy, than in congressional politics, which is crucial in the elaboration and distribution of the budget.

Relative Economic Stability

Historically, Colombia has been characterized as one of the least volatile economies in Latin America. Table 6.4 provides information on inflation and growth for the region's largest economies. In all subperiods, Colombia had the third lowest inflation rate. In terms of volatility, except during 1960-69, Colombia also had the most stable rate of inflation. However, the table indicates that Colombia's relative stability occurred in the context of macroeconomic results that were not particularly impressive.

Economic volatility depends on several factors, particularly external conditions (i.e., terms of trade and capital flows) and economic policy. Table 6.5 shows that with regard to the terms of trade, Colombia's external environment has not been particularly stable. Yet over 1970-92, Colombia had by far the most stable economic policy of 22 countries in the region, according to an analysis by the Inter-American Development Bank (1995).

It is important to acknowledge that, for present purposes, stability has a very precise dimension. With regard to prices, Colombia is a remarkable case of stability of the rate of inflation.[12] That relative stability has been achieved in the context of moderate rather than low inflation is not independent of political economy issues—there is evidence

---

[12] Dornbusch and Fischer (1993) refer to Colombia as the "moderate-inflation country par excellence." Williamson (1996, p. 34) writes: "Colombia provided the best example of a country that seemed to have learned to live with inflation."

Table 6.4. Inflation and Growth in Latin America

Country	Variable	1960-69	1970-79	1980-89	1990-96
Argentina	Inflation (%)	22.9	132.9	565.7	361.3
	Ranking: level[1]	4	5	6	5
	c.v.	1	5	6	6
	Growth (%)	4.04	2.66	-0.75	4.85
	Ranking: level[1]	1	2	1	5
	c.v.	6	5	1	3
Brazil	Inflation (%)	45.9	30.5	319.6	1,329.6
	Ranking: level[1]	6	4	5	6
	c.v.	3	2	5	5
	Growth (%)	9.19	8.01	3.11	1.60
	Ranking: level[1]	6	6	4	1
	c.v.	5	3	3	6
Chile	Inflation (%)	25.1	174.6	21.4	14.7
	Ranking: level[1]	5	6	1	1
	c.v.	4	6	2	3
	Growth (%)	4.51	2.22	3.67	6.83
	Ranking: level[1]	2	1	6	6
	c.v.	4	6	5	1
Colombia	Inflation (%)	11.2	19.3	23.4	24.9
	Ranking: level[1]	3	3	3	3
	c.v.	5	1	1	1
	Growth (%)	4.92	5.77	3.40	4.14
	Ranking: level[1]	3	4	5	4
	c.v.	1	1	2	2
Mexico	Inflation (%)	2.7	14.7	69.1	21.6
	Ranking: level[1]	2	2	4	2
	c.v.	2	4	3	4
	Growth (%)	7.16	6.48	2.26	2.60
	Ranking: level[1]	5	5	3	2
	c.v.	2	2	4	5
Venezuela	Inflation (%)	1.2	6.6	23.0	52.2
	Ranking: level[1]	1	1	2	4
	c.v.	6	3	4	2
	Growth (%)	5.64	5.19	0.2	3.12
	Ranking: level[1]	4	3	2	3
	c.v.	3	4	6	4

Note: Annual percentage change in CPI and in GDP, respectively.
[1] An entry of 1 (6) indicates the lowest (highest) level of the variable and of the coefficient of variation (c.v., computed as the ratio between the standard deviation and the mean).
Source: Authors' calculations based on figures from the International Monetary Fund.

Table 6.5. Terms of Trade in Latin America

Country		1960-69	1970-79	1980-89	1990-96
Argentina	Coefficient of Variation	0.16	0.20	0.21	0.14
	Ranking[1]	6	3	3	6
Brazil	Coefficient of Variation	0.07	0.09	0.13	0.12
	Ranking	2	1	2	5
Chile	Coefficient of Variation	0.08	0.26	0.09	0.04
	Ranking	3	5	1	3
Colombia	Coefficient of Variation	0.11	0.22	0.31	0.03
	Ranking	4	4	6	2
Mexico	Coefficient of Variation	0.14	0.18	0.22	0.03
	Ranking	5	2	4	1
Venezuela	Coefficient of Variation	0.04	0.43	0.25	0.10
	Ranking	1	6	5	4

[1]An entry of 1 (6) indicates the lowest (highest) level of the variable or coefficient of variation.
Source: IMF, "Supplement on Trade Statistics", Supplement Series, 15, and World Bank, "World Development Indicators on CD-Rom," 1997.

that the inflation tax has helped finance the deficit, itself partially the result of the resolution of conflicts between the country's economic and political interests.[13]

Institutional History

Table 6.6 shows the phases of central banking in Colombia. The *Banco de la República* was established as a private and autonomous entity in 1923, and it remained so until 1963. Until 1931, Colombia adhered to the gold standard, maintaining a fixed (and stable) exchange rate until 1949. In 1951, the bank's objectives were expanded to include not only price stability but also "economic development." In the early 1960s, the bank was nationalized and in 1963 the monetary board was created. Composed solely of members of the government and an appointed governor, the board was given control of monetary, credit and exchange rate policies.[14]

---

[13] Suescún (1992) shows that Colombia's inflation and devaluation rates exhibit the time-series properties derived from an "optimal financing" model (Phelps, 1973). On the uses of the inflation tax, see Steiner et al. (1992) and Carrasquilla (1996).

[14] As is mentioned below, the board's actual role in the formulation of exchange rate policy was rather limited.

Table 6.6. Central Banking Phases in Colombia

Period	Nature of the board	Main objective
1923-1951	Private and independent from government	Price stability
1951-1963	Private and independent from government	Price stability and economic development
1963-1991	Official and dependent on government	Monetary, exchange and credit management
1991-	Official and independent from government	Price stability

Source: Meisel (1996).

The 1991 Constitution overhauled the central banking regime. The *Banco de la República* was organized as an autonomous state institution, independent from the government, with the sole objective of achieving price stability. Its Board of Directors is in charge of monetary, credit and exchange rate policies. The board is composed of seven members: the Governor of the Bank, the Minister of Finance and five full-time members appointed by the government for staggered fixed terms.

In 1967, Colombia adopted a crawling peg exchange rate system. Any analysis of stability in Colombia's key economic variables has to take into account the fact that since 1967, and at least until 1991, the country maintained the same exchange rate regime.[15] The stability of the exchange rate regime has coincided with remarkable institutional stability. Table 6.7 shows that since 1960, the central bank has had only six governors, with an average tenure of 6.5 years, well above the regional average suggested in Table 6.8, borrowed from Cukierman (1992). If the tenure of the central bank governor has been noteworthy, it still pales in comparison to that of the General Manager of the National Federation of Coffee Growers (Fedecafé–*Federación Nacional de Cafeteros*). Since 1937, Fedecafé has had only three general managers.

---

[15] It is revealing to note that in 1987, the central bank organized a well-attended international seminar to commemorate the 20th anniversary of the *Estatuto Cambiario*, the 1967 legislation that laid the foundation for the crawling peg system.

Table 6.7. Tenure of Central Bank Governors in Colombia

Starting Date	Name	Tenure (years)
15/Dec/1960	Eduardo Arias	8.8
22/Oct/1969	Germán Botero	8.8
24/Aug/1978	Rafael Gama	4.0
26/Aug/1982	Hugo Palacios	3.1
26/Sep/1985	Francisco Ortega	7.4
22/Feb/1993	Miguel Urrutia	
Average tenure		6.4

Source: Banco de la República.

Table 6.8. Turnover Rate of Central Bank Governors in Latin America

Country	Turnover rate[1]
Argentina	0.93
Honduras	0.13
Chile	0.45
Colombia	0.20
Mexico	0.15
Panama	0.24
Brazil	1.33
Uruguay	0.48
Venezuela	0.30
Averge rate	0.48

[1] Average changes per year.
Source: Cukierman (1992).

The Coffee Revenue Distribution Mechanism

During the first half of the 20th century, coffee producers and the government realized that it was in their mutual interest to stabilize the coffee revenue stream. To do so, two interrelated decisions were jointly adopted. On the external front, Colombia decided to vigorously support multilateral agreements seeking to regulate prices and quantities in the world coffee market through the International Coffee Agreement (ICA). On the domestic front, in the 1940s the government and the coffee sector embarked on a revenue stabilization scheme. Under this mechanism, the government taxed coffee exports at variable rates, which were broadly related to world prices and the exchange rate, transferring the resulting collections to a stabilization fund (the National Coffee Fund, or FNC), administered by Fedecafé.[16] In turn, Fedecafé used FNC resources to finance stock accumulation during periods of high world supplies and guarantee a minimum price to producers when world prices were low. Collections over and above those needed for these purposes were held by the FNC in assets of varying liquidity or used to finance social and infrastructure projects in Colombia's coffee regions. In periods of very high world prices, government and coffee growers agreed to pass on to the treasury part of the revenues.

The FNC largely succeeded in its stabilization role. In terms of exchange rate policy, the relation between prices paid to producers and external prices determined an implicit exchange rate applicable to coffee. Over 1950-88, this implicit rate was more stable than the general effective real exchange rate (Ocampo, 1989). Prices paid to coffee growers, rather than the exchange rate, became the politically sensitive variable affecting coffee-producing households.[17] Of course, the sustainability of a high price to producers is enhanced through a weak exchange rate.

This highlights the fact that the coffee sector could obtain a desired goal by adjustments in other variables as long as the exchange rate was not excessively out of line. When the latter did occur, jeopardizing the financial stability of the FNC, the coffee sector became quite vocal. Coffee sector representatives had ways of obtaining stable effective exchange rates without getting themselves involved in the sensitive issues surrounding exchange rate policy (Urrutia, 1981). Nelson et al. (1971, p. 251) probably put it best: "The coffee sector will be more inclined to use its political influence to change the domestic support price and the ex-

---

[16] This explanation is highly stylized. Taxes on coffee exports took various (frequently complicated) forms, ranging from less favorable exchange rates applicable to coffee exports to direct taxes accruing to the national treasury, charged on an ad valorem basis. Other taxes were levied on coffee production or exports, earmarked for use solely in the country's coffee-growing regions. Finally, there was the *retención cafetera* (retention), a charge applied to coffee exports. In principle, it was designed to finance coffee stocks as a result of the ICA. In practice, though, this charge had a wider practical scope, i.e., absorbing changes in external prices and in the exchange rate when domestic coffee prices were fixed.

[17] This fact notwithstanding, Cárdenas and Partow (1998) have recently provided some econometric evidence in the sense that the domestic price of coffee does not depend on electoral or partisan cycles.

Table 6.9. Partisan Orientation of Executive Directors of Fedesarrollo

Executive Director	Partisan orientation	Partisan orientation of the government in place
Rodrigo Botero	Liberal	Conservative
Roberto Junguito	Conservative	Liberal
Carlos Caballero	Liberal	Conservative
José Antonio Ocampo	Liberal	Conservative-Liberal
Guillermo Perry	Liberal	Liberal
Miguel Urrutia	Conservative	Liberal
Eduardo Lora	Independent	Liberal
Mauricio Cárdenas	Conservative	Liberal
Juan José Echavarría	Liberal	Conservative

Source: Fedesarrollo.

change rate differential–specific coffee sector policy–than to lobby for a higher exchange rate structure, a strategy that would put it in direct conflict with other special interest groups."

The Role of Technocrats

Some authors have emphasized the role of "technocrats" in Colombia's economic decisionmaking process. To be sure, though, that was not always the case. Rivera (1976) persuasively argues that in the early 1960s, Colombian technocrats were not considered as valuable as their counterparts elsewhere in Latin America. When their role in policymaking was enhanced during the Lleras administration (1966-70), they were vehemently opposed by some politicians.

Edwards (1995, p. 117) has also highlighted the role of technocrats in explaining Colombia's relative economic stability: "Fedesarrollo (a private research institution) has been the intellectual breeding ground of an amazingly large number of those in charge of economic policy. *It could be argued that Fedesarrollo's bipartisan and nonideological positions is a good reflection of Colombia's implicit pact according to which Liberals and Conservatives share power*" [emphasis added].

Fedesarrollo has been home to many Colombian policymakers. More interesting than its clout, however, is its nonpartisan orientation. Of its nine directors, five have been Liberals, three Conservatives, and one independent (Table 6.9). In all instances but one, the director has been

Table 6.10. Organized Labor

Year	Membership rate[1] (%)	Number of unions	Number of members
1939	2.80	571	76,274
1947	5.50	809	102,023
1965	15.80	892	165,595
1980	15.70	3,781	600,000-700,000
1984	9.32	2,172	873,442
1990	7.80	2,265	880,155

[1] Unionized labor as percent of total labor force.
Sources: Urrutia (1976), Londoño (1986) and Ministry of Labor and Social Security.

affiliated with a different party than that of the government in power. The same individuals sometimes act as government officials and at other times as independent analysts. It can be argued that the institution is a facilitator for achieving consensus, not because of its intellectual power, but rather because it credibly internalizes policy options that are politically viable.

For better or worse, Colombian economic technocrats, regardless of party affiliation, have frequently been inclined to reach broad consensus on economic policy. This was illustrated by a Colombian Bankers' Association symposium held in early 1978, during the peak of the coffee boom and in the midst of a huge accumulation of reserves. Wiesner (1978) reports that of the 17 young economists who expressed their views during the discussions, only one suggested doing away with exchange controls. The rest, in one way or another, endorsed the then-accepted economic policy paradigm: without exchange controls the economy would repeatedly enter into stop-go cycles that would curtail growth, hamper export-oriented industries and promote capital flight. The voices of these economists were not simply those of academia. Six of the speakers would eventually become finance ministers, three would hold ministries in other economic areas, and seven would become either advisors to the monetary board or members of it successor institution, the central bank board. Only in the 1990s did this trend toward consensus begin to dissipate.

Labor Unions

Colombia's labor movement does not appear to be particularly important. While in 1965 close to 16 percent of the labor force belonged to a labor organization, that number dropped to 9.3 percent in 1984 and to

Table 6.11. Labor Union Membership Rate by Economic Sector
(In percent)

	1984	1990
Agriculture	1.8	1.5
Mining	12.7	4.9
Manufacturing	8.1	8.2
Public utilities	53.2	42.0
Construction	3.9	3.0
Commerce	3.0	2.6
Transportation and communications	51.4	27.4
Financial intermediaries	12.8	14.3
Services	19.6	18.4
Total	9.3	7.8

Source: Ministry of Labor and Social Security.

only 7.8 percent in 1990. Affiliation numbers are small and have barely increased (Table 6.10).

In 1990, the utilities sector (generally publicly owned) had the highest percentage of workers belonging to a labor union, with an affiliation rate of 42 percent. Affiliation rates were as low as 1.5 percent in agriculture and 8.2 percent in manufacturing. The importance of the labor movement is thus restricted to the public sector, and even there percentages have been declining (Table 6.11).

Of course, the actual importance of organized labor might differ from what affiliation figures suggest. In that respect, Wiesner (1998) argues that the rent-seeking practices of organized labor in key public sector services such as health and, especially, education, have played a crucial role in slowing much-needed structural reforms.

Exchange Rate Policy Phases

The stability of the exchange rate regime after 1967 was systematically accompanied by the fine-tuning of other variables. When stability was not justified by economic conditions, its maintenance resulted from compromises that sheltered affected groups. Because of the polity and the institutions described above, these compromises could be credibly made.

Figure 6.1 presents an index of the real effective exchange rate

Figure 6.1. Colombia: Phases of the Real Exchange Rate
(1975 = 100)

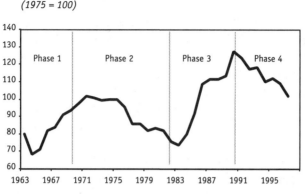

Source: Authors' calculations based on Banco de la Republica.

Figure 6.2. Annual Rate of Nominal Devaluation, 1951-97
(In percent)

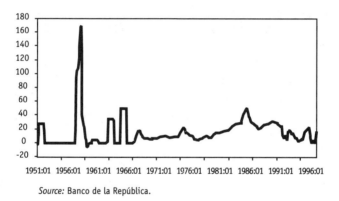

Source: Banco de la República.

for Colombia between 1962 and 1997. During two periods (1962-70 and 1983-90), the exchange rate tended to depreciate; in two other periods (1970-82 and 1990-onwards), the exchange rate tended to appreciate. Figure 6.2 shows the corresponding rate of nominal devaluation. Discussed below are these main phases and the private sector's reaction to exchange rate management.

Phase 1: The 1960s—Instability and Exchange Controls

Until 1967, the instability of export earnings and shortcomings in domestic policies periodically led to abandonment of the exchange rate peg and to attempts to establish a new parity. During the 1960s Colombia experienced three such episodes. The unsatisfactory results of the first two paved the way for less ad hoc approaches to exchange rate management.

The first episode took place in 1962. A significant real appreciation had accumulated over several years, and the necessity for a parity adjustment was evident. The form that the adjustment was to take led to heated discussions, both in Congress and within the administration. After several months, the adjustment was finally made, accompanied by loose monetary policy and an increase in wages advocated by the Minister of Labor. Inflation, however, eliminated most of the effects of the parity change.[18] Memories of the 1962 debacle would linger for a long time, complicating the handling of the subsequent crisis, as summarized by Díaz-Alejandro (1976, p. 195):

> ...[It] can easily be seen why memories of [the devaluation's] impact were a major obstacle facing those who later attempted to use a more flexible exchange rate as a policy tool. The argument that the event was a textbook example of how *not* to manage a devaluation made little impression. The feelings of most Colombians were accurately reflected by the then President Valencia, who throughout 1963 and 1964 would warn his economic advisors not to mention the abominable word in his presence...

The second episode took place in 1965-66. Despite persistent foreign exchange shortages, the central bank defended a fixed rate while simultaneously expanding domestic credit.[19] The resulting loss of reserves became unsustainable, leading to the adoption of increasingly stringent quantitative import restrictions (QRs). In October 1964, the central bank decided to let the market determine the rate, which depreciated by almost 90 percent,

---

[18] Congress compounded the damage by granting general wage increases over and above those decreed by the executive branch. Despite the upsurge in inflation, for the whole of 1963 real wage rates were 7 percent above those for 1962. See Díaz-Alejandro (1976) and Ocampo et al. (1987).

[19] Among the main components of this expansion in domestic credit were loans to Fedecafé (Gómez, 1978).

[20] Imports increased 39 percent in 1966, and the current account deficit reached 5.3 percent of GDP (García-García and Jayasuriya, 1997).

before fixing it again in the second half of 1965. QRs were again eliminated and tariffs raised to curb import demand. These measures were accompanied by a standby arrangement with the International Monetary Fund.

By mid-1966, when the Lleras administration took office, practically all imports had been freed from licensing requirements and an import boom had ensued. As coffee prices were declining, a large current account deficit again developed.[20] The standby reserve target was not met, and the IMF pressed for a new devaluation. The 1962 fiasco was still fresh in the minds of the new policymakers, who feared that without effective monetary and fiscal instruments a new parity change would simply initiate another stop-go cycle (López, 1987a). The end result was the breakdown of negotiations with the IMF. The president moved to muster domestic support for the administration's position, issued emergency legislation imposing comprehensive exchange controls, and re-established QRs. He then persuaded Congress to grant him authority to legislate on exchange rate matters.[21] On March 22, 1967, the Lleras administration issued Decree-Law 444, which came to be known as the "exchange statute." This measure became the basic legislation governing exchange rate policy over the next quarter century.

The new exchange rate regime imposed far-reaching controls. All foreign exchange receipts had to be surrendered to the central bank, which in turn sold them only to those showing an "acceptable need." In addition, multiple exchange rate schemes were replaced by a unified rate that would remain in place for the next nine years.[22] Several transparent mechanisms were adopted as a substitute for multiple exchange rates: the exchange rate differential for coffee was replaced by an ad valorem tax; direct subsidies were granted to nontraditional exports; and a subsidized credit scheme, funded with a surtax on imports, was directed at nontraditional exports. The nominal exchange rate consequently moved in tandem with declining inflation rates, achieved through fiscal discipline and monetary policy. As the real exchange rate depreciated, nontraditional exports surged, imports were reined in, and the balance of payments delivered surpluses. Growth rebounded to over 6 percent per year. Although protection for domestic production increased in comparison to the levels of 1966, import substitution policies were placed on a back burner.

---

[21] A detailed account of the evolution of the debates in Congress is presented in López (1987b).
[22] A temporary two-tiered system was initially established: one for most transactions, which was adjusted periodically, and another, limited to capital transactions, which was fixed at a more depreciated level. It was agreed that when the two rates coincided, the two-tiered system would disappear, which occurred 15 months later.

Phase 2: The 1970s—Coffee Boom and Capital Inflows

In July 1975, cold weather in Brazil destroyed coffee crops, causing world prices to increase fivefold and suddenly rendering the peso undervalued at the existing (managed) exchange rate. Viewing the shock as short term, the government opposed an exchange rate policy shift. Exchange and import restrictions were thus maintained, while other policies were designed to increase savings and sterilize the increase in reserves.[23] The political decision to pass on the boom proceeds to coffee growers through higher domestic coffee prices, a variable traditionally controlled by the government, rendered this policy course untenable.[24] Pressure on the domestic currency to appreciate was accentuated by the increasing supply of external capital made available through the recycling of surpluses from oil exporting countries.

To deal with the policy contradictions, multiple exchange rates were once again put in place, with a more competitive rate applied to nontraditional exports. At the same time, a vast array of administrative controls was implemented to deal with rising inflation and capital inflows.[25] Inflation passed the 30 percent threshold in early 1977 and rose to over 40 percent by mid-year. Tight monetary policy attracted even more capital inflows, which the central bank attempted to keep at bay through cumbersome administrative restrictions on foreign borrowing.[26] The direct intervention measures, complemented by a degree of fiscal restraint, finally arrested the momentum of inflation. The government had delivered a clear signal that it would not tolerate a dramatic increase in inflation. In all, between 1975 and early 1978, the coffee boom led to a real appreciation of the peso of over 20 percent.[27]

---

[23] Banco de la República, August 1976.

[24] This policy decision was summarized in a single phrase, made famous by then President López: "La bonanza es de los cafeteros" ("The boom is for the coffee-growers"). In time, policy would have to part from this dictum. See Ocampo and Revéiz (1980).

[25] For a steadfast defense of this policy mix, see Sarmiento (1978).

[26] QRs were maintained, under the pretext that low import price elasticities precluded the search for domestic price stability by increasing the availability of foreign goods (Sarmiento, 1978).

[27] Almost a decade later in 1986, world coffee prices again surged, propelled this time by drought in Brazil. This sudden change again moved the fundamentals in the direction of a more appreciated currency. On this occasion, however, and in contrast to the 1975-77 episode, a clearer agreement was reached between the government and the coffee growers to avoid drastic increases in domestic coffee prices. The coffee sector's resulting surplus was thus largely saved, and its financial counterpart was invested in medium-term government-backed securities. As a result, domestic spending was kept in check and the exchange rate did not significantly appreciate, as had happened in 1977-78.

By 1978, coffee prices had declined, but income from coffee exports remained high as Colombia's export volumes increased significantly (Caballero, 1987).[28] Currency appreciation continued to be reinforced by abundant financial resources in international markets and by Colombia's increasing involvement in illicit drug markets (García-García and Jayasuriya, 1997). Finally, the administration that took office in 1978 viewed the abundance of foreign exchange as a longer-term trend and moved towards a more liberal trade regime, a position consistent with the objective of increasing public investment, financed with external credit. Higher levels of public investment, however, eroded the country's fiscal position, which declined from virtual equilibrium in 1978 to a deficit of 6 percent of GDP in 1982. As QRs were reduced, imports reached record highs and the current account changed from a surplus of 1.4 percent of GDP in 1978 to a 7.4 percent deficit in 1982. In the meantime, GDP growth declined from almost 8.5 percent in 1978 to less than 1 percent in 1982.

Phase 3: The 1980s—The Debt Crisis

In August 1982, only weeks before the Mexican foreign debt moratorium, the Conservative Betancur administration (1982-86) took office in the midst of a significant economic slowdown. High on the new government's agenda was to jump-start the economy, without acknowledging that a fundamental change in the external economic environment had led to the virtual shutdown of international capital markets and that, under the new circumstances, the financing of the twin fiscal and external deficits was not viable.[29] Not surprisingly, the central bank began to rapidly lose reserves.

The real exchange rate had appreciated significantly between 1975 and the early 1980s (see Figure 6.1). By late 1982, there was no clear decision as to the preferred policy course. As explained by Montenegro (1997) and Palacios (1997), many analysts were recommending expansionary policies. For example, Fedesarrollo insisted on the need for fiscal stimulus, and the planning department advocated the

---

[28] High domestic prices provided the incentive to modernize coffee plantations, apply increasing amounts of labor for crop maintenance, and intensify the use of fertilizers. As a result, production went from about 8 million 60k bags in 1975 to about 13 million in 1980, and exports from about 7 to 11 million bags over the same period. See Junguito and Pizano (1991).

[29] This had been the case since 1978. In an article extraordinary for its candor, Hugo Palacios, then central bank governor, presented a lucid assessment of the policy miscalculations made at the time by the government's leading policymakers. See Palacios (1997).

mobilization of resources towards housing construction. Only a few scattered voices in the private sector, and fewer still within the public sector, insisted on the need to pursue a major parity adjustment before attempting to stimulate aggregate demand.

As external credit dried up and the economy came to a virtual standstill, pressure mounted to facilitate resources to ease the cash flow problems of many (particularly industrial) firms. The monetary board made available subsidized credit that would be largely used by the private sector to pay debts abroad and by many to take long positions in dollars. The policy amounted to a self-inflicted wound that accelerated the loss of reserves. The central bank, for its part, publicly expressed its preference for gradually correcting the overvaluation through an increase in the rate of crawl. It favored export subsidies and QRs as temporary mechanisms until competitiveness was restored.[30] Reflecting the economic slowdown, the fiscal accounts deteriorated despite a major tax hike. As external credit dwindled, the central bank moved to further restrict sales of foreign exchange for all but the most basic needs.

By early 1984, it had become evident that without the support of international financial institutions external credit sources would remain unavailable. The administration thus drastically changed its policy course, engineering a significant fiscal adjustment and reaching a monitoring agreement with the IMF. Export subsidies were sharply reduced, while the rate of crawl was accelerated. By the end of 1985, the real exchange rate had depreciated by over 30 percent, commercial credit flows were normalized, reserves began to increase, and restrictions on imports were gradually reduced to pre-crisis levels. These measures allowed Colombia to avoid a moratorium on external debt.

Phase 4: The 1990s—The Resurgence of Capital Inflows

After the 1985 adjustment, the real exchange rate remained rather stable until mid-1989, when the collapse of the ICA led policymakers to expect a sharp decline in coffee prices, suggesting the need for a more depreciated rate. In addition, the government sought to use a weaker currency as a means of reducing opposition to lifting the QRs. The rate of crawl was thus accelerated while the government committed itself to tightening fiscal policy and gradually liberalizing trade. The government's fiscal stance, however, proved less restrained than planned, and trade liberalization moved at a

---

[30] President Betancur, who had been Labor Minister during the 1962 devaluation-cum-wage inflation debacle, was rather reticent to consider an exchange rate adjustment.

slower pace than originally envisioned. Furthermore, after 1989 capital markets continued to brush aside the debt crisis. Resources became increasingly available and capital began to return, though the authorities were slow to acknowledge this changing external environment. At the same time, the value of coffee exports did not decline, as increased volume compensated for the decline in prices. Consequently, while market forces were moving in the direction of a real appreciation of the currency, the government and the central bank were seeking to depreciate. As in 1975, real appreciation came about through an acceleration of inflation.

Structural reforms also tended to appreciate the peso. First came the authorization of a free market for foreign exchange transactions below a certain limit. Although the official market continued to operate, the existence of a non-regulated segment effectively eliminated the reach of exchange controls. This relaxation was followed by a fiscal amnesty for capital resources held abroad by Colombian nationals.[31] Both changes promoted the repatriation of flight capital. Finally, trade liberalization, which should have depreciated the equilibrium exchange rate, temporarily produced the opposite effect, as the announcement of gradual reductions in tariffs prompted importers to postpone their purchases abroad.

Capital inflows continued to exert pressure on the exchange rate. By the end of 1991 it had become evident that the policy of sterilized intervention was futile, as it was not supported by fiscal adjustment.[32] In order to generate a nominal appreciation, the authorities, as in 1977, made use of exchange certificates. Intervention points established by the central bank in its transactions in the market for certificates created a de facto exchange rate band, and a band was explicitly adopted in early 1994.[33]

Private Sector Reactions to Exchange Rate Management

Throughout the period analyzed, economic sectors reacted differently over time to similar exchange rate policies. These reactions largely depended on the presence or absence of measures to compensate for the adverse effects of these policies. During the 1970s, for example, com-

---

[31] The ethical implications of this policy were questioned, but in general the approach was accepted. Nevertheless, the possibility that such a mechanism could serve as a means to launder drug-related resources was a far more serious matter.

[32] Although the overall public sector deficit did not increase, public expenditures increased significantly from 23.7 percent of GDP in 1990 to 26.9 percent in 1992 and 27.6 percent in 1994.

[33] The band had a width of 7.5 percentage points above and below a mid-point rate and was depreciated at a pre-announced rate.

pensatory measures were adopted that favored the industrial sector (via preferential access to external credit), nontraditional exports (via a preferential exchange rate), and the agricultural sector (via access to subsidized local credit). During the 1990s, however, these sectors received little relief or preferential treatment, and their reactions to similar policy changes differed sharply.

Manufacturing sector. During the coffee boom of the 1970s, the industrial association, ANDI, did not take a position on the exchange rate, which affected industrial firms in a variety of ways. Rather, it sought protection for domestic production through import tariffs and, above all, through quantitative import restrictions, while aggressively advocating the use of direct subsidies and drawback mechanisms for exporting firms. ANDI repeatedly warned against "indiscriminate" import liberalization and pushed for an industrial policy that would completely free imports of capital goods, while imposing tariffs and strict QRs on consumer goods.[34] ANDI's demands largely coincided with government policy, at least until 1979, and this was reflected in the industrial sector's support for official economic policy during the second half of the 1970s.

The manufacturing sector's preferences on economic policies, however, did not seem to keep pace with changing circumstances. By 1984, almost two years into the debt crisis, ANDI insisted on further fiscal stimulus and warned against the "perils of fiscal adjustment." The group advocated an expansion of public spending financed by the central bank, arguing that the decline in reserves created "room" for central bank credit.[35] The policy advocated by the industrial sector was exactly the same as it had advocated (and the government had adopted) during the reserve build-up of 1976-79.[36] In spite of a looming balance of payments crisis during the first two years of the Betancur administration, ANDI's proposals were largely implemented.

During the first stages of the import liberalization process initiated in 1989, the industrial sector again favored existing restrictions and repeatedly expressed its opposition to the idea that QRs could be replaced by a new tariff structure and a more depreciated exchange rate. Industry frowned upon permitting the exchange rate to replace direct protection for local production. This

---

[34] See ANDI's Magazine (issues 24-27 of 1975 and issues 28 and 32 of 1976).

[35] See Montenegro (1997) in reference to the position adopted by Fedesarrollo.

[36] One exception was the proposal to restructure external public debt and to grant government guarantees for private debt. None of these proposals prospered: public sector debt would be refinanced on a voluntary basis and private sector debt was handled through a mechanism by which the exchange rate risk was removed and replaced by a domestic interest rate risk. The mechanism was applicable only to those debts that banks voluntarily agreed to restructure, and it did not convey a public guarantee of the obligations.

downplaying of exchange rate policy ended when, after 1991, the industrial sector was no longer able to maintain import liberalization at bay. From then on, the sector became very vocal in arguing for a "competitive" exchange rate.[37]

Coffee growers. During the real appreciation of the peso in the second half of the 1970s, coffee producers supported exchange rate management and did not resist the creation of a dual exchange rate scheme designed to curtail part of their windfall. To some extent this reflected the fact that the sector's exports were the main cause of the peso's real appreciation. As explained previously, however, coffee growers, rather than arguing for a preferred exchange rate policy, concentrated their lobbying efforts on other variables that directly affected their income. This approach would change by the end of 1991, when the breakdown of the ICA made further adjustments to non-exchange rate variables impossible. At this time, Fedecafé decided to voice concern over the persistent appreciation. This concern was again manifested in 1993, as the financial situation of the FNC continued to deteriorate, and in 1996, for the first time in decades, Fedecafé adopted an explicit position regarding exchange rate policy. In the words of Fedecafé management, the appreciation was "the most serious threat ever faced by the coffee industry."[38] Fedecafé's policy proposal amounted to a return to the regime prevailing before 1991 and included a request for temporary subsidies.[39] More remarkable than the policy proposal as such was the fact that Fedecafé modified its traditional low-key attitude regarding exchange rate policy.

Non-coffee export sector. During the period of appreciation in the 1970s, exporters of nontraditional goods (associated through ANALDEX) were not vocal on exchange rate management. Their silence was due largely to government policies that attempted to shield nontraditional exports from the appreciating peso. Like ANDI, non-coffee exporters showed a clear preference for subsidies, which they obtained either through the budget or by way of preferential exchange rates.[40] ANALDEX did become critical of exchange rate management during the 1990s,

---

[37] ANDI, (1991, issue 107).

[38] Informe del Gerente de la Federación Nacional de Cafeteros al Congreso Cafetero, December, 1996.

[39] Fedecafé noted that during periods of high coffee prices, the coffee sector had historically made huge transfers of resources to the rest of the economy. The organization argued, not without reason, that it was now time for reciprocity, noting the difficult situation faced by the FNC, while elsewhere (i.e., in oil) there was an evident boom.

[40] Another reason why exporters were not vocal about the overvalued peso was that many of them were highly indebted in foreign currency (Urrutia, 1981).

consistently arguing in favor of a more depreciated currency[41] when the government adopted market-oriented policies that dismantled existing subsidy schemes.

Agricultural sector. The non-coffee agricultural sector did not share the industrial sector's protectionist views. The differences between the two sectors regarding exchange rate policy followed the patterns one would expect a priori: a preference for protection by the relatively inefficient import substitution sector, in contrast with an emphasis on cost controls and efficiency advocated by the more export-oriented agricultural sector. Thus, in the late 1970s and early 1980s, the farmers' association (SAC) openly advocated a more depreciated exchange rate as the way to recover competitiveness, and noted that the sustainability of that policy depended on fiscal restraint. In contrast to ANDI, the agricultural sector questioned the benefits of import restrictions, viewing such a policy as biased against exports, and expressed skepticism regarding subsidies as an alternative to a competitive exchange rate. SAC also advocated a strong anti-inflation stance. In the 1990s, SAC similarly became increasingly critical of the real appreciation of the peso. SAC argued that controls should have been imposed on capital inflows to halt the appreciation trend, noting that revenues from illicit drug exports were being brought into the country through the capital account.[42]

Financial sector. Perhaps as a result of the draconian restrictions imposed by DL 444, whereby capital flows were severely restricted for over a quarter century, the banker's association (*Asociación Bancaria*, or AB[43]) seldom voiced an opinion regarding exchange rate management, except perhaps through papers or conferences of an academic nature. When exchange controls were lifted in the 1990s, AB became more vocal regarding exchange rate management. In commenting on the peso's appreciation, the AB pointed out that if "fundamentals" had appreciated the real exchange rate, then government policy was correct in allowing part of the adjustment to be done through nominal appreciation (with certificates of exchange), and not solely through inflation. However, it was criti-

---

[41] It argued, for example, that interest rates and public sector tariffs—which did not enter into the price calculations used to estimate the real exchange rate, but which had increased more than general inflation—were significant costs confronted by exporters.

[42] It is noteworthy that the issue of illicit drug money was very seldom mentioned as a contributing factor to the peso's appreciation, despite the fact that yearly revenues from this trade probably amounted to 5 percent of GDP during the 1980s and 2-3 percent in the early 1990s (Steiner, 1998).

[43] Revista Banca y Finanzas, no. 20 (April 1991) and no. 23 (January 1992).

cal of attempts to curtail capital inflows by establishing a ceiling on interest rates. The association argued that such a policy would exacerbate appreciation expectations, stimulating capital inflows even more.

The central bank also changed its declared policy stance during the 1990s.[44] For the first time in decades, the bank asserted that maintaining the real exchange rate would cease to be the primary objective of exchange rate policy. In the bank's view, its new charter, which made price stability the bank's primary objective, precluded active exchange rate management.[45]

At this point, two questions arise. Given Colombia's tradition of moving very cautiously on reform policy, how was it possible to implement the ambitious reform program of the late 1980s and early 1990s, which apparently did away with many compensation mechanisms? Second, how was it possible to have a significant real exchange rate appreciation, without using compensatory mechanisms, as had been the case in previous experiences?

With regard to reform, Edwards (1998) offers several reasons why President Gaviria embarked on a structural reform program. First, even though Colombia was not in the midst of an economic crisis, it was going through severe political and social turmoil, as warfare with leftist guerrillas intensified and drug traffickers went on an all-out terrorist rampage. In that sense, Colombia complied with the argument that views crisis as a prerequisite to reform, according to Bates and Krueger (1993) and Williamson (1994). Second, multilateral institutions, unlike in the past, were indeed highly influential, in particular in promoting import liberalization. Third, on close examination, the reform process was quite incomplete, and in certain aspects it was tailored to shield important interest groups.[46]

With regard to appreciation without compensation, two issues

---

[44] Whether the declared and actual policy stances coincided is another issue.

[45] Changes extended to the monetary board. In the board minutes corresponding to late 1991, a discussion of exchange rate policy is documented. More noteworthy than the issues discussed was the fact that the issue was a matter of deliberation. Since the creation of the board in 1963, exchange rate policy discussions were traditionally held between the governor of the central bank and the Minister of Finance but were seldom, if ever, a matter analyzed within the board.

[46] Many public servants, including the powerful teachers' and oil sector unions, were excluded from labor reform. Second, pension reform did not do away with the public pension fund. Third, tariffs on key agricultural products were determined through a "price band" mechanism, with tariffs increasing as world prices declined. Fourth, the central bank was granted independence, but the Finance Minister was the President of its Board of Directors.

are worth highlighting. First, GATT restrictions now curtailed the use of subsidies as a compensating mechanism for a strong exchange rate; this constraint was publicly acknowledged. Second, and more importantly, the appreciation of the early 1990s came after the substantial and deliberate weakening of the peso in 1989 and 1990 (Cárdenas and Steiner, 1997). As mentioned above, the undervaluation of the peso was an integral part of trade liberalization from its very beginning. Of course, any subsequent appreciation is more palatable if the starting point is a weak currency.

Quantitative Analysis and Evidence

There are several studies regarding the determinants of the real exchange rate in Colombia, and even a few on the determinants of the nominal exchange rate. A recent summary of the most relevant work appears in Cárdenas (1997). While nominal variables such as relative money supplies between Colombia and the United States or relative price indexes satisfactorily explain the nominal exchange rate, real variables such as the terms of trade and relative factor productivity explain variations in the real exchange rate (RER). These results are, of course, clearly supported by several theories on exchange rate determination.

The most important econometric work regarding political determinants of economic outcomes is that of Escobar (1996). He focuses on the political business cycle governing fiscal and monetary policy, not explicitly addressing issues of exchange rate management. Moreno (1998) reports that the real exchange rate seems to follow a political business cycle, appreciating throughout a presidential period. He does not, however, perform a similar analysis for the nominal exchange rate, which is, after all, the control variable. Both authors use annual data (1950-95), perhaps not the ideal frequency for analyzing political business cycle issues (see below).[47]

The usual approach to exchange rate determination can be complemented by including, in addition to the usual "fundamental" variables, others that should capture elements of political economy. In most cases, dummy variables are used (i.e., to distinguish between a Liberal and a Conservative government). In other instances, continuous variables (i.e., the "fiscal incentive to depreciate") are employed.

---

[47] Political economy analysis of exchange rate policy based on descriptive rather than on econometric analysis is undertaken by Nelson et al. (1971), Díaz-Alejandro (1976) and Wiesner (1978).

Motivation of Political/Institutional Dummy Variables

The new political economy literature, surveyed in Alesina (1994), suggests the possible existence of two types of political cycle models:

1. Political-business cycle. According to early models of political business-cycles (Nordhaus, 1975, 1980) parties manipulate policy in order to maximize their chances at reelection, stimulating economic activity prior to elections and stabilizing afterwards. This theory is questionable and has found little supporting evidence. Rogoff and Sibert (1988) and Rogoff (1990) offer a model in which informational asymmetries between government and citizens produce a political-business cycle. According to this model, support at elections might be related to the government's delivery of short-term benefits.[48] In this strand of the literature, governments, in order to gain re-election for their party, manage economic policy in such a way that policy is expansionary during the last year in office, and contractionary in the first year after elections. In terms of four-year governments, this is captured through a dummy variable that is -1 the first year, +1 the last, and 0 for other years.

While Nordhaus and Rogoff and Sibert mainly refer to fiscal policy, this analysis indicates that in Colombia such a pattern might be observed in regard to exchange rate policy, under the assumption that, at least since 1967, a weak currency seems to have been politically appealing.[49] It should be noted that there is an important time-dimension difference between fiscal and exchange rate policy. While the stance in the former is well approximated by the yearly budget, the stance in the latter cannot be captured with low-frequency observations.

2. Partisan theory. The original formulation is by Hibbs (1977). Alesina (1988) proposed an alternative model, in which parties are rational and in which differences in behavior can be ascribed to differences in the underlying party coalitions. In both cases, ideology is the driving force. Parties left of center implement policies that favor growth as opposed to stability, while right of center parties favor low inflation. Empirically, if the dependent variable is in nominal terms (i.e., the rate of devaluation) the dummy variable is 0 during a right-of-center government and 1 otherwise.

---

[48] Recent work on political business cycles in reference to Latin America includes Stein and Streb (1998, 1999).

[49] This hypothesis is in sharp contrast to the intuition in Nelson et al. (1971, p. 248), according to whom "the identification of the exchange rate with national prestige is a phenomenon found in virtually every country. Devaluation is never a popular act with the electoral majority, although it may be in the interests of certain minority groups."

Other Political Dummy Variables

In addition to the above models, some additional political/institutional dummy variables should be considered in the case of Colombia. First, a distinction should be made between National Front and non-National Front governments to capture the fact that in the former there was no active political competition. Second, differences among exchange rate regimes (fixed until 1967, crawling peg until 1993, and crawling band thereafter) should be taken into account. A third variable worth considering is the nature of the central bank's board (private until 1963, fully controlled by the government until 1991, and "independent" since 1991).

Descriptive Analysis of Political/Institutional Phases

A brief description of the evolution of the dependent variables is useful in introducing the results of the econometric analysis. Table 6.12 uses monthly data to calculate the means for the nominal rate of devaluation and the real exchange rate. This examines whether the variables considered exhibit important differences throughout four of the five political/institutional dummy variables mentioned above.[50]

The data in the table are quite revealing. Regarding the rate of devaluation, it has been higher during Conservative than Liberal administrations, and much higher after the National Front political arrangement. In addition, the rate was similar during the period of fixed (but frequently adjusted) parities and during the crawling peg, but smaller during the crawling band years. Finally, nominal devaluation has been smaller during the tenure of an independent central bank.[51]

With regard to the RER, it has been weaker (higher) during Liberal administrations and since the National Front. In addition, the RER was lower during the fixed exchange rate regime, coinciding with the private nature of the central bank's board. The RER estimated by the central bank has an upward

---

[50] The political business cycle model analyzed below uses monthly data, not annual averages based on monthly data.

[51] Certainly a similar and maybe indistinguishable story can be told with regard to the rate of inflation. In the context of a heavily indexed economy, the linkages (in both directions) between inflation and devaluation are obvious. In the context of this study, lack of concern for nominal stability refers to the acceptance of a high rate of inflation and/or of a high rate of nominal devaluation, regardless of which one causes which. Of course, there might be cases in which devaluation "comes first" (i.e., as a reaction to a decline in the terms of trade), and others in which it "comes last" (i.e., a fiscal deficit might be monetized, producing inflation and inducing a nominal depreciation).

Table 6.12. Political/Institutional Phases of Dependent Variables
(Annual average of monthly data)

Phase	Nominal devaluation	RER (Dec. 86=100)
Partisan model		
1. Liberal	12.69	82.05
2. Conservative	19.88	71.81
Political competition		
1. National Front (1958.08-74.07)	10.22	69.32
2. Post-National Front (1974.08-)	18.24	87.44
Exchange rate regime		
1. Fixed (1951.01-67.03)	15.79	63.38
2. Crawling peg (1967.04-93.12)	16.84	82.89
3.1. Crawling band (1994.01-97.12)	9.98	94.78
3.2. Crawling band (1994.01-94.12)	5.19	96.18
Central bank board		
1. Private (1951.01-63.03)	15.52	62.69
2. Official (1963.04-91.08)	17.08	78.69
3.1. Independent (1991.09-97.12)	11.43	98.16
3.2. Independent (1991.09-94.12)	11.3	101.54

Source: Authors' calculations based on Appendix 6.1.

trend (Figure 6.1).[52] All other things being equal, then, any political or institutional event occurring towards the end of the sample period will be associated with a weaker real exchange rate. This upward trend is not a matter of concern, since the econometric exercises reported below use "RER misalignments" as the dependent variable.

Empirical Analysis

Before presenting the econometric estimations, it is interesting to discuss the possible existence of a political business cycle (PBC) in two key variables: devaluation and inflation.

Figures 6.3 and 6.4 show the average monthly nominal rate of devaluation and the average monthly rate of inflation. The exact month of each of the last 10 presidential elections (from 1958 until 1994) was identified. Elections

---

[52] Estimations not reported confirm that it is a nonstationary variable.

Figure 6.3. Monthly Rate of Devaluation, Election Year vs. Average Year, 1958-98

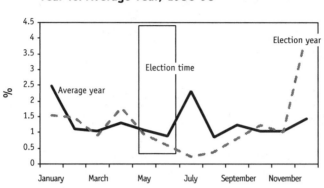

Source: Authors' calculations based on Banco de la Republica.

Figure 6.4. Monthly Rate of Inflation, Election Year vs. Average Year, 1958-98

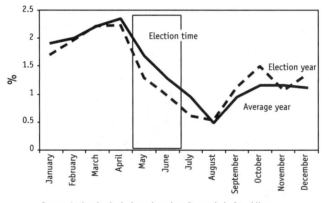

Source: Authors' calculations, based on Banco de la Republica.

took place either in May or June ("election time" in the figures). For both variables, two averages were calculated for every month of the year: one average includes all years in the sample (i.e., every January from 1958 until 1994, yielding the "average year" line in the figures); the other average includes only months of election years (i.e., every fourth January from 1958 until 1994, yielding the "election year" line in the figures).

For both variables, the months prior to an electoral period are similar regardless of whether it is an election year or an average year. After

Figure 6.5. Structural Change in the Rate of Inflation
(Monthly data)

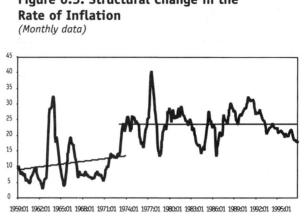

Source: Departamento Administrativo Nacional de Estadística (DANE).

controlling for seasonal elements (which seem to be quite relevant in the case of inflation), there seems to be no particular change in exchange rate policy or in inflation in the months leading to an election.

Differences do emerge, however, in the monthly pattern of exchange rate policy in the months *following* an election. Figure 6.3 shows that in an election year, the nominal rate of devaluation is lower than in an average year during the two to three month period between an election and the presidential inauguration in early August. Consequently, in the two to three months following inauguration, the nominal rate of devaluation is higher than during an average year.

One can therefore argue that although exchange rate policy does not seem to change as a function of a presidential election, outgoing administrations still prefer to strive for nominal stability in the months prior to transferring power. In Colombia, as in many other countries, the new administration is generally left with the responsibility of correcting for (some degree of) exchange rate overvaluation.

These results are reflected in the econometric exercises, where two dependent variables have been considered. Table 6.13 presents the (quarterly) nominal rate of devaluation of the Colombian peso against the U.S. dollar, and in Table 6.14 the dependent variable is the deviation from the trend of a PPP-version of the real exchange rate.

Nominal devaluation. The OLS estimation uses quarterly data for the 1960:2-1997:4 period. The strictly exogenous explanatory variables are the terms of trade (TOT); the lagged values of Venezuela's nominal inflation

Table 6.13. Determinants of the Nominal Rate of Devaluation
Dependent variable: Devnom
(Quarterly data, 1960.2-1997.4, OLS estimations)

Explanatory variable	(1)	(2)	(3)	(4)	(5)
Constant	11.610	9.410	9.380	8.310	8.130
	(2.81)**	(3.594)***	(3.59)***	(3.48)***	(3.43)***
TOT	-0.02	-0.02	-0.02	-0.01	-0.01
	(-1.97)*	(-1.88)*	(-1.89)*	(-1.74)*	(-1.69)*
INFVEN	-0.007				
	(-0.182)				
TBILL	-0.21				
	(-0.652)				
RERMISALIG[1]				-0.70	-0.73
				(-5.34)***	(5.95)***
DPBC	0.48	0.42			
	(0.275)	(0.242)			
DFN	-6.46	-5.70	-5.66	-3.80	-3.33
	(-2.80)***	(-2.84)***	(-2.84)***	(-2.4)**	(-2.42)**
DCONS	3.89	3.82	3.81	0.94	
	(2.42)**	(2.45)**	(2.45)**	(0.61)	
DFIXED	0.57	1.03	1.01		
	(0.276)	(0.523)	(0.512)		
DIND	-3.95	-3.31	-3.29	-3.41	-3.47
	(-1.47)	(-1.71)*	(-1.71)*	(-1.93)*	(-1.97)**
DEVCOL(-1)	0.67	0.68	0.68	0.75	0.76
	(10.95)***	(11.42)***	(11.48)***	(13.51)***	(15.27)***
Adjusted R2	0.65	0.66	0.66	0.71	0.72
Durbin Watson	1.62	1.62	1.63	2.18	2.21

Notes: t-statistics in parentheses. *Significant at 90% **Significant at 95% ***Significant at 99%.
[1] Difference between "observed" and "permanent" RER, using a Hodrick-Prescott filter.

(INFVEN), Venezuela being Colombia's most important non-coffee trading partner; and foreign interest rates (proxied by TBILL, the nominal rate of interest on 3-month U.S. Treasury bills).[53]

Several dummy variables are included. DPBC is the "political business cycle" dummy. In non-presidential election years it is equal to zero in every quarter. In presidential election years it is 0 in the first and fourth quarters, 1 in the second and -1 in the third, in order to capture the fact that elections always take place between April and June. DFN is the "National Front" dummy (1 during Front administrations, 0 otherwise); DCONS is the "partisan" dummy (1 during Conservative administra-

---

[53] For details on the precise definition of all variables, including sources, see Appendix 6.1.

tions, 0 otherwise); DFIXED is the "exchange rate regime" dummy (1 if fixed, 0 otherwise); and DIND is the "central bank" dummy (1 if independent, 0 otherwise). In addition, RERMISAILG captures the degree of misalignment in the RER, as defined above.[54]

In the five estimations reported, no less than 65 percent of the variance of the nominal rate of devaluation is explained by the variables under consideration. The inclusion of the lagged dependent variable removes any problems of first-order serial autocorrelation. Consistently, TOT is significant and has the expected negative sign. Neither the foreign interest rate nor the Venezuelan inflation rate showed up as significant.

Turning to the political/institutional dummy variables, two consistently do not appear as significant, DPBC and DFIXED. The latter result suggests that the fixed but unsustainable peg regime in place from 1960-67 yielded average quarterly rates of devaluation that were no different than those obtained during the crawling peg and crawling band periods.

In all but one estimation, the nature of the board of the central bank was significant. In particular, controlling for all other variables, the nominal rate of devaluation is lower during the tenure of the independent central bank. This result is not very surprising, especially as the independent central bank has as its sole objective the control of inflation. This mandate has prompted it to adopt policies that have included a deliberate strengthening of the currency.

More interestingly, DFN is highly significant in all the estimations and has the expected negative sign. In the spirit of Bates (1997), the smaller the degree of political competition, as during the National Front period, the more likely governments are to pursue policies that do not compromise economic stability. In the two years before the National Front formally ended in 1974, world oil prices had dramatically increased and several indexation mechanisms were introduced in Colombia, including an indexed unit of account for certain financial transactions and the consolidation of yearly adjustments of the minimum wage. In addition, after allegations of fraud, the president elected in 1970 pushed for an important increase in public expenditure, an increase that later became permanent. Since these events

---

[54] It is important to note that certain obvious explanatory variables have been excluded. In particular, the domestic rate of inflation and the stance in terms of monetary and/or fiscal policy have been excluded. This was done because it is precisely through these variables that all political economy determinants express themselves. For example, if it is the case that DCONS is positive and significant, then it follows that during Conservative administrations control variables such as fiscal and monetary policy are set in such a way as to accommodate a higher rate of nominal devaluation. It is highly unlikely that, if these control variables were explicitly included in the estimations, any political economy dummy variable would show up as significant.

have been considered possible determinants of the increase in Colombia's rate of inflation from single to double digits in the first half of the 1970s, the DMFN variable may actually capture these events.

Nonetheless, commitment to nominal stability faltered precisely when political competition became a reality. While most countries faced the same shock as Colombia, most saw only temporary rather than permanent increases in the growth rate of key nominal variables. If the cause of these increases is uncertain, the propagation mechanisms, including most prominently the generalization of indexation, can be understood as a political reaction designed to minimize the adverse redistributive effects usually ascribed to inflation.

Finally, DCONS is significant and positive in three of four estimations. As observed above, corroboration that Conservative administrations have witnessed higher nominal devaluations might have something to do with politics (i.e., in spite of the apolitical nature of the coffee growers' federation, the Conservative Party has always been dominant in the more traditional and religious coffee-growing region).

During the sample period, there were very few Conservative administrations, and one of them (Betancur, 1982-86) engineered the most important nominal depreciation in recent memory in order to correct for a highly overvalued exchange rate and avoid an imminent balance of payments crisis. It would be highly inappropriate to suggest that this event was motivated by the Conservatives' lack of commitment to nominal stability. In fact, when controlling for the misalignment in the RER (estimation 4), DCONS is no longer significant.[55] It is still possible, however, to argue that when confronted with an overvalued exchange rate, Conservative administrations are readily willing to implement a nominal depreciation, and that readiness has to do with the fact that the party's most important constituents are the main beneficiaries of a weak currency.

Real Exchange Rate Deviations from Trend

The difference between the "observed" RER and the forecast RER is computed from an estimation in which the RER level depends on the terms of

---

[55] In this case, the misalignment is computed at every point in time (i.e., for every quarter) as the difference between the (log of) RER and its permanent component, the latter constructed with a Hodrick-Prescott filter. One certainly feels more comfortable with an "RER misalignment" that is derived from the residuals of a well-specified regression in which the dependent variable is the RER. While it is possible to follow this procedure in the case of annual data (as in Table 6.14), it cannot be done when dealing with quarterly data, since many of the right-hand side "fundamentals" are not available at this frequency.

Table 6.14. Determinants of Real Exchange Rate Misalignment
Dependent variable: MISALIGN
(Annual data 1961-94, OLS estimations)

Explanatory variable	(1)	(2)
Constant	-0.10	-0.08
	(-0.98)	(-1.98)**
FISINCENT	0.021	0.02
	(2.19)**	(2.37)**
XMXT	0.01	
	(0.231)	
DFN	0.07	0.07
	(2.26)**	(2.42)**
DCONS	-0.01	
	(-0.04)	
DMIND	-0.09	-0.09
	(-1.80)*	(-1.98)**
DFIXED	-0.13	-0.14
	(-2.05)**	(-3.83)***
Adjusted R2	0.47	0.51
Durbin Watson	1.37	1.37

Note: t-statistics in parentheses.*Significant at 90% **Significant at 95% ***Significant at 99%.
MISALIGN = RER-RER(forecast)
RER(forecast) = f (TOT, PFT, PFNT, KAC, DEFICIT)

trade, productivity in the tradables and nontradables sectors, the fiscal deficit, and the capital account balance. The misalignment is positive when the observed RER is above (i.e., more depreciated than) its forecast value.

OLS estimations using annual data for the 1961-94 period are reported in Table 6.14. The first result that should be highlighted is that the misalignment is positively correlated with fiscal incentive (FISINCENT).[56] This finding suggests that when tailoring exchange rate policy, the fiscal consequences of a devaluation are taken into account. As described in Appendix 6.1, the fiscal incentive is affected both by stocks (government foreign assets and liabilities) and by flows (public sector imports and exports and trade-related taxes).

While the nominal rate of devaluation was lower during National

---

[56] FISINCENT is computed as the following ratio: import taxes + taxes on coffee exports + annual change in external public debt - interest on external public debt + Ecopetrol net exports + coal exports/GDP. See Appendix 6.1.

Front administrations, the RER misalignment was positive. This might suggest that, nominal exchange rate policy notwithstanding, other determinants of the RER (in particular, fiscal policy) probably served to enhance competitiveness. In any case, if the exchange rate is already depreciated in real terms, there is less need to increase the nominal rate of devaluation.

As expected, given the results reported in Table 6.13, DCONS does not show up as significant in Table 6.14. It is important to recall that Table 6.13 used quarterly data, whereas Table 6.14 uses yearly observations. If it is true that Conservative administrations actively use nominal exchange rate policy to correct (quarterly) misalignments in the RER, then it should be the case that yearly RER misalignments do not depend on which political party holds power.

The MISALIGN variable is negatively correlated with DIND, a result that is hardly surprising, given the discussion presented above. Similarly, the fact that DFIXED shows up as negative and significant suggests that, as is generally accepted, one of the drawbacks of a fixed exchange rate regime in the context of moderate inflation is that it tends to strengthen the currency in real terms (in the present context, it keeps the RER below its forecast value).

The 1994 Presidential Election

As was noted above, the National Front's bipartisan coalition for all practical purposes lasted until 1990. In that sense, during the last 40 years, Colombia has only witnessed truly contested presidential elections in 1990 and 1994. The first was a landslide for Liberal candidate César Gaviria. Besides running on the coattails of slain anti-drug campaigner Luis Carlos Galán, he faced a divided Conservative opposition.

The 1994 contest was certainly more interesting, featuring Liberal Ernesto Samper, Conservative Andrés Pastrana, and Antonio Navarro from AD-M19, a leftist coalition. In addition, the 1991 Constitution mandated that the winner had to command an absolute majority, a requirement that necessitated a run-off election. The 1994 contest featured Samper, the eventual winner, and Pastrana.

Table 6.15 presents a brief summary of the candidates' positions regarding key economic issues. While ideological differences had all but vanished during the previous three decades, these differences were quite explicit in 1994. Colombians clearly were faced with a left of center option in Samper and a right of center alternative in Pastrana. While Samper favored growth promotion through nominal policies, Pastrana ran on a supply-side oriented platform. More specifically, Samper fa-

Table 6.15. The Economics of the 1994 Presidential Election

Policy	Samper	Pastrana
Exchange rates	Avoid exchange rate revaluation by investing Cusiana oil revenues and maintaining part of this abroad. Revaluation is the country's major risk. Because of the negative consequences of revaluation on economic activity, the government in accordance with the Central Bank must avoid it.	Consolidate structural reforms and liberalization of the economy. Create a foreign account for oil revenues, stimulate private savings and investment by reforming the financial system. Clear pro-market orientation.
Wages	Social agreement: All salaries, in real terms, will increase in proportion to productivity growth. Wages and pensions must keep at least their purchasing power.	Wages will be determined independently from other prices in the economy, according to conditions of the labor market, taking into account labor productivity. There must be agreements between all actors to achieve goals of reducing inflation, macroeconomic stability and productivity gains.
Coffee	Separate coffee policies from macroeconomic performance. Finance infrastructure and social investment with fiscal resources instead of using coffee revenues. Promote a deregulated and aggressive commercial policy. Use the National Coffee Fund for price and income stabilization of coffee producers.	The evolution of international prices must be the point of reference for determining internal prices. During unfavorable conditions and for the short term, the government can provide credit to the National Fund to avoid fluctuations or falls in producer income. It is more appropiate to support producers with technology, marketing and credits than with subsidies.

Source: *El Tiempo*, April 1994.

vored enhancing international competition through active management of the nominal exchange rate. On that basis, Liberal candidate Samper should presumably have done better in those parts of the country that are more outward-oriented in their productive structure, while Pastrana should have done relatively better in those parts more heavily dependent on production of nontradables.

Table 6.16 presents two sets of data. Columns (1)-(5) report the results of presidential elections at the department level, and column (6) indicates the degree of tradability of each department's output (according to the 1992 National Accounts; see note to the table). Columns (1)-(3) show the ratio of the Conservative to the Liberal vote for the 1986, 1990 and 1994 elections,[57] column (4) reports the average for this ratio for 1986/1990, and column (5) indicates the change in the ratio between 1994 and the 1986/1990 average. Even though the Liberal candidate won all three

---

[57] During the 1990 elections Conservatives were divided. There was an "official" as well as an "independent" candidate. For the present purposes, the sum of the two is the relevant outcome.

Table 6.16. Electoral Results and Composition of GDP

	Conservative/Liberal					Output
				Average		
	1994	1990	1986	1986/90	((1) - (4))*100	Tradable GDP
Department	(1)	(2)	(3)	(4)	(5)	(6)
Antioquia	1.32	1.01	0.74	0.87	44.77	43.29
Risaralda	1.23	0.48	0.69	0.58	64.82	49.43
Caldas	1.41	1.02	0.96	0.99	42.46	46.78
Quindío	0.82	0.65	0.45	0.54	28.04	50.56
Tolima	0.85	0.70	0.54	0.62	23.45	49.70
Huila	1.39	0.84	0.95	0.89	49.36	46.61
Córdoba	0.67	0.50	0.50	0.50	16.78	57.67
Sucre	0.60	0.44	0.50	0.47	13.23	50.58
Bolivar	0.76	0.63	0.46	0.54	22.14	41.47
Atlántico	0.67	0.57	0.47	0.52	15.49	38.56
Magdalena	0.78	0.57	0.42	0.49	28.33	43.44
Cesar	0.84	0.73	0.47	0.59	25.34	56.88
Guajira	0.81	0.65	0.56	0.60	20.96	59.62
Chocó	0.54	0.33	0.33	0.33	20.74	51.77
Valle del Cauca	0.93	0.76	0.59	0.67	26.10	38.95
Cauca	0.72	0.53	0.58	0.56	16.63	53.65
Nariño	1.28	0.77	0.98	0.87	41.17	41.08
Norte de Santander	1.38	1.06	0.85	0.95	42.58	37.22
Santander	0.92	0.74	0.67	0.70	21.25	51.06
Boyacá	1.27	1.05	0.87	0.96	30.86	43.90
Cundinamarca	0.90	0.77	0.52	0.63	27.05	51.56
Meta	0.88	0.79	0.58	0.68	19.84	51.12
Caquetá	0.99	0.60	0.55	0.58	41.04	50.31
Total	0.96	0.71	0.62	0.66	29.67	48.05

Column (2): Independent candidate considered as Conservative vote.
Column (6): As percent of total in 1992. Tradable GDP is the sum of agriculture, mining and industry.
Source: Authors' calculations based on Registraduría Nacional del Estado Civil and DANE.

elections (the average for the Conservative/Liberal ratio for the entire country was always below 1), it is quite evident that Conservatives made consistent, significant progress at the national level as well as in most departments. Certainly, one would like to control for this general trend. That is the purpose of column (5), which shows that the average improvement by Conservatives at the national level between 1986/90 and 1994 was 29.7 percent. Of course, in some departments the improvement was larger than this average, while in others it was smaller.

In seven of the 10 departments when the improvement by Conservatives in 1994 was above average, the share of tradables in GDP was below the national average (48.05 percent). Correspondingly, in 10 of the 13 departments where the 1994 improvement by Conservatives was below average, the share of tradables in GDP was above the national average. After correcting for an improving trend by Conservatives since 1986, the table shows that whether the marginal improvement in 1994 was above or below average seems to be associated with the expected economic impact of announced exchange rate policy on departmental economic well-being, given each department's productive structure. This was true in 17 of 23 cases.

Conclusions

By regional standards, since the 1960s Colombia has exhibited remarkable economic stability and institutional continuity. Until recently, the political system was based on an entrenched bipartisan coalition, with little ideological confrontation between the Liberal and Conservative parties. Power sharing, which was mandatory during the National Front period (1958-74), effectively lasted until 1991. Extreme economic positions seldom emerged, reflecting the nonideological character of the political coalition.

Coffee, the main export, is a labor-intensive activity, taking place in thousands of family-owned small plots. Coffee producers' income depends on the domestic price of coffee, which is the result of a complex arrangement with the government, and of which the exchange rate is but one component. Overall, the relevance of labor unions has been declining, although in key public sector activities their importance has probably been enhanced. Following a 1968 constitutional amendment, the role of Congress in economic issues has been limited to fiscal policy, with the tailoring of the budget being its main concern.

A survey of key economic episodes from 1962 to 1997 indicates that efforts have generally been geared towards delivering a moderate rate of inflation and a competitive real exchange rate. Widespread indexation has made this arrangement palatable to most interest groups. Historically, exchange rate policy was conducted in tandem with commercial, financial and fiscal policies. The latter were used as compensatory mechanisms, designed to garner private sector support for the chosen path of the exchange rate. More recently, when market-oriented structural reforms were introduced, most compensatory mechanisms disappeared, and interest groups became vocal regarding exchange rate policy. This description holds true for all business associations, including the coffee growers' federation.

Institutional continuity and the longevity of the exchange rate regime, which basically remained unaltered during the 1967-91 period, suggest that political considerations might not be relevant in explaining the stable pattern of key economic variables. This intuition, though, is not fully supported by the numbers. Econometric estimations indicate that the nominal rate of devaluation was lower during National Front administrations and higher during Conservative governments. The first result supports the notion that political competition might imply less concern for stability. The second could be partially explained by the political influence of the Conservative Party in the coffee-growing region and to the willingness of Conservative administrations to accelerate the nominal rate of depreciation to correct for currency overvaluations.

In addition, the nominal rate of devaluation seems to depend on the nature of the central bank board. In particular, it has been mainly during the tenure of an "independent" central bank that exchange rate policy has been actively used to bring down inflation.

References

Alesina, A. 1994. Political Models of Macroeconomic Policy and Fiscal Reforms. In S. Haggard and S. Webb (eds.), *Voting for Reform: Democracy, Political Liberalization, and Economic Adjustment.* Oxford: Oxford University Press.

_____. 1988. Macroeconomics and Politics. In S. Fischer (ed.), *NBER Macroeconomics Annual.* Volume 3. Cambridge, MA: MIT Press.

Archer, R.P., and M. Soberg Shugart. 1997. The Unrealized Potential of Presidential Dominance in Colombia. In S. Mainwaring and M. Soberg Shugart (eds.), *Presidentialism and Democracy in Latin America.* Cambridge, UK: Cambridge University Press.

Asociación Bancaria de Colombia. *Revista Banca y Finanzas.* Various issues.

Asociación Nacional de Exportadores (ANALDEX). *Exponotas.* Various issues.

Asociación Nacional de Industriales. (ANDI) *Revista ANDI.* Various issues.

Banco de la República. 1993. *Principales Indicadores Económicos 1923-1992.* Bogota: Banco de la República.

_____. *Revista del Banco de la República.* Various issues.

Bates, R. 1997. Instituciones y Desarrollo. In D. Pizano and J. Chalarca (eds.), *Café, Instituciones y Desarrollo Económico.* Bogota: Federación Nacional de Cafeteros de Colombia.

Bates, R., and A.O. Krueger. 1993. *Political and Economic Interactions in Economic Policy Reform: Evidence from Eight Countries.* Cambridge: Blackwell.

Caballero, C. 1987. *50 Años de Economía: de la Crisis del Treinta a la del Ochenta.* Bogota: Editorial Presencia.

Cárdenas, M. 1997. La Tasa de Cambio en Colombia. Cuadernos Fedesarrollo 1, Bogota.

Cárdenas, M., and R. Steiner. 1997. El Flujo de Capitales Privados en Colombia. *Cuadernos de Economía* 34(103): 309-37.

Cárdenas, M., and Z. Partow. 1998. *Oil, Coffee and the Dynamic Commons Problem in Colombia.* Working Paper Series 5, Fedesarrollo, Bogota.

Carrasquilla, A. 1996. Dimensiones Fiscales de una Inflación Moderada. Banco de la República, Bogota. Mimeo.

Cukierman, A. 1992. *Central Bank Strategy. Credibility and Independence: Theory and Evidence.* Cambridge, MA: MIT Press.

Díaz-Alejandro, C. 1976. *Foreign Trade Regimes and Economic Development: Colombia.* New York: National Bureau of Economic Research/Columbia University Press.

Dix, R.H. 1990. Social Change and Party System Stability in Colombia. *Government Opposition* 25: 98-114.

_____. 1980. Consociational Democracy. *Comparative Politics* 12(3): 303-21.

_____. 1978. The Varieties of Populism: The Case of Colombia. *The Western Political Quarterly* 31(3): 334-51.

Dornbusch, R., and S. Edwards. 1991. The Macroeconomics of Populism. In R. Dornbusch and S. Edwards (eds.), *The Macroeconomics of Populism in Latin America*. Chicago: National Bureau of Economic Research/University of Chicago Press.

Dornbusch, R., and S. Fischer. 1993. Moderate Inflation. *World Bank Economic Review* 7(1): 1-44.

Echeverry, J.C. 1996. The Rise and Perpetuation of Moderate Inflation: Colombia, 1970-1991. *Borradores Semanales de Economía* 50, Banco de la República, Bogota.

Edwards, S. 1998. The Political Economy of Incomplete Market-Oriented Reform: The Case of Colombia. University of California at Los Angeles/National Bureau of Economic Research. Mimeo.

_____. 1995. Un Cuarto de Siglo de Fedesarrollo: una Perspectiva Personal. In H. Gómez (ed.), *Economía y Opinión*. Bogota: TM Editores/Colciencias.

Escobar, A. 1996. Ciclos Políticos y Ciclos Económicos en Colombia: 1950-1994. *Coyuntura Económica* 26(1): 115-41.

Findley, R., F. Cepeda, and N. Gamboa. 1983. *Intervención Presidencial en la Economía y el Estado de Derecho en Colombia*. Bogota: CIDER/Universidad de los Andes.

García-García, J., and S. Jayasuriya. 1997. *Courting Turmoil and Deferring Prosperity - Colombia Between 1960 and 1990*. Washington, DC: World Bank.

Gómez, H. 1978. Comentarios al Artículo de E. Wiesner. In E. Wiesner (ed.), *Política Económica Externa de Colombia*. Bogota: Asociación Bancaria de Colombia.

Haggard, S. 1994. Inflation and Stabilization. In G. Meier (ed.), *Politics and Policy Making in Developing Countries: Perspectives on the New Political Economy*. San Francisco: ICS Press.

Haggard, S., and S. Webb. 1994. Introduction. In S. Haggard and S. Webb (eds.), *Voting for Reform: Democracy, Political Liberalization, and Economic Adjustment*. Oxford: Oxford University Press.

Hartlyn, J. 1993. *La Política del Régimen de Coalición*. Bogota: Tercer Mundo Editores/Universidad de los Andes/CEI.

Hibbs, D. 1977. Political Parties and Macroeconomic Policy. *American Political Science Review* 7: 1467-87.

Inter-American Development Bank. 1995. Overcoming Volatility. In *Economic and Social Progress in Latin America*. Washington, DC: Inter-American Development Bank.

Junguito, R., and D. Pizano. 1991. *Produccion de Café en Colombia*. Bogota: Fondo Cultural Cafetero/Fedesarrollo.

Krugman, P. 1992. Target Zones and Exchange Rate Dynamics. *Quarterly Journal of Economics* 106(3).

Leal, F. 1995. *En Busca de la Estabilidad Perdida*. Bogota: Tercer Mundo Editores/ IEPRI/Colciencias.

Lijphart, A. 1977. *Democracy in Plural Societies: A Comparative Exploration*. New Haven, CT: Yale University Press.

Lleras, C. 1987. Discurso de Instalación. In *Colombia: 20 Años del Régimen de Cambios y de Comercio Exterior*. Vol. 2. Bogota: Banco de la República.

Londoño, R. 1986. La Estructura Sindical Colombiana en la Década del 70. In H. Gómez, R. Londoño and G. Perry (eds.), *Sindicalismo y Política Económica*. Bogota: Fedesarrollo/Fescol.

López, A. 1987a. El Estatuto Cambiario y el Gobierno. In *Colombia - 20 Años del Régimen de Cambios y de Comercio Exterior*. Vol. 1. Bogota: Banco de la República.

_____ 1987b. El Estatuto Cambiario, el Ambiente Político y el Congreso. In *Colombia - 20 Años del Régimen de Cambios y de Comercio Exterior*. Vol. 1. Bogota: Banco de la República.

Maullin, R. 1967. The Colombia I.M.F. Disagreement of November-December, 1966: An Interpretation of its Place in Colombian Politics. Rand Corporation, Santa Monica, CA. Mimeo.

Meisel, A. 1996. Autonomía de la Banca Central e Inflación: La Experiencia Colombiana, 1923-1995. *Borradores Semanales de Economía* No. 49. Banco de la República, Bogota.

Montenegro, A. 1997. Lecciones de la Crisis y el Ajuste Macroeconómico de la Administración Betancur. In C. Caballero (ed.), *La Pasion de Gobernar*. Bogota: ANIF/Tercer Mundo Editores.

Moreno, A.M. 1998. Ciclo Político y Política Económica: Un Análisis del Caso Colombiano 1930-1995. *Informe Financiero*. Bogota: Contraloría General de la República.

Musalem, A. 1971. *Dinero, Inflación y Balanza de Pagos: la Experiencia Colombiana en la Post-Guerra*. Bogota: Banco de la República.

Nelson, R.R., T.P. Shultz, and R.L. Slighton. 1971. *Structural Change in a Developing Economy: Colombia's Problems and Prospects*. Princeton, NJ: Princeton University Press.

Nordhaus, W. 1980. Alternative Approaches to the Political-Business Cycle. *Brookings Papers on Economic Activity* 2: 1-68.

_____. 1975. The Political Business Cycle. *Review of Economic Studies* 42: 169-90.

Ocampo, J.A. 1989. Ciclo Cafetero y Comportamiento Macroeconómico en Colombia, 1940-1987. *Coyuntura Económica* 19(4): 147-83.

Ocampo, J.A., and E. Revéiz. 1980. Bonanza Cafetera y Economía Concertada. In E. Reveiz (ed.), *La Cuestión Cafetera*. Bogota: CEDE/Universidad de los Andes.

Ocampo, J.A., J. Bernal, M. Avella, et al. 1987. La Consolidación del Capitalismo Moderno–1945-1986. In J.A. Ocampo (ed.), *Historia Económica de Colombia*. Bogota: Fedesarrollo/Siglo XXI Editores.

Palacios, H. 1997. Estabilización Económica con un Banco Central Intervenido: la Experiencia del Gobierno Betancur. In C. Caballero (ed.), *La Pasión de Gobernar*. Bogota: ANIF/Tercer Mundo Editores.

Phelps, E. 1973. Inflation in the Theory of Public Finance. *Swedish Journal of Economics* 75: 67-82.

Reveiz, E., and M.J. Pérez. 1986. Colombia: Moderate Economic Growth, Political Stability, and Social Welfare. In J. Hartlyn and S.A. Morley (eds.), *Latin American Political Economy: Financial Crisis and Political Change*. Boulder, CO: Westview Press.

Rivera, A. 1976. The Politics of Development Planning in Colombia. State University of New York at Buffalo. Doctoral dissertation.

Rogoff, K. 1990. Political Budget Cycles. *American Economic Review* 80(1): 1-36.

Rogoff, K., and A. Sibert. 1988. Elections and Macroeconomic Policy Cycles. *Review of Economic Studies* 55(1): 1-16.

Sánchez, F., J.I. Rodríguez, and J. Núñez. 1996. Evolución y determinantes de la productividad en Colombia: Un análisis global y sectorial. In R. Chica (ed.), *El Crecimiento de la Productividad en Colombia*. Bogota: Tercer Mundo Editores.

Sarmiento, E. 1978. Estabilización de la Economía Colombiana, Diciembre 1976-Junio 1978. *Revista del Banco de la República:* 1108-121.

Soberg Shugart, M., and D.L. Nielson. 1997. Constitutional Change in Colombia: Policy Adjustment through Institutional Reform. In *Comparative Political Studies*.

Stein, E., and J. Streb. 1999. Elections and the Timing of Devaluations. Inter-American Development Bank Research Department Working Paper 396, Washington, DC.

_____. 1998. Political Stabilization Cycles in High Inflation Countries. *Journal of Development Economics* 56(1): 159-80.

Steiner, R. 1998. Colombia's Income from the Drug Trade. *World Development* 26(6): 1013-31.

Steiner, R., H. Rincón, and L.A. Saavedra. 1992. Utilización del Impuesto Inflacionario en Colombia. *Monetaria* 15(2): 195-212.

Suescún, R. 1997. Bonanzas, Enfermedad Holandesa y Ciclo Económico Real en Colombia. *Coyuntura Económica* 27(2): 124-49.

_____. 1992. Inflación y Devaluación como un Fenómeno Fiscal: la Financiación Óptima del Gobierno a través de la Tributación, el Senoraje y las Utilidades por Compraventa de Divisas. *Ensayos Sobre Política Económica* 22: 7-50.

Supelano, A. 1992. The Political Economy of Latin America: The Colombian Experience During the 1980s. *Journal of Economic Issues* 26(3): 845-64.

Urrutia, M. 1991. On the Absence of Economic Populism in Colombia. In R. Dornbusch and S. Edwards (eds.), *The Macroeconomics of Populism in Latin America*. Chicago: NBER/University of Chicago Press.

_____. 1981. Experience with the Crawling Peg in Colombia. In J. Williamson (ed.), *Exchange Rate Rules*. New York: St. Martins Press.

_____. 1976. *Historia del Sindicalismo en Colombia*. Medellin: Editorial La Carreta.

Wiesner, E. 1998. Transaction Cost Economics and Public Sector Rent-Seeking in Developing Countries: Toward a Theory of Government Failure. In R. Picciotto and E. Wiesner (eds.), *Evaluation & Development: The Institutional Dimension*. New Brunswick, NJ: World Bank/Transaction Publishers.

_____. 1978. Devaluación y Mecanismo de Ajuste en Colombia. In E. Wiesner (ed.), *Política Económica Externa de Colombia*. Bogota: Asociación Bancaria de Colombia.

Williamson, J. 1996. *The Crawling Band as an Exchange Rate Regime: Lessons from Chile, Colombia, and Israel*. Washington, DC: Institute for International Economics.

_____. 1994. *The Political Economy of Policy Reform*. Washington, DC: Institute for International Economics.

Yanovich, D. 1997. Regionalismo y Déficit Fiscal en Colombia: 1930-1995. Universidad de los Andes, Bogota. M.A. thesis.

Appendix 6.1. Database

Year	Inflation rate (%)	Nominal exchange rate (%)	Nominal devaluation (%)	RER (1975=100)	Public expenditure (% of GDP)	Fiscal deficit (% of GDP)	Money growth (M1) (%)	Capital flows (% of GDP)	Terms of trade (1975=100)	External coffee price (USc/pound)
	(1)	(2)	(3)	(4)	(5)	(6)	(7)	(8)	(9)	(10)
1951	2.8	2.5	28.1	58.9	9.1	0.1	16.4	-0.2	158.1	58.7
1952	2.6	2.5	0.0	58.1	8.7	1.4	16.9	0.3	163.5	57.0
1953	6.8	2.5	0.0	54.8	10.0	1.1	18.3	-0.1	167.9	59.8
1954	4.4	2.5	0.0	50.9	10.3	0.2	19.3	1.6	209.9	80.0
1955	2.3	2.5	0.0	50.4	11.5	1.2	4.7	2.2	178.6	64.6
1956	7.8	2.5	0.0	48.6	10.7	2.0	24.9	0.6	184.6	74.0
1957	20.2	5.4	114.3	60.0	9.5	3.4	13.6	-5.1	172.9	63.9
1958	8.1	6.4	19.0	87.5	9.0	0.3	20.9	-1.9	164.6	52.3
1959	7.9	6.4	0.0	73.0	8.5	-0.0	12.0	-1.0	123.4	45.2
1960	7.2	6.7	4.7	75.4	8.6	-0.1	10.4	2.1	87.8	44.9
1961	5.9	6.7	0.0	75.4	9.0	1.7	24.6	2.9	87.8	43.6
1962	6.4	9.0	34.3	79.1	9.0	4.2	20.7	3.0	65.9	40.8
1963	32.6	9.0	0.0	79.9	8.7	1.9	12.2	3.3	75.3	39.6
1964	8.9	9.0	0.0	68.4	8.3	2.2	20.9	2.3	94.1	48.8
1965	14.6	13.5	50.0	71.3	8.4	3.0	15.7	0.6	82.4	47.4
1966	13.0	13.5	0.0	81.6	9.4	0.5	14.0	5.2	65.9	44.1
1967	7.3	15.8	16.9	83.9	10.2	2.1	21.9	2.0	83.8	41.1
1968	6.5	16.9	7.0	90.8	9.9	0.7	14.8	2.6	81.1	41.3
1969	8.6	17.8	5.6	93.6	10.5	2.0	19.5	3.5	75.3	41.8
1970	6.8	19.0	6.7	97.2	14.5	2.2	17.2	4.8	99.3	54.0
1971	13.6	20.8	9.4	101.6	17.1	3.0	10.9	4.6	92.5	47.0
1972	14.0	22.7	9.1	100.7	14.8	3.0	24.4	2.7	97.3	52.3
1973	23.5	24.7	8.6	99.5	17.4	2.8	29.3	2.2	103.9	64.3
1974	26.0	28.3	14.6	99.7	14.1	3.1	19.6	2.5	108.1	67.8
1975	17.7	32.5	15.1	100.0	14.1	3.2	27.8	0.9	100.0	66.2
1976	25.7	36.2	11.2	95.4	14.4	0.7	34.7	1.4	140.5	144.8
1977	28.4	37.7	4.2	85.7	18.5	1.8	30.4	-0.1	194.8	236.7
1978	18.8	40.8	8.1	85.5	16.2	0.1	30.3	0.6	145.4	164.8
1979	28.8	43.8	7.4	81.7	14.1	1.5	27.8	3.6	129.9	175.5
1980	26.0	50.6	15.5	83.5	14.4	2.3	34.7	3.0	132.1	156.2
1981	26.3	58.6	16.0	81.6	18.5	5.5	30.4	6.0	111.4	130.2
1982	24.0	69.6	18.7	75.6	16.2	6.0	30.3	6.2	108.1	142.1
1983	16.6	87.8	26.2	73.6	21.2	7.4	26.0	4.1	110.8	134.1
1984	18.3	112.8	28.4	79.9	20.0	5.9	23.4	2.8	114.6	146.6
1985	22.5	169.2	50.0	91.4	19.7	4.4	28.2	7.6	113.5	148.1
1986	20.9	217.0	28.2	108.5	18.0	0.3	22.8	3.4	138.3	196.7
1987	24.0	262.1	20.8	111.2	17.6	1.9	32.9	-0.0	106.7	116.1
1988	28.1	333.0	27.0	111.3	18.5	2.5	25.8	2.7	107.3	142.9
1989	26.1	429.3	28.9	113.5	18.7	2.4	29.1	1.4	85.2	116.2
1990	32.4	563.4	31.2	127.4	16.8	0.5	25.8	-0.0	92.3	95.1
1991	26.8	630.4	11.9	123.7	17.3	-0.0	30.6	-1.9	89.6	90.8
1992	25.1	733.4	16.3	117.4	19.1	-0.1	41.0	0.3	84.2	69.0
1993	22.6	803.5	9.6	118.2	18.4	-0.1	30.0	4.8	85.2	76.8
1994	22.6	829.2	3.2	109.8	23.4	-0.0	25.3	4.0	101.3	157.3
1995	19.5	988.2	19.7	111.7	0.4	20.2	5.8	99.0	158.4	29.3
1996	21.6	1000.4	1.2	109.1	1.9	16.5	8.2	95.8	131.2	36.7
1997	17.7	1296.9	29.6	101.9	3.1	21.7	6.7	96.4	194.3	32.6

(1) Percentage growth in CPI.
(2) End of period. *Source:* Banco de la República.
(3) Percentage growth in nominal exchange rate.
(4) From 1951 to 1974, this corresponds to the RER calculated with information for 10 trading partner countries. From 1975 to 1994, it corresponds to the RER published by the Banco de la República. *Source:* Revista del Banco de la República, IMF Statistics and authors' calculations.
(5) Consumption and investment expenditures of public administrations. *Source:* Herrera and Steiner (1997) and Dane.
(6) *Source:* Banco de la República (1993) and Dane.
(7) *Source:* Banco de la República (1993) and Revista del Banco de la República.
(8) Capital account of the balance of payments. *Source:* Banco de la República (1993), Revista del Banco de la República and DANE.
(9) *Source:* IMF.

Appendix 6.1. (cont.)

Mining exports (% of total exports)	Import tariffs (%)	Import licences (1951=100)	Productivity of nontradables (1951=100)	Productivity of tradables (%)	Venezuelan inflation (%)	Venezuelan devaluation (against the D-Mark)	Dollar appreciation (%)	Treasury bill rate (3 month)	U.S. inflation (% of GDP)	Fiscal incentive to devaluate
(11)	(12)	(13)	(14)	(15)	(16)	(17)	(18)	(19)	(20)	(21)
15.2	25.0	25.0	100.0	100.0	6.3	0.0	0.0	1.6	10.6	
14.8	19.4	20.0	98.2	100.1	0.0	0.0	0.0	1.8	-2.9	
12.6	21.0	15.0	95.0	100.4	-2.0	-3.5	0.0	1.9	-1.0	
11.4	21.8	10.0	95.9	98.2	2.7	14.5	0.0	1.0	0.2	
10.7	23.8	15.0	95.6	98.9	0.8	-12.0	0.4	1.8	0.2	
13.2	21.1	22.1	96.1	99.0	-2.4	0.4	-0.4	2.7	3.4	
15.9	16.7	29.1	97.3	98.4	0.4	3.4	0.1	3.3	2.7	
16.6	18.3	42.2	97.2	97.8	1.4	-0.0	-0.6	1.8	1.5	
17.3	18.5	39.0	96.9	95.0	2.6	-0.0	-0.2	3.4	0.2	
18.8	17.8	40.1	95.0	95.5	0.8	-0.0	0.0	2.9	0.2	
16.8	16.4	39.4	95.6	94.1	1.5	0.0	-4.2	2.4	-0.4	4.4
14.6	15.5	47.4	95.4	94.4	4.9	-0.0	0.1	2.8	0.2	3.9
18.1	13.7	62.4	94.7	94.6	3.1	0.0	-0.6	3.2	-0.4	4.1
15.0	12.7	62.7	95.1	93.1	4.2	34.4	0.1	3.6	0.2	3.8
17.7	15.8	84.9	94.5	94.8	3.4	-0.0	0.7	4.0	2.0	3.3
15.8	22.7	43.6	94.2	95.0	1.3	-0.0	-0.7	4.9	3.4	5.9
14.4	16.1	96.2	93.6	94.7	1.3	0.0	0.6	4.3	0.2	5.3
8.8	12.9	83.0	93.2	93.3	1.7	-0.0	0.0	5.3	2.4	5.3
11.8	14.1	82.8	92.5	92.3	1.6	0.0	-7.8	6.7	3.9	5.7
9.8	15.6	81.0	90.5	93.3	1.5	-0.0	-1.1	6.5	3.6	5.9
9.9	15.7	71.7	89.4	93.3	3.5	0.1	-10.4	4.3	3.3	5.0
7.1	16.7	71.9	89.5	90.9	3.4	-2.2	-2.0	4.1	4.4	5.3
4.9	15.9	68.8	87.2	91.0	6.4	-2.2	-15.6	7.0	13.1	5.5
7.8	12.8	56.4	87.0	89.4	16.5	-0.5	-10.9	7.9	18.8	4.5
7.1	13.0	57.2	87.8	89.8	14.3	0.0	8.8	5.8	9.3	4.4
4.0	12.8	60.2	86.9	90.2	7.2	0.1	-9.9	5.0	4.6	3.0
3.9	13.4	58.8	87.4	90.8	10.5	0.1	-10.9	5.3	6.1	3.3
4.2	12.7	57.2	87.1	88.3	7.3	0.0	-13.2	7.2	7.8	2.9
3.9	12.6	55.6	86.4	87.7	9.3	0.0	-5.3	10.0	12.5	3.6
2.6	12.0	56.0	86.0	87.6	19.9	0.0	13.1	11.6	14.2	3.6
1.3	11.4	47.8	86.4	88.9	13.9	0.0	15.1	14.1	9.1	3.4
7.0	11.4	45.3	85.3	90.5	8.1	0.0	5.4	10.7	2.0	2.7
15.3	10.7	58.6	86.0	90.6	6.9	0.1	14.6	8.6	1.2	2.6
14.6	10.4	71.9	86.5	88.2	17.5	63.3	15.6	9.6	2.4	3.9
15.1	16.1	85.2	85.9	88.1	15.2	6.9	-21.8	7.5	-0.5	4.8
15.9	18.9	57.6	86.3	83.5	17.6	7.8	-21.1	6.0	-2.9	9.8
31.1	24.0	54.7	88.1	80.0	44.8	79.4	-18.5	5.8	2.6	6.5
26.7	21.1	52.8	87.6	80.8	19.3	0.0	-0.1	6.7	4.0	4.1
33.5	19.5	55.3	88.8	78.5	97.5	139.2	7.4	8.1	5.0	5.0
39.3	18.0	38.3	87.7	77.7	27.2	35.2	-12.0	7.5	3.6	5.9
31.4	5.9	11.8	89.4	77.1	22.3	21.1	1.5	5.4	0.2	3.6
30.1	6.4	10.0	88.1	78.6	23.6	20.3	6.5	3.5	0.6	1.6
28.0	6.4	9.0	83.3	78.9	34.9	32.8	0.8	3.0	1.5	3.0
23.4	6.4	8.0	78.8	79.2	78.1	63.5	-4.8	4.3	1.3	3.7
6.4	57.8	19.1	-7.4	5.5	3.6	4.2				
6.4	103.2	136.0	8.5	5.0	2.3	5.8				
6.4	29.3	20.6	15.3	5.2	0.1	4.9				

(10) *Source:* Federación Nacional de Cafeteros de Colombia, Boletín de Información Estadística sobre Café, several issues, and Junguito and Pizano (1997).

(11) Includes oil, coal and ferroniquel exports. *Source:* Banco de la República Source: Banco de la República (1993).

(12) *Source:* Sánchez, Rodriguez and Nuñez (1996).

(13) Imports under licence requirement as percentage of total imports. From 1992 to 1994, it is assumed that this percentage decreased gradually. *Source:* Ocampo (1989b).

(14) and (15) *Source:* Suescún (1997).

(16) to (20): IMF.

(21) Computed as the following ratio: Import taxes + tax on coffee exports + annual change in external public debt - interests on external public debt + Ecopetrol net exports + coal exports/PIB. *Source:* Banco de la República, Ecopetrol and Musalem (1971).

CHAPTER SEVEN

Exchange Rates and Interest Groups in Peru, 1950-96

Alberto Pascó-Font
Piero Ghezzi[1]

A review of Peruvian exchange rate policies over the past 50 years prompts several questions. First, why did governments choose some exchange rate regimes over others? Second, why did governments target certain exchange rate levels? Third, why, during certain episodes, did governments refuse to abandon an exchange rate peg?

With respect to the choice of the exchange rate regime, the obvious extreme alternatives are fixed and pure floating, with several intermediate categories such as fixed rates with discrete realignments, crawling pegs, bands, and dirty floats. By choosing one exchange rate regime, a government simultaneously selects other underlying objectives. The most common tradeoff mentioned in the literature is that between volatility and flexibility. A fixed exchange rate is assumed to reduce volatility in the real exchange rate (RER) to the extent that prices are one order of magnitude less volatile. But this limits government's ability to counteract unanticipated real shocks. On the other hand, a flexible exchange rate allows the implementation of a discretionary policy to react to real shocks. This policy, however, is usually associated with a higher degree of RER volatility.[2]

In countries such as Peru that have experienced high chronic inflation, the relationship between real and nominal exchange rate volatility apparently breaks down: an increase in the volatility in the nominal ex-

---

[1] Alberto Pascó-Font is a researcher at the Grupo de Análisis para el Desarrollo in Lima. Piero Ghezzi is an economist at the Deutsche Bank.
[2] See Obstfeld (1997).

change rate does not necessarily imply an increase in volatility of the real exchange rate.[3] So the volatility-flexibility tradeoff is mitigated, and other factors need to be taken into account to explain such choices. Most notably, to the extent that inflation does not necessarily converge to international levels, the choice is not primarily between volatility and discretion, but between competitiveness and inflation. A fixed exchange rate provides a nominal anchor that can help to build the credibility necessary to fight inflation. At the same time, however, a pegged rate more often than not results in a real exchange rate appreciation that can jeopardize the viability of external accounts.

Peru's experience with the adoption of exchange regimes over the past 50 years has been particularly interesting because almost every type of system has been implemented. Two episodes, however, deserve special attention. The first was the adoption of a fixed exchange rate—de facto in the late 1950s and de jure in 1961—at a time when the country was experiencing high GDP growth rates. Factors contributing to this choice included a growing urban population, disenchantment with laissez-faire policies after years of terms of trade volatility, and the adoption of inward-oriented policies by other countries in the region. The second episode was the adoption of a flexible exchange rate in the 1990s, when most high-inflation countries had opted for exchange rate-based stabilization. This choice of exchange rate regimes apparently resulted from initial economic conditions, such as the lack of reserves to commit to a credible peg, and indirect pressure by the International Monetary Fund (IMF). It also seems that the system has been maintained until now mainly because of the political costs—and risks—of switching regimes.

A discussion of the second question—why governments have targeted certain exchange rate levels—assumes that government has some discretion over the exchange rate level. Empirical studies show that even if in the longer run the RER converges to purchasing power parity (PPP)—probably adjusted by productivity gains—in the short run there are important deviations from productivity-adjusted PPP. This suggests that short-term monetary and fiscal policies can affect the exchange rate level. To target a more depreciated exchange rate to increase competitiveness or to solve a balance of payments crisis is usually done at the expense of higher inflation. Peru's history of exchange rate policy shows certain periods—most of the 1960s and early 1970s, the mid-1980s and most of the 1990s—when the

---

[3] See Bufman and Leiderman (1995).

RER seems to be appreciated with respect to its equilibrium value. Thus, one of the main objectives of this chapter will be to understand why and how the government endured, or sometimes induced, such misalignment.

The third relevant question is related to the appropriate timing for abandoning an exchange rate peg. There are at least two approaches. One requires a devaluation, followed by fixing at a new level, and another is to introduce a more flexible system. In general, those shifts are associated with huge political costs because they have short-term contractionary implications. For this reason, pegs are in several cases abandoned too late.

There are at least three episodes in Peru over the past 50 years when needed exchange rate adjustments were postponed: in the 1960s, in the early 1970s and from 1985 to 1987. While econometric techniques cannot readily test an exchange rate switch, a narrative section below discusses the first of these episodes in detail.

The history of Peruvian exchange rates demonstrates that interest group pressures, as well as overall policy orientation, help to explain both the choice of exchange rate regime and the degree of misalignment. The industrial sector oriented to the domestic market (both entrepreneurs and unions) pushed for a protectionist tariff level, a fixed exchange rate regime and a stronger (appreciated) currency. When tariffs were low, however, the sector was less prone to accept an overvalued real exchange rate. The results also suggest that export subsidies played a role in compensating the export sector, reducing pressures for a more depreciated currency. These results must be viewed with caution, however, due to the difficulty of estimating from relatively small samples and the limited capacity of the measures used to proxy for underlying economic variables.

Exchange Rate Policies

Peru has experimented over the past 50 years with numerous exchange rate regimes established by policies with a variety of purposes. These have included providing a nominal anchor to fight inflation, an instrument to promote international competitiveness, and an important relative price within a set of policies aimed at industrializing the country.

By any standards, Peru was an outward-oriented economy in the 1950s. For example, the ratio of exports plus imports to GDP exceeded 45 percent in 1960. Exports were concentrated in agricultural and mining products, and economic policies were basically laissez-faire. Unlike most Latin American nations, which had a fixed nominal exchange rate, Peru opted for a floating exchange rate regime. This had followed a negative experience with fixed exchange rates in the mid-1940s.[4] This regime was maintained until 1954, when the central bank increased its intervention in the foreign exchange market. During most of the 1950s, however, exchange rate policy was designed to maintain a weak (i.e., depreciated) real exchange rate in order to raise the domestic currency price of exportables (most of which were commodities). Thus, when the terms of trade deteriorated in 1957, generating a balance of payments crisis, the currency was devalued by 20 percent in January 1958. This devaluation was followed by a large-scale and by-the-book stabilization program in 1959.

However, in the mid-1950s, a development paradigm based on exporting raw materials was already being questioned. The instability of raw material prices, along with the theories put forth by the Economic Commission on Latin America and the Caribbean (ECLAC), encouraged a gradual policy shift in favor of the incipient manufacturing sector as opposed to the still-powerful export sector. As Thorp and Bertram (1978, p. 262) stated: "A turning point for industrialization can thus be identified in the last year or so of the Odria government, as a new generation of manufacturing ventures came on to the scene. The new firms of the 1950s represented the first steps in a diversion of the local elite interest away from export activities and toward non-export sectors, including manufacturing."

In addition to the stabilization package, the Industrial Promotion Law was also enacted in 1959. This law, originally proposed in 1955, could be considered the first effort to promote industrialization by means of an import substitution strategy.

Within this new development paradigm, exchange rate intervention was increased, and the exchange rate was finally fixed in February 1961. As discussed further below, an appreciated rate was consistent with the need to provide cheap foodstuffs to the growing urban population as well as cheap inputs and equipment to the industrial sector. The exchange rate regime was also linked to other policies. For example, tariffs were raised substantially in order to protect manufacturers of final goods for the domestic market. Simultaneously, though, tariff exemptions were granted to intermediate and capital goods demanded by the industrial sector. These measures were complemented by an agrarian reform that was timidly launched in the southern part of the country.

A fixed exchange rate, coupled with an inflation rate of 83 percent between 1961 and 1967—well above international levels and with-

---

[4] Peru was the only Latin American country that did not introduce exchange rate controls after the Great Depression. See Rojas (1996).

out major changes in productivity–generated a very strong appreciation of the real exchange rate. The strong anti-export bias was reflected in a deterioration of the trade balance. This time the government was reluctant to devalue, but a speculative attack forced a 44.3 percent devaluation in September 1967.

Economic failure–made obvious by the exchange rate devaluation–prompted a military coup in 1968. The new military government considered the previously implemented import substitution measures insufficient and embarked on a package of reforms that constituted one of the most radical import substitution programs in Latin America. The agrarian reform and a far-reaching nationalization of mining and oil companies seriously affected those economic groups that could push for a higher RER, and Peru's economy entered a stage of maintaining a strong RER as a precondition for achieving industrialization.

The agrarian reform and the nationalization of mining and petroleum companies severely affected the ability of exporters, concentrated in agriculture and mining, to pressure the government for a devalued exchange rate; the new policies displayed a marked pro-industrial bias. In addition, land reform in the coastal region implied the transfer of vast *haciendas* to workers who were not ready to manage them; sugar and cotton exports consequently began to decline. The new agricultural cooperatives, for their part, were never able to organize themselves into a pressure group. At the same time, the administration of the state mining companies followed political imperatives rather than economic principles, subsidizing the emerging industrial sector through low energy prices and an overvalued exchange rate.

The new government kept the nominal exchange fixed, enacted a new industrial law (*Ley General de Industrias*) in 1970, and increased protection even further. A favorable evolution in the terms of trade and the discovery of oil in Peru's interior during the first oil shock nonetheless allowed the country to access international financial markets, which were glutted with petrodollars at the time. As a consequence, during 1973 and 1974 the government could subsidize oil and foodstuffs without adjusting the exchange rate. The gradual increase in the manufacturing share of GDP, as well as the growing process of urbanization, contributed to shaping new powerful economic groups interested in keeping a strong RER and a highly restrictive tariff structure.

Once favorable international prices and lending disappeared, the economy's weaknesses became apparent. In addition, oil reserves proved to be much lower than initially expected. A steep deterioration in the terms of trade, which began in 1974, along with a fiscal deficit, produced a balance of payments crisis in 1975. These conditions forced a change in the military government, which imposed adjustment measures that included a 45 percent devaluation after eight years of fixed rates.

Peru's economic difficulties exacerbated the country's social tensions. While industrialists supported the regime, labor unions organized the first general strike. It was during this period that the central bank regained control of economic policymaking, at least partially as a result of pressure from foreign creditors and the IMF. Subsequent adjustment measures included a new devaluation in June 1976, followed by the implementation of a crawling peg system. In July 1977, the exchange rate was fixed again, followed by a very short period of dirty float and the implementation of a pre-announced crawling peg system in 1978. Current account deficits of 8.9 percent in 1976 and 7.7 percent in 1977 forced the government to implement other policies to reduce aggregate demand. Nonetheless, given that the government could still access some foreign funds, it did not implement a coherent stabilization program until 1978.

Over 1975-77, the government was reluctant to apply a drastic stabilization program because of the social cost of such a package. The resulting use of partial or incomplete measures generated growing imbalances. It is interesting to compare the unwillingness to adjust in this period with the relative ease with which stabilization packages were implemented during the 1950s. As mentioned above, when terms of trade deteriorated in 1957, the government was quick to undertake a by-the-book stabilization program. However, after more than a decade of import substitution, the industrial sector and urban workers, accustomed to subsidized food and energy prices, would not readily accept either a devaluation or a tax increase. Indeed, 1978 was one of the country's worst years for strikes. Even public school attendance was suspended for several months because of a general strike organized by the teachers' union.

The first serious stabilization program aimed at reducing the level of expenditure was implemented in 1978, when political discontent, the critical situation of the external sector, and the lack of access to external credit allowed no other option. In that year, the military government announced a timetable to amend the Constitution and hold democratic elections in 1980.

During those years, the promotion of nontraditional exports, a process begun in the 1960s, was intensified. Between 1976 and 1978, the real exchange rate depreciated 60 percent while, from 1975 to 1979, nontraditional exports increased eightfold.

The dramatic improvement in the terms of trade in 1979-80 helped to reverse the current account situation and almost automatically solved the public sector deficit. Silver prices quadrupled between 1978 and 1980, and the second oil shock occurred shortly after Peru had opened an oil pipeline from the interior to a coastal port. A 17 percent export tax, introduced as part of the 1978 stabilization package, allowed the government to acquire a substantial share of export boom revenues and improve public sector accounts.

While capital inflows had not changed substantially, international reserves accumulated. The sudden export boom, and the related inflow of foreign exchange, both occurring while the crawling peg system was maintained, forced an appreciation of the real exchange rate. As Peru's financial markets were quite underdeveloped at that time, the central bank lacked the instruments to sterilize the sudden inflow of foreign exchange, and monetization of foreign reserves neutralized previous government efforts to reduce inflation. The government prepaid some foreign debt, which had been refinanced in previous years, and began to liberalize imports in order to reduce inflationary pressures.

As the external disequilibrium was corrected, exchange rate policy was redirected towards fighting inflation. In 1980, the newly elected Belaúnde administration launched an aggressive investment plan based on the assumption that the improvement in terms of trade was largely permanent. Peru's position at the time was enviable, with a favorable external context and a newly elected democratic government. It was therefore easy for Belaúnde's government to launch an ambitious foreign indebtedness plan that was aimed mainly at the construction sector, including both roads and housing.

The favorable external situation of 1979 and 1980 was reversed in 1981 and 1982, however, as the Peruvian economy experienced negative terms of trade shocks and higher international interest rates. Again, the government was reluctant to adjust, apparently hoping that the reversal in the terms of trade was only temporary. It devoted a substantial part of foreign lending to cushioning the situation without taking any serious stabilization measures. Trade tariffs were also increased as a way to cope with the external situation.

In 1981, the current account deficit reached 8 percent of GDP. When the external and internal disequilibria were no longer tolerable, the government ended up undertaking drastic measures to increase government savings and pursue real exchange rate devaluation. In 1983, when Peru's economy was hard-hit by the El Niño climatic effect, GDP decreased by more than 13 percent. Much of this recession, though, stemmed from underlying economic imbalances rather than climatic factors. Again, the reluctance to adjust to a negative external shock increased the magnitude of the imbalances, eventually increasing the costs of adjustment. After the 1983 El Niño, the government hit bottom. It stopped servicing international banks' foreign debt and was forced to negotiate several refinancing deals, as well as enter into IMF monitoring, which prompted an adjustment plan.

Exchange rate policy went basically unmodified from the end of 1983, when the crawl was accelerated, until the end of Belaúnde's term in July 1985, as the government maintained a high real exchange rate to ensure the country's competitiveness. This approach, however, generated inflationary pressures, and the real term prices of basic items such as gasoline, water and electricity substantially increased in a context of growing inflation. In the first months of 1985 inflation rose to an annual rate of around 250 percent, and the country was immersed in an inflation-devaluation spiral. As a result of restrictive fiscal and monetary measures, however, Peru achieved both fiscal and external balances. By the end of Belaúnde's term the country had $1.5 billion in foreign reserves and the public sector was running a surplus.

In August 1985, the newly elected García administration launched a heterodox stabilization program in the spirit of the Austral and Cruzado Plans in Argentina and Brazil, respectively, using the exchange rate as one of several anchors to reduce inflation. As expected, freezing prices of most products helped to reduce inflation. In addition, expansive fiscal policies encouraged growth, as GDP grew by 9.3 percent in 1986 and 8.3 percent in 1987. However, the government did not undertake major adjustments to the underlying sources of inflation, which remained substantially above international levels. Favorable starting conditions such as a relatively high stock of foreign reserves and healthy public sector finances delayed a crisis. But the maintenance of price controls and a fixed exchange rate eventually generated major distortions in the economy, especially as García limited foreign debt payments in order to direct resources to domestic public expenditures. By 1987, the underlying disequilibria were evident. The country was running out of foreign reserves, there was a drastic current account deficit, and the public deficit reached 5.7 percent of GDP.

A multiple exchange rate system was introduced in subsequent years. This system had two objectives that, under the circumstances, were inconsistent in the short run: keeping inflation under control and avoiding an excessive deterioration of external accounts. As expected, the system failed and a sharp reduction in aggregate demand, serving as an automatic stabilizer, proved the only way to reduce the external deficit.

From early 1987 until the first months of 1990, the government implemented several incomplete stabilization packages. A strong official rate for certain transactions maintained the role of the exchange rate as an anchor to fight inflation. Although the stabilization measures were somehow successful in regaining the external balance, a growing public sector deficit continued to fuel inflation. In an attempt to boost the chances of the official candidate toward the end of its term, the government tried to generate a small consumption boom with its remaining reserves. The attempt was a failure. While international reserves were depleted, the recession continued, and inflation in the 12 months before July 1990 was almost 5,000 percent.

In August 1990, newly elected president Alberto Fujimori launched a comprehensive stabilization program. Unlike other successful stabilization programs in the region, the exchange rate was not pegged. On the contrary, the rate was allowed to float with a certain degree of intervention, and the somewhat contractionary monetary policy contributed to the appreciation of the real exchange rate.[5] The real exchange rate generally remained strong in the years that followed. The central bank undertook limited sterilized interventions with the objective of depreciating the RER, or at least avoiding further appreciation, but without major success. These interventions were, moreover, undertaken only to the extent that they were consistent with the objective of containing inflation; following the international financial crisis in the late 1980s, the real exchange rate depreciated and monetary policy was aimed at limiting the negative effects of excessive exchange rate volatility. These measures were accompanied by Fujimori's abandonment, after almost two decades of failure, of Peru's previous industrialization-based paradigm of development. This model was replaced by a new scheme in which markets played a central role. International pressures, represented by the World Bank and the IMF, played a crucial role in this transformation.

Potential Determinants of Exchange Rate Policies

External Shocks

As Peru is a small and open economy, external factors are likely to directly and indirectly affect both the type and level of its exchange rate policies. As is well known, deterioration of the terms of trade usually requires a depreciation of the real exchange rate. If the exchange rate is

---

[5] The fact that real appreciation was widespread in Latin America during the 1990s leads one to believe that it was more related to external factors, as suggested by Calvo, Leiderman and Reinhart (1993).

fixed, the required real depreciation could be achieved either by reducing the domestic price level or devaluing the local currency. The first option is usually difficult due to downward nominal rigidities prevailing in the economy. Therefore, a sustained and significant deterioration in the terms of trade usually forces the devaluation of the local currency. Of course, the more diversified the export base is, the less shock-prone the economy will be. Thus, changes in the structure of exports could indirectly affect the exchange rate regime and level.

Fluctuations in international interest rates can also affect exchange rate policy. Two of the most important effects of these fluctuations are their impacts on fiscal accounts and capital flows. The impact on fiscal deficits is positively correlated with the level of foreign debt, while the effect on capital inflows is largely affected by the degree of openness of the capital account.

Intellectual Climate, Overall Policy Orientation and Other External Constraints

The international environment is certainly relevant to the adoption of exchange rate policies. Sustainable exchange rate policies need to be consistent with a general policy orientation and the international environment. For example, floating rates operate better when capital and goods are free to move. Furthermore, a fixed exchange rate can impose severe risks in countries with relatively weak financial institutions and open capital accounts. This is consistent with the evidence that a larger percentage of countries have more flexible exchange rates now than 20 years ago (see Obstfeld and Rogoff, 1995).

In Peru, when the economy has been more liberalized, the exchange rate has tended to float, while in periods of greater government intervention in the economy, the exchange rate has been more fixed. For example, during the 1950s the floating exchange rate system worked better in an environment of high capital mobility of factors and very low protection. Once the government started to intervene more heavily, promoting the manufacturing sector, the exchange rate was fixed. Similarly, in the 1990s the process of structural reforms and the complete liberalization of capital and current accounts made a flexible system more natural.

Another related instrument is trade policy. It is very easy to draw links between trade and exchange rate policies. For example, for the import-competing sector, exchange rate and trade policies can be substitutes. Different combinations of levels of the real exchange rates and tariffs or quotas can equally protect the sector. In the Peruvian experience, this can be seen in the

1960s and 1970s, when the low exchange rate, consistent with low food prices and cheap inputs and capital goods, was accompanied by a tariff structure that granted high protection to manufacturers of final goods. Similarly, the export sector was compensated with export subsides that averaged 20 percent.[6]

Distributional Issues and Interest Groups

As the world grows more integrated, both in terms of goods and financial assets, the exchange rate becomes the key price of an economy. As a consequence, various groups are affected by exchange rate policies and try to influence it. Frieden (1994) maintains that, in general, tradables producers will prefer a weak (i.e., depreciated) exchange rate while nontradables producers will favor a strong (i.e., appreciated) RER. Similarly, domestic producers can be expected to favor more flexible exchange rates. However, it is necessary to take into account heterogeneity within the tradables sector. In general, one would expect the import-competing sector and the export-oriented sector to favor a more depreciated currency. However, for years the import-competing manufacturing sector has been protected by high tariffs on final manufactured goods, which makes the sector nontradable, de facto. If that is the case, the domestically oriented manufacturing sector would favor an appreciated currency in periods of high levels of protection, while demanding a more depreciated currency when protection is low.

Similarly, the extent to which the export-oriented sector is affected depends on its cost structure. Ex ante, one would expect the mining sector to be less affected by the real exchange rate due to its highly dollarized cost structure, while more labor-intensive nontraditional exporters should be more RER sensitive. It is thus hypothesized that nontraditional exporters represented by the *Asociación de Exportadores* (ADEX) are more concerned with the evolution of the real exchange rate.

Another issue related to interest groups is the effect of the degree of dollarization. One would expect creditors to be more concentrated than depositors and, to that extent, more able to exert pressure to avoid a devaluation or a high real exchange rate depreciation (in the case of a floating system). One caveat related to the importance of interest groups as an explanatory variable of exchange rate policy choices is that some of the most prominent economic groups are widely diversi-

---

[6] See Rojas (1996).

fied. Thus, while certain members of the group lose as a result of a particular policy, others gain. The need to favor or fight a particular policy could thus be substantially lessened.

Political and Institutional Variables

Exchange rate policy is often used as a mechanism to provide short-term benefits to the electorally significant urban population. For example, one should expect that, ceteris paribus, the real exchange rate would be more depreciated when governments take office and more appreciated towards the end of their term. It is very likely, for instance, that the probability of devaluation decreases significantly when elections are imminent. This is partially because the negative income effect of the devaluation, as a result of the reduction of real wages, is in the short run larger than the positive substitution effect. In the same spirit, one would expect that on average democratic governments would have a more appreciated currency than dictatorships, since the former are account-able for their actions.

Also worth noting is the effect of different political bases of gov-ernment on exchange rate policies. While some suggest that the degree of political stability can affect exchange rate policy, this effect can go both ways. On the one hand, a more stable government can more easily obtain support for fixing the exchange rate. On the other, a more unstable govern-ment may want to fix the exchange rate to gain credibility. Determining which effect is likely to dominate is an empirical problem.

The role of the central bank and its willingness to finance fiscal deficits definitely affect the exchange rate outcome. As the central bank becomes more independent, one should expect a more contractionary monetary policy and, as a result, a more appreciated exchange rate.

Methodology and Data

One challenge of studies involving institutional and political factors is to accurately capture the variables that are considered important. The ob-jective here is to provide some statistical tests of exchange rate policy choices. Of course, given the small sample size and the fact that institu-tional variables change very slowly over time, the results can only sug-gest the significance of certain factors. More importantly, it is difficult to accurately measure some of the effects suggested in the preceding dis-cussion. The statistical analysis of this section is thus followed by a more detailed description of particular episodes.

Regime Choice

The objective in this case is to explain the choice of exchange rate regime. The dependent variable here is discrete according to the different exchange rate regimes available. It is worth mentioning at this point that the choice of a particular exchange rate regime usually represents underlying preferences about the degree of volatility, the level of the real exchange rate, and the level of inflation, among other factors. These preferences are taken into account in an effort to capture regime choice.

A multinomial logit model is thus proposed.[7] The variable Y takes the value $0, 2 \ldots j$, where $j + 1$ is the number of exchange regimes available. The probability of a particular exchange regime's occurring will be:

$$Prob \ (Y \ = j \ ) = \frac{e^{\beta_j' x_i}}{1 + \sum_{k=1}^{j} e^{\beta_k' x_i}}$$

where the likelihood ratios can be computed by:

$$\ln(\frac{P_{ij}}{P_{iK}}) = x_i' (\beta_j - \beta_K)$$

and the estimates can be obtained from the log likelihood function:

$$\ln L \ = \sum_{i=1}^{n} \sum d_{ij} \ \ln Prob(Y_i = j)$$

With regard to the exchange rate regime variable, there are different possible classifications of exchange rate regimes. One approach is the IMF classification, which encompasses the following regimes: i) currencies pegged to a single currency or a composite of currencies; ii) currencies whose flexibility is limited in terms of a single currency or a group of currencies; and iii) managed and independent floating currencies.

The classification is not useful for the present objective because it does not distinguish, within the second group, between systems intended to control inflation and those intended to maintain a desired RER level. In

---

[7] See Greene (1997).

order to take that distinction into account, the following classification is proposed: i) currency pegged to another currency or to a group of currencies; ii) forward-looking crawling peg; iii) backward-looking crawling peg; iv) floating (including dirty floating); and v) periods of collapse or crisis.

As mentioned above, at least theoretically, the choice of a regime implies certain preferences regarding underlying objectives, particularly the degree of inflation and the level of appreciation. The exchange rate has been used in Latin America in general and Peru in particular on several occasions as an instrument to fight inflation, generally at a cost of real appreciation. At other times the exchange rate has been used to enhance competitiveness at the cost of higher inflation. This is the basic tradeoff in exchange rate policy.

In order to illustrate this point, Table 7.1 shows the average levels of inflation and real exchange rates for the different exchange rate regimes. Not surprisingly, the fixed exchange rate is associated with the lowest level of inflation and with the more appreciated real exchange rate, whereas the periods of backward-looking pegs are associated with the highest inflation (if periods of collapse or crisis are excluded) and a more depreciated currency. Other variables that affect the level of inflation or the real exchange rate are not included.

The results suggest an ordered estimation. For example, periods of backward-looking crawling pegs are associated with relatively high inflation and real exchange rate levels. This is not surprising, since, in general, these systems are aimed at achieving a depreciated real exchange rate, usually at the cost of inflation. Similarly, periods of a fixed exchange rate usually are characterized by low inflation and an appreciated real exchange rate

Due to these characteristic and the small sample size, regimes 0 and 2 have been regrouped, and regimes are reclassified in the following order: regime 0–fixed and forward-looking crawling pegs; regime 1–pure and dirty floating; regime 2–crisis; and regime 3–backward-looking crawling pegs.

In order to account for regime choice, the following explanatory variables are proposed:

i) Log of level of inflation lagged (inflation(-1)). This variable is expected to have a negative sign, which implies that fixed exchange rates are consistent only with low inflation.

ii) Share of exports over GDP as a proxy of the power of this group to influence the exchange rate policy. Here a distinction is made between mining and nonmining exporters (XMIN(-1)) and XNMIN(-1)). Both variables are expected to have a positive sign, although the variable that reflects the mining sector should be less important. The tests thus focus

Table 7.1. Inflation and Real Exchange Rates under Different Regimes

Regime	Inflation (%)	Real exchange rate
Fixed	18.5	93.03
Collapse	2,500.0	122.12
Forward-looking crawling peg	67.8	108.53
Backward-looking crawling peg	107.0	136.59
Floating	25.2	104.27

on the share of the export sector in GDP as opposed to the size of the tradables sector in general due to the lack of reliable data.

iii) Share of the domestically oriented manufacturing sector (approximated by total industrial output less manufacturing exports) in total output, as a measure of the ability of this group to influence economic policy. This assumes that the exchange rate affects the manufacturing sector in two ways: first, the exchange rate affects the price of inputs, and second, competition with foreign products affects the price of final goods. MAGDP (-1) is manufacturing output as a percentage of total output lagged one period. MAGDPTAR (-1) results from multiplying the previous variable by a dummy that takes the value of 1 when tariffs are below 30 percent. Thus, MAGDPTAR (-1) equals MAGDP (-1) if tariffs are below 30 percent, and 0 otherwise. As a result, when the economy is closed due to high tariffs or quantitative restrictions, the manufacturing sector will benefit from a more appreciated currency and will favor fixed regimes or forward-looking crawling pegs.

iv) A dummy that qualifies the type of government (DICT=1 if dictatorship, 0 otherwise). As mentioned before, one should expect that the variable has a negative sign, as dictatorships should be less concerned with keeping an appreciated real exchange rate.

v) Percentage of the population in the urban sector, measured by URB. One should expect a larger urban population to be more concerned with an appreciated real exchange rate. The sign of the coefficient is expected to be positive.

The results appear in the first row of Table 7.2.

Before interpreting the coefficients, one should notice that the effect of an increase in the explanatory variables on the probabilities of a particular exchange rate system is not unambiguously determined by the coefficients (see Greene, 1997). Indeed, it can only be determined with extra calculation. Nevertheless, the sign of the effects of the explanatory

Table 7.2. Ordered Logit Regressions for Regime

	(1)	(2)	(3)*
INFLATION	.41		
	(0.92)		
INFLATION1		0.58	.52
		(1.94)	(1.27)
MAGDP (-1)	-75.58	-68.56	-155.95
	(-2.61)	(-2.38)	(-3.02)
MAGDPTAR (-1)	7.93	10.06	19.90
	(1.88)	(2.38)	(2.69)
XMIN (-1)	30.84	36.45	125.4
	(0.86)	(0.99)	(2.32)
XNMIN (-1)	-72.55	-71.9	-133
	(-1.82)	(-1.8)	(-2.42)
DICT	1.58	1.74	1.93
	(1.93)	(2.12)	(1.73)
URB	8.94	11.98	25.04
	(0.94)	(1.24)	(1.95)

*Excludes periods of exchange rate collapse.
Note: t-statistics in parentheses.

variables on the two ends of the ordered choices is correctly determined by the coefficients of the above equation.

The sign of the coefficient of inflation is not significant, although the sign is as expected. The sign of the manufacturing sector is also as predicted, and it is significant: for high tariff levels, the manufacturing sector will favor a fixed exchange rate system, whereas low tariff levels may cause manufacturers to be more concerned with a high real exchange rate. For the export sector, either in mining or other activities, coefficients are not significant. The variable for urbanization (URB) is not significant and has the opposite sign. The variable for type of government (DIC) suggests a relation opposite to what was expected.

The lack of significance of the inflation coefficient is not totally surprising. This is probably due to the non-linearity of the relation, which even the smoothing filter fails to remove.[8] In column (2) inflation is smoothed differently (the smoother variable is now called INFLATION1).

---

[8] The inflation variable is measured log $(1 + \pi)$, where π is the rate of inflation.

The results of this modification appear in column (2). While the coefficients of the other variables are basically unaltered, inflation becomes significant at 5.3 percent.[9]

Column (3) excludes periods of exchange rate collapse, since during those periods there is not an explicit choice of regime. The results do not change significantly, although the coefficient of mining exports becomes significant, whereas other nonmining exports are significant, but with the opposite sign.

These results are counterintuitive. Two explanations, though, may be offered. First, the proxy of the export sector's strength may be poorly captured by its share of GDP. Its degree of cohesion, for example, can be equally important. Second, the export sector can be less concerned about the exchange rate system if it is compensated through other mechanisms.

It is worth mentioning that the variable that measures the effect of the type of government on the regime choice enters with the unexpected sign, and at the borderline of significance. These results could be explained by the fact that, unlike other military governments in Latin America, the Peruvian regime had a socialist orientation.

Real Exchange Rate Targeting

A second line of research will try to explain the level of the exchange rate. As stated above, the government can affect the level of the exchange rate, at least in the short run, even if in the long run the rate is going to return to its equilibrium value.

The real exchange rate is affected by both fundamental and nonfundamental variables. Fundamental variables include terms of trade, nonpolicy induced openness, a measure of productivity, and long-term capital flows. Changes in these variables affect the real exchange rate, though changes in the equilibrium exchange rate do not necessarily reflect an explicit objective of the government with regard to the level of the real exchange rate. The theory clearly states the expected effects of each fundamental variable on the RER.[10] Thus, an improvement in the terms of trade could be the result either of an increase in the demand for domestic output or a reduction in the relative supply of domestic output. In both scenarios the exchange rate

---

[9] The use of dummy variables for hyperinflation was also attempted, but the likelihood function failed to converge.
[10] See Edwards (1988) and Williamson (1995).

is going to be appreciated. An increase in domestic productivity relative to the rest of the world also appreciates the exchange rate as a result of the Balassa-Samuelson effect, and an increase in capital inflows increases the demand for domestic output and results in an appreciation of the RER. Finally, a reduction in tariff levels reduces the demand for domestic output and results in the depreciation of the RER. Other nonfundamental variables will also affect real exchange rate levels. Those variables will be similar to the RHS variables used in the ordered logit model of the previous section.

The following model is estimated:

$$LnRER = X_F \beta_F + X_{NF} \beta_{NF} + \varepsilon \qquad (1)$$

where X_F and X_{NF} represent fundamental and nonfundamental variables respectively and ε is an error term, probably autocorrelated.

Alternatively, equation (1) could have been estimated directly by following two steps: first, estimating the degree of misalignment and, second, explaining it as a function of political or institutional variables that reflect government action. The level of misalignment would be the error term in the regression of the fundamental variables on the real exchange rate. Thus it would be possible to estimate:

$$LnRER - X_F \beta_F = X_{NF} \beta_{NF} + \varepsilon$$

which would be equivalent to the previous one if at the small sample level the regressors X_F and X_{NF} are orthogonal, which is not necessarily the case.

In order to estimate equation (1), it is necessary to determine whether series are stationary. Existing unit root tests are generally of low power for a short sample and very often fail to reject the hypothesis of a unit root. The existing literature finds that the RER converges to its long run trend. For example, Frankel and Rose (1996), using a panel for 150 countries, found that the average half time of deviation from PPP (once time trends are adjusted) is approximately four and a half years. Other studies have been consistent with those estimations.

This suggests that exchange rates are trend-stationary as opposed to difference-stationary and, therefore, more traditional econometric techniques of estimation can be used. In line with this, it is assumed that variables are stationary and Generalized Least Squares are used, due to the existence of autocorrelation on the residuals, to estimate the equation above. The estimates appear in Table 7.3. The variables are similar to the ones used in the previous subsection. Two extra variables are introduced as well: capital inflows (Kflows) and productivity measured by the Solow residual (Solow).

The results indicate that among the fundamental variables both productivity and capital inflows are significant. Among the nonfundamental variables, again the variables that capture the manufacturing sector are significant.

It should be kept in mind that the derivative of an increase in the importance of the manufacturing sector is:

$$\beta_3 + \beta_4 d$$

where d is a dummy variable that takes the value of 1 when tariffs are below 30 percent. Therefore, the results confirm the priors, as well as the priors in the previous section that β_3 is negative and β_4 is positive. This is not surprising. High tariffs in place in Peru from 1964 until 1990, except for a short interval in the late 1970s, implied that most of the manufacturing sector would be nontradable and, therefore, favoring more appreciated currency. On the other hand, in the 1950s and 1990s—years of low protection—the manufacturing sector faced competition from imported goods, and its stance toward exchange rate policy was less clear.

Similar to the estimations in the ordered logit, the effect of the importance of the export sector on the real exchange rate is not significant, which raises doubts regarding how well the variable captures the export sector's ability to exert pressure.

One variable that has not been used, and may have potential importance, is export subsidies (CERTEX). Loosely speaking, exporters that receive these subsidies will have a total profitability, which will be affected by:[11]

$$ln((RER)(1+certex)) = ln\, RER + ln(1+certex)$$

which implies that in the presence of the RER as a left-hand side variable, the existence of export subsidies will reduce pressures by the export sector for a higher real exchange rate. The intuition is that compensation CERTEX reduces pressure for a more depreciated currency. Since those subsides did not exist before 1970 and were eliminated at the beginning of the Fujimori administration in 1990, they cannot be included in the full sample. The regression is therefore run for the sub-sample 1970-89. The results appear in column (2) of Table 7.3.

---

[11] The equation is not exact because the RER also affects the price of imported inputs; however, as long as technological coefficients are constant, the equation will hold.

Table 7.3. Estimation of the Real Exchange Rate

	(1)	(2)
Constant	5.46	8.54
	(.44)	(7.13)
Kflows	-2.81	-3.90
	(-2.58)	(-1.12)
Solow	-0.93	-.57
	(-3.13)	(-1.10)
MAGDP(-1)	-3.68	-10.38
	(-2.07)	(-4.91)
MAGDPTAR (-1)	0.51	1.49
	(2.07)	(3.24)
XMIN (-1)	-0.02	-4.10
	(-.01)	(-1.12)
XNMIN(-1)	-0.67	-2.70
	(-0.53)	(-1.15)
CERTEX		-2.04
		(-1.81)

Note: t-statistics in parentheses.

Of course, results with a very small sample must be interpreted with caution. Still, the results regarding the preferences of the manufacturing sector hold. CERTEX has the correct sign and is significant at 10 percent. This can be seen as mildly supporting the hypothesis that the existence of export subsidies reduces pressure for a more depreciated exchange rate, in an environment in which economic groups are highly diversified and to that extent might prefer a direct export subsidy.

As in previous estimations, the coefficients that attempt to measure the export sector interests are not significant, either for mining or other export activities. This contradicts the prior that the nonmining export sector should press for a depreciated currency.

Elections and the Real Exchange Rate

It was hypothesized above that on several occasions the exchange rate has been manipulated for electoral purposes. One would expect an appreciated real exchange rate before elections for a variety of reasons. First, an appreciated exchange rate is usually consistent with low inflation, which

Figure 7.1. Elections and the Real Exchange Rate

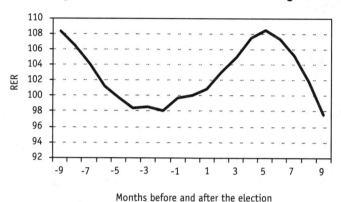

Months before and after the election

governments might be interested in delivering. Second, a nominal depreciation usually leads to a real depreciation and is contractionary in the short
term (see Agenor and Montiel, 1996). For that reason, governments may
be reluctant to devalue before elections, and this reluctance can contribute
to an appreciated RER. Third, governments tend to spend more before
elections and that per se appreciates the real exchange rate. After elections,
depreciations are less costly in political terms.

Figure 7.1 shows the real exchange rate nine months before and
after presidential elections. Even though it is necessary to be cautious about
drawing general conclusions from a small number of elections—Peru has
held only six elections in the last 50 years—the almost picture-perfect political business cycle is nonetheless surprising: a continuous appreciation consistently occurs before elections and a depreciation immediately afterward.

Complementary Analysis

To complement the previous econometric analysis, this section analyzes
three particular episodes of Peruvian exchange rate policy in order to illustrate how the choice of regime is also affected by noneconomic variables.

Adoption of a Fixed Exchange Rate in 1959:
Preference for a Strong Currency and Reluctance to Devalue

As previously mentioned, the government switched from a floating exchange
rate to a de facto fixed exchange rate in the late 1950s and de jure in 1961.

Since average annual economic growth during the 1950s was 5 percent and exchange rate volatility was not particularly high, the question is why was the change in policy made.

It is important to highlight that a floating exchange rate was consistent with overall policy orientation in the 1950s, when goods and capital were free to move in response to market forces. Thus, adoption of the fixed exchange rate is better understood if one takes into account the abandonment of the laissez-fare paradigm that prevailed in the 1950s and the adoption of a development paradigm aimed at promoting industrialization.

There are several possible explanations for why the development paradigm based on exporting raw materials was questioned during the mid-1950s. First, there was an important decline in the profitability of exports. As Thorp and Bertram (1978, p. 218) show, while total returned value in the mining sector as a percentage of gross value of output was 72 percent in 1952, it fell to 53 percent in 1960, due mainly to high repatriation rates. Similarly, there were signs that natural resources were being depleted. This was very clear in petroleum, but it was also true for other nonmineral exports such as cotton and sugar.

Second, the external environment was a very important factor. ECLAC's theories about economic development encouraged a gradual policy shift aimed at benefiting the incipient manufacturing sector, as opposed to the still powerful export sector. Similarly, researchers such as Singer, Lewis, Hirshman and Myrdal questioned the free trade paradigm and proposed the idea of balanced growth and the need for import substitution. Indeed, the Industrial Promotional Law of 1959 was prepared with the "encouragement" of an ECLAC mission.

Third, major social and institutional changes were occurring. Population growth rose from 1.9 percent in the 1940s to 2.2 percent in the 1950s, reaching 2.7 percent by 1961. This development was accompanied by urbanization, as populations in cities larger than 2,500 inhabitants rose from 18 percent in 1940 to 39 percent in 1961. During this period, Lima grew from half a million to two million people. Increased white-collar employment produced by urbanization resulted in the emergence of a middle class and a shift in politics.

Peru's political life was further reshaped by an increase in literacy rates, which tripled the number of voters between 1950 and 1956. The election of President Prado in 1956, thanks to a *convivencia* with the middle-class APRA political party, was an effort by the traditional oligarchic system to extend its basis of political support in a time of change. However, as Fitzgerald (1978) states: "...[It] was the last of the traditional oligarchic administrations: it was a regime which preserved, in the context of urbanization and industrialization which had taken place in the previous two decades, a serious divergence between the traditional political and emerging social structures." The new forces started to question the export orientation of the oligarchic system, and the newly important urban population demanded a strong currency in order to contain the prices of foodstuffs, most of which were imported.

Another significant issue is that even in the mid-1950s there were some joint ventures between the local elite and foreign firms in the manufacturing sector. While these at first primarily involved export processing, they were followed relatively soon by other joint ventures dedicated to pure import substitution. These ventures were stimulated by the belief that industrialization was necessary to increase employment and growth. Thus, the local elite was more willing to support the promotion of industrial growth. Thorp and Bertram (1978, p. 255) also mention that the withdrawal of the local elite from the export sector implied that their allies, foreign firms in the export sector, lost leverage with the government in an increasingly nationalistic environment.

As seen above, the adoption of a fixed exchange rate, coupled with an inflation rate above international levels, implied an appreciation of the exchange rate beyond what any reasonable gain in productivity could warrant. While the balance of payments was healthy until 1965, mainly because of the country's fishing boom, the balance of payments deteriorated steeply in 1966 as a result of worsening terms of trade and a policy-induced real appreciation. This situation was aggravated by a reduction in capital inflows.

The reduction of the unsustainable current account deficit though the usual method of expenditure switching and reduction policies was more complicated than in previous crises, as Belaúnde's political base was largely resistant to devaluation. These sectors benefited from postponing a devaluation, which at least in the short term kept food, input and industrial equipment prices low and contained the government's external debt burden. Thus, unlike a previous episode in 1957, when devaluation was undertaken without major opposition, the perceived political losses of devaluation in the mid-1960s were substantial, as some of the most important players were against it. The government only devalued in 1967, when there was no other choice. Possible alternatives such as raising taxes and imposing exchange controls were unacceptable to the IMF and to the APRA, which dominated the Congress.

The 1990s: Adoption of Floating Exchange Rates and Appreciation of the Exchange Rate

In August 1990, the newly elected government of Alberto Fujimori launched a stabilization program aimed at eliminating hyperinflation inherited from the previous regime. Unlike other successful stabilizations in the region, the program did not fix the exchange rate but controlled the money supply after an initial reliquification. In the years that followed, the central bank intervened only to try to depreciate the currency to a degree that was consistent with the objective of reducing inflation.

The government's initial choice of exchange rate regime seemed to be more the result of the absence of reserves to credibly commit to a peg and the reluctance of international institutions to provide funds before the adjustment was made. In that sense, initial conditions inherited by Fujimori's government largely explain its choice of exchange rate regime. Furthermore, given this initial decision, it is relatively easy to understand why such a regime has continued. To the extent that stylized facts show that exchange rate-based stabilizations are expansionary at the beginning and contractionary afterwards, while money-based stabilizations display opposite effects, it seemed reasonable to maintain the flexible regime once the main economic costs (the initial contraction) had been paid.

Given the relatively low volatility of the nominal and real exchange rate in Peru in the 1990s, there was certainly no consensus for switching to a more fixed regime. The country was receiving benefits usually associated with a fixed exchange rate, without bearing the costs.

Conclusions

A variety of factors have affected exchange rate policymaking in Peru over the past 50 years. Besides the economic variables that theoretically determine optimal exchange rate policies, political economy and institutional variables figure prominently. In fact, Peruvian exchange rate policies have been very much related to the government's overall policy stance. Exchange rate polices have generally been used, and very often misused, to achieve such changing objectives as reducing inflation, sustaining an appreciated real exchange rate that supports industrialization, and promoting exports.

These goals have been apparent not only in the choice of exchange rate regime, but also in the targeting of exchange rates, and the timing of devaluations or other nominal adjustments. Quantitative and qualitative analysis suggest that, besides the usual fundamentals, exchange rate policymaking can be seen as the interaction of several factors rather than the product of factors isolated from one another.

For example, the results support the hypothesis that in an environment of high protection, the manufacturing sector would prefer a fixed exchange rate, usually an appreciated one, that reduces the domestic currency prices of imported inputs and machinery. The domestic prices of final goods should not be affected by the real exchange rate, since by virtue of the high levels of protection of final goods, manufacturing goods become de facto nontradables. In a more open and competitive environment with low tariffs, the exchange rate preferences of manufacturers are less clear. Similarly, though less conclusively, it has been found that export subsidies, which Peru employed for 20 years, reduce political pressures on exchange rate policy. This is consistent with findings on preferences of the manufacturing sector, given that export subsidies have been aimed at manufactured exports.

Regarding other export groups, two factors can explain why the export share of GDP is not a good measure of their lobbying power. One is the difficulty of developing a variable that can appropriately capture the political pressures that the export sector could have exerted in regard to exchange rate policy. In this case, the export share of GDP does not seem to provide a good measure of exporters' power to influence macroeconomic policy. A second factor is that export groups were dismantled at an early stage of the period analyzed, neutralizing their political strength. The drastic agrarian reform implemented by the military government in the late 1960s, which transferred property on coastal *haciendas* to workers, destroyed the ability of sugar and cotton exporters to exert political pressure. Similarly, the nationalization of mining and oil enterprises prevented any other major group of exporters from shaping economic policy. These transformations may also explain why, although the export share of GDP remained relatively high during the whole period, that variable serves as a poor proxy for the ability of exporters to influence economic policy. Of course, one must be cautious in drawing strong conclusions from one country time series study. Nevertheless, the results are consistent with those obtained by the cross-country study on this matter.

The statistical analysis was complemented by a description of two exchange rate-related episodes. In the first, the shift towards a fixed (and in general more appreciated) exchange rate in the late 1960s resulted from growing interest in industrialization and an increase in the size of the urban population. These developments made devaluations more costly in political terms. In the second episode, the adoption of a floating exchange rate in Peru in the 1990s was initially due to the scarcity of reserves that could have been used to stabilize the exchange rate with a credible peg. Switching to a more active exchange rate policy was not viable, since the social preferences favored low inflation rates. Further evidence that exchange rate policies are determined largely on the basis of noneconomic considerations is the behavior of the real exchange rate around presidential elections. In Peru, the RER tends to appreciate before elections and depreciate after.

References

Agenor, P.R., and P. Montiel. 1996. *Development Macroeconomics.* Princeton, NJ: Princeton University Press.

Alesina, A. 1989. Politics and Business Cycles in Industrial Democracies. *Economic Policy* 8: 57-59.

Alesina, A., and A. Drazen. 1992. Why Are Stabilizations Delayed? *American Economic Review* 81: 1170-88.

Alesina, A., and L. Summers. 1993. Central Bank Independence and Macroeconomic Performance: Some Comparative Evidence. *Journal of Money, Credit and Banking* 25: 151-62

Asea, P., and E. Mendoza. 1994. The Balassa-Samuelson Model: A General Equilibrium Appraisal. *Review of International Economics* 2(3): 244-67.

Banco Central de Reserva del Peru. *Anual.* Various issues. Lima: Memoria.

Bufman, G., and L. Leiderman. 1995. Searching for Nominal Anchors in Shock-Prone Economies in the 1990s: Inflation Targets and Exchange Rate Bands. Paper prepared for the Sixth Annual Meeting of the International Forum on Latin American Perspectives.

Calvo, G., L. Leiderman, and C. Reinhart. 1993. Capital Inflows and Real Exchange Rate Appreciation in Latin America. *IMF Staff Papers* 40(1): 108-51.

Collins, S. 1996 On Becoming More Flexible: Exchange Rate Regimes in Latin America and the Caribbean. *Journal of Development Economics* 51: 117-38.

Dixit, A. 1996. *The Making of Economic Policy: A Transaction-Cost Politics Perspective.* Cambridge, MA: MIT Press.

Edwards, S. 1996. *The Determinants of the Choice between Fixed and Flexible Exchange Rate Regimes.* NBER Working Paper 5756, National Bureau of Economic Research, Cambridge, MA.

_____. 1989. *Real Exchange Rates, Devaluation and Adjustment.* Cambridge, MA: MIT Press.

_____. 1988. *Exchange Rate Misalignment in Developing Countries.* Baltimore: Johns Hopkins University Press.

Eichengreen, B. 1996. *Globalizing Capital: A History of the International Monetary System.* Princeton, NJ: Princeton University Press.

Eichengreen, B., J. Frieden, and J. von Hagen. 1995. The Political Economy of European Integration: Introduction. In B. Eichengreen, J. Frieden and J. von Hagen (eds.), *Monetary and Fiscal Policy in an Integrated Europe.* New York: Springer.

Fischer, S., R. Sahay, and C. Végh. 1996. *Stabilization and Growth in Transition Economies–The Early Experience.* Working Paper WP/96/31, International Monetary Fund, Washington, DC.

Fitzgerald, E.V.K. 1978. *The Political Economy of Peru 1956-78: Economic Development and the Restructuring of Capital.* Cambridge, UK: Cambridge University Press.

Frankel, J., and A. Rose. 1996. A Panel Project on Purchasing Power Parity: Mean Reversion Within and Between Countries. *Journal of International Economics* 40: 209-24.

Frieden, J. 1994. Exchange Rate Politics: Contemporary Lessons from American History. *Review of International Political Economy* 1(1): 81-103.

Greene, W. 1997. *Econometric Analysis.* New York: Prentice Hall.

Grilli, V., D. Masciandaro, and G. Tabellini. 1991. Political and Monetary Institutions and Public Financial Policies in Industrial Countries. *Economic Policy* 13: 342-92.

Heckman, J., and B. Singer. 1984. Econometric Duration Analysis. *Journal of Econometrics* (January): 63-132.

International Monetary Fund (IMF). *Exchange Arrangements and Exchange Restrictions.* Various issues. International Monetary Fund, Washington, DC.

Klein, M., and N.P. Marion. 1994. *Explaining the Duration of Exchange Rate Pegs.* NBER Working Paper 4651. National Bureau of Economic Research, Cambridge, MA.

Lyons, R.K. 1992. Floating Exchange Rates in Peru, 1950-54. *Journal of Development Economics* 38: 99-118.

Obstfeld, M. 1997. *Open-Economy Macroeconomics: Developments in Theory and Policy.* NBER Working Paper 6319. National Bureau of Economic Research, Cambridge, MA.

_____. 1995. International Currency Experience: New Lessons and Lessons Relearned. *Brookings Papers of Economic Activity* 1: 119-96.

Obstfeld, M., and K. Rogoff. 1996. *Foundations of International Macroeconomics.* Cambridge, MA: MIT Press.

_____. 1995. The Mirage of Fixed Exchange Rates. *Journal of Economic Perspectives* 9: 73-96.

Paredes, C. 1988. *Política Económica, Industrialización y Exportaciones de Manufacturas en el Perú.* GRADE Documento de Trabajo 1. Grupo de Análisis Para el Desarrollo, Lima.

Paredes, C., and J. Sachs. 1991. *Peru's Path to Recovery.* Washington, DC: Brookings Institution.

Pastor, M., Jr. 1992. *Inflation, Stabilization and Debt: Macroeconomic Experiments in Peru and Bolivia.* Boulder, CO: Westview Press.

Rogowsky, R. 1987. Trade and the Variety of Democratic Institutions. *International Organization* 47: 1-39.

Rojas, J. 1996. *Políticas Comerciales y Cambiarias en el Perú: 1960-1995*. Lima: Fondo Editorial, Universidad Católica del Perú.

Sachs, J. 1996. The Transition at Mid-Decade. *American Economic Association Papers and Proceedings* 86(2): 128-33.

_____. 1985. The Dollar and the Policy Mix. *Brookings Papers on Economic Activity* 1: 117-85.

Thorp, R., and G. Bertram. 1978. *Peru 1890-1977: Growth and Policy in an Open Economy*. New York: Columbia University Press.

Williamson, J. 1995. What Role for Currency Boards? *Policy Analyses in International Economics* No. 40, Institute for International Economics, Washington, DC.